Kasparov's Opening Repertoire

Kasparov's Opening Repertoire

LEONID SHAMKOVICH
and
ERIC SCHILLER

B. T. Batsford Ltd, *London*

First published 1990

© Leonid Shamkovich and Eric Schiller 1990

ISBN 0 7134 5718 X

A CIP catalogue record for this book is available from the British Library

Typeset by W. Turner & Son Ltd, Halifax, Yorks
and printed in Great Britain
by Dotesios (Printers) Ltd, Trowbridge, Wilts
for the publishers, B. T. Batsford Ltd,
4 Fitzhardinge Street, London W1H 0AH

A BATSFORD CHESS BOOK

Adviser: R. D. Keene GM, OBE

Technical Editor: Ian Kingston

Preface

World Champions exert a strong influence on fashion in opening play, and Gary Kasparov is no exception. His advocacy of such variations as the Tarrasch, Catalan and Grünfeld has brought these openings from the back pages of opening manuals into the forefront of theoretical discussion. The purpose of this book is to explore the development of Kasparov's opening repertoire and to present the core of a repertoire which the reader can apply in his own games. All recent theoretical developments have been incorporated into the work, so that the most important variations of these openings are critically up to date as at 30 May 1988.

It is not our intention to present deep analysis of the middlegame and endgame portions of Kasparov's games. The World Champion has done that himself in a number of places. We will, on occasion, add our own corrections and improvements to the published canon, but the games are included primarily to illustrate the themes of the openings. It is interesting to note the number of top players who have adopted portions of this repertoire. Jan Timman, Tony Miles and Valery Salov are just three of the players whose games will be examined in our book. We have attempted to analyze critically all important positions, and have introduced a number of new ideas in familiar positions.

The authors have worked together over many months to collect and analyse the relevant material. Some of the analysis by Grandmaster Shamkovich first appeared in the American publication *Chess Life*. Older material on the Tarrasch was used in our book *Play the Tarrasch* (Pergamon Press, 1984). Both the first and second editions of Eric Schiller's *Catalan* (Chess Enterprises, 1983 and 1988) and *Grünfeld Defense: Russian Variations* (Chess Enterprises, 1985 and 1988) were used for the preparation of this work, as well as research notes and analysis for his forthcoming works on the Closed Spanish and Hedgehog openings. We are grateful to Bob Dudley for permission to use all Chess Enterprises materials. To sort out the web of transpositions in the Spanish and Hedgehog lines, the remarkable piece of software from Bookup was employed. ChessBase was consulted to keep the manuscript up to date. Chessworks Unlimited provided the special software used in preparation of the manuscript on its Macintosh computers. The manuscript underwent a thorough proofreading at the hands of Ian Kingston.

Contents

1 Introduction

What is an opening repertoire?
An opening repertoire is the set of opening lines which a player feels comfortable playing at any time against any level of opposition. At amateur levels it often consists of only a single approach for White, say, 1 d4, and a few basic defences, for example the Sicilian and the Benoni. At professional levels there is usually an additional system held in reserve in the event that one's main weapon misfires and important games need to be played before there is time to remedy the defect.

How is the repertoire built? At all levels of play the repertoire is generally constructed by calculating all probable responses to the moves one chooses and determining a variation which will be an effective reply to each.

We can offer a few guidelines which should be observed while building one's repertoire. Naturally, the advice given here is just a set of guidelines. There is plenty of room for individual variation. But there are certain principles which should always be followed:

DON'T RELY ON UNUSUAL AND TRAPPY OPENINGS. They may earn points in tournaments but will not provide a good base on which to build your repertoire.
DON'T BLINDLY COPY THE REPERTOIRES OF THE BEST PLAYERS. Some middlegames must not be entered without a great deal of knowledge of certain pawn structures and endgames.
DON'T BE LAZY. If an opening involves complicated lines which must be learned, that should not scare you. These lines can be assimilated quickly without embarrassment if one has access to a chess computer. In fact, software is being developed for microcomputers with the specific goal of teaching openings! If you do not have access to such technological marvels, study the lines the same way you prepare(d) for tests at school.
DON'T LIMIT YOUR STUDY OF GAMES TO MATERIALS INVOLVING JUST THE OPENINGS YOU PLAY. One day you will want to change openings, and the more experience you have with a wide range of variations

the easier that task will be. DON'T BLINDLY FOLLOW ANALYSIS FROM BOOKS. This even applies to our own writings! Examine everything you read with a critical eye. If the author claims that one side has an advantage, try to find out what it is. In fact, when you are learning an opening from a book it is a good idea to scribble notes in the margins articulating the advantages and disadvantages of certain positions. Keep in mind that some annotators, especially in *Informant*-type publications, give incorrect analysis to mislead future opponents! IGNORE 'STATISTICS'. Some books provide statistical analyses of openings. Remember, 'there are lies, damned lies and statistics'! Many of these books count a game played between two beginners as having the same statistical value as a World Championship game, or a game between a GM and a beginner.

How is it maintained?

There are a number of ways of staying current with the latest opening trends. There are reliable journals, such as *Chess Informant* and *New In Chess,* which can supply not only raw data but also Grandmaster opinions. Of course, one must be careful, as sometimes 'recommendations' are actually traps which are baited with exclamation marks to catch the unwary. Trust no-one but yourself, and double check every move you intend to incorporate into your repertoire. Faster access to new ideas is available via tele-communications networks like LeisureLINC, which can be accessed from all over the world and which tries to provide information and games as soon as events are finished. There are several computerized databases which are available to the public and which contain a great deal of useful information. Finally, there is the seemingly endless flow of monographs on the openings, produced by theoreticians all over the world. Books by active grandmasters are likely to contain the most accurate information, although there is always the possibility that some material, especially original analysis, has been withheld for personal use. Valuable research is also carried out by less exalted players, but one should keep in mind that their ability to evaluate positions is more limited.

When should it change?

Some players stick with a small repertoire throughout their career. Grandmaster Lev Alburt, for example, has rarely strayed from his combination of Alekhine Defence and Benkö Gambit as Black, Wolfgang Uhlmann was slavishly devoted to the French Defence, and a number of players have made a living off the Sicilian Dragon.

Other players change openings almost as frequently as they change their clothes. Universal players such as Boris Spassky, Oleg Romanishin, Bent Larsen and Mikhail Tal can never be predicted in the early stages of the game. Gary Kasparov falls into this group.

Most players, however, maintain a preference for a small group of openings while experimenting on occasion with a select group of alternatives. We recommend this approach to most players. No player should deny himself some experience of the classic openings such as the Spanish Game or Queen's Gambit, preferably on both sides of the board.

Nevertheless, some personalities are better suited toward the hypermodern play of the Pirc, or quiet handling of the Caro-Kann, or wild complications of the Sicilian Defence. With White, the strategic tranquility of the Catalan may be more appealing than the brawling nature of the king pawn games.

The time to change openings is signalled by a change in overall attitude toward the game and a certain boredom with familiar positions. Nothing rekindles the chess fires like an abrupt change of scenery, which can be brought about by a radical change in approach to the openings. One should not fear the complexity of a new variation, or the accumulated mass of theory. Many openings can be handled quite well with only a basic knowledge of the principles of the opening. This applies to variations as different as the Modern Defence and the Closed Spanish. Of course not all openings are amenable to this kind of treatment. One can hardly recommend an innocent foray into the jungle of the Poisoned Pawn variation of the Najdorf Sicilian, or the Marshall Attack!

Kasparov's Opening Repertoire

In the following sections we will discuss the development of Kasparov's opening repertoire. For the moment, let us consider the overall composition of his repertoire. Viewed without regard to colour, the chart overleaf shows the distribution of openings throughout his career. We have chosen to use pictures rather than words because we don't put much stock in mere statistics. After all, many openings are chosen for a particular occasion or opponent, and the exact number of times an opening has been played is not of great significance.

The overall picture reflects a reliance on the more orthodox Sicilian Defence and Queen's Gambits, despite considerable experimentation on the flanks.

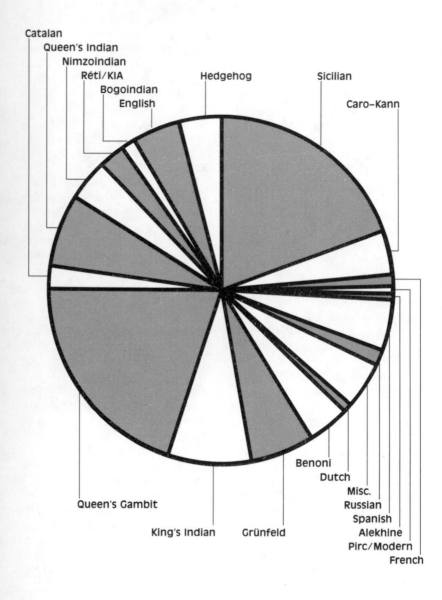

Catalan
Queen's Indian
Nimzoindian
Réti/KIA
Bogoindian
English
Hedgehog
Sicilian
Caro–Kann

Benoni
Dutch
Misc.
Russian
Spanish
Alekhine
Pirc/Modern
French

Queen's Gambit

King's Indian   Grünfeld

When Kasparov has the advantage
of the first move, the picture is a
bit different:

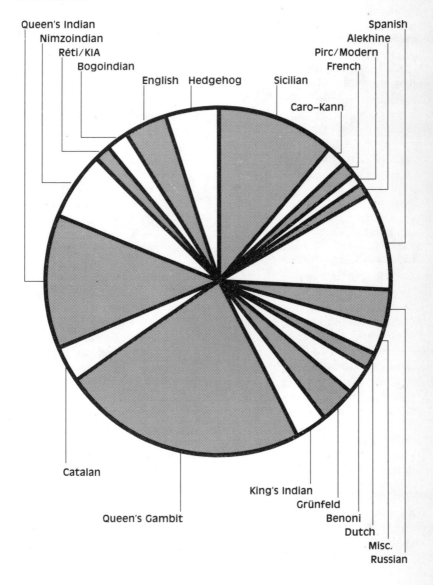

Queen's Indian
Nimzoindian
Réti/KIA
Bogoindian
English Hedgehog
Spanish
Alekhine
Pirc/Modern
French
Sicilian
Caro–Kann

Catalan
Queen's Gambit
King's Indian
Grünfeld
Benoni
Dutch
Misc.
Russian

His reliance on 1 d4 has reduced the proportion of Sicilian Defences, and there is a broader range of Semi-Open games even when 1 e4 does occur. The Queen's Indian figures more prominently.

When playing Black the Sicilian Defence is dominant. The seemingly large number of games in the King's Indian reflects his preference in the past, but we cannot tell how he feels about it now because few players would adopt that opening against Karpov, though Kasparov did risk it once in their fourth match, coming away with a draw.

Kasparov's early development: Becoming a Grandmaster

No great player of the present era can disclaim the influence of Bobby Fischer. In Kasparov's case, the most obvious ramification of Fischer's play can be seen in Gary's use of the King's Indian Defence. This fighting opening has brought Kasparov numerous spectacular victories. He enriched the theory of the opening with new moves and new ideas, but temporarily abandoned it for more classical defences. Here are a few impressive examples:

Tukmakov – Kasparov, USSR 1981: 1 d4 ♘f6 2 c4 g6 3 ♘c3 ♗g7 4 e4 d6 5 ♗e2 0-0 6 ♗g5 c5 7 d5 b5?! 8 cb a6 9 a4 h6 10 ♗d2 e6 11 de ♗xe6 12 ♘f3 ab 13 ♗xb5 ♘a6 14

0-0 ♘c7 15 ♖e1 ♘xb5 16 ♘xb5 d5 17 ed ♘xd5 18 ♘e5 ♖e8 19 ♖c1 ♗f5 20 ♘c6 ♕d7 21 ♖xc5 ♖xe1+ 22 ♕xe1 ♖e8 23 ♕c1 ♘b6 24 b3 ♖e2 25 ♗a5 ♗e4 26 ♘e5 ♕e7! 27 ♘d4? (27 ♕f1±) 27 ... ♖a2 28 ♗xb6 ♗xe5 29 ♕e3? (29 ♕e1 =) 29 ... ♕xc5! 0-1.

Vaiser – Kasparov, USSR 1981: 1 d4 ♘f6 2 c4 g6 3 ♘c3 ♗g7 4 e4 d6 5 f4 0-0 6 ♘f3 c5 7 d5 e6 8 ♗e2 ed 9 e5 ♘g4 10 cd de 11 h3 e4 12 hg ef 13 gf ♖e8 14 f5! ♕b6? 15 ♗h6 ♕xb2 16 ♗xg7 ♔xg7 17 f6+? (17 ♖c1!) 17 ... ♔g8! 18 ♕c1! ♕b4! 19 ♔f1? (19 ♕d2!) 19 ... ♘d7 20 ♗b5 ♕d4! 21 ♔g2 ♖e3! 22 ♘e2 ♕e5 23 ♔f2 ♖xe2+ 24 ♗xe2 ♘xf6 and White's attack ran out of steam (0-1, 40). For exceptionally deep and incisive commentary on this game, see *Fighting Chess* (Kasparov and Wade), where Kasparov and Vaiser conduct an analytical dialogue.

Kavalek – Kasparov, Bugojno 1982: 1 c4 g6 2 ♘c3 ♗g7 3 d4 ♘f6 4 e4 d6 5 ♘f3 0-0 6 h3 e5 7 d5 ♘a6! 8 ♗e3 ♘h5 9 ♘h2!? (9 ♘d2) 9 ... ♕e8 10 ♗e2?! (10 g4 ♘f4 11 ♕d2) 10 ... ♘f4 11 ♗f3 f5 12 h4 ♕e7! (Typical of Kasparov's style. Timman pointed out that a positional player would probably prefer 12 ... ♘c5 with a comfortable game.) 13 g3 ♘b4!! 14 ♕b3?! ♘fd3+ 15 ♔e2 f4 16 ♗d2 fg?! (Co-author Schiller was present at this game, and saw this move shoot out without using even a full minute of thought.

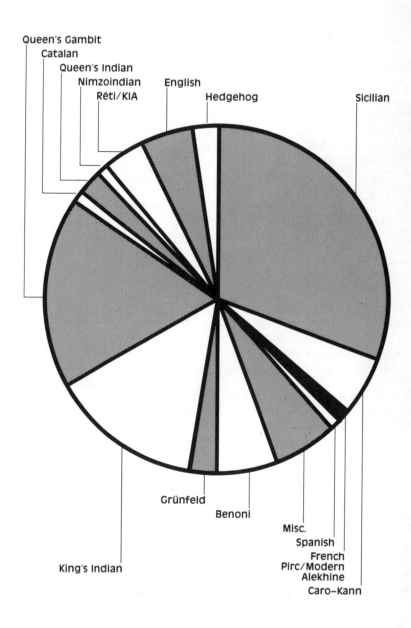

Such rashness was the source of immediate frustration, as the brilliant and effective 16 ... ♘xf2!! presented itself to Kasparov as soon as he let go of his pawn.) 17 fg ♖xf3! (Kasparov regained his balance quickly, and found the best move.) 18 ♘xf3 ♗g4 19 ♖af1 ♖f8 20 ♘d1? (Kavalek could have saved the game with 20 ♗e3!) 20 ... ♕f7! 21 ♗e3! ♗xf3+ 22 ♔d2! ♕d7 23 ♖hg1 ♕h3! 24 a3 ♗xe4 25 ♖xf8+ ♗xf8 26 ab ♕h2+ 27 ♔c3 ♘c1! 0-1.

Belyavsky – Kasparov, Moscow (m/8) 1983: 1 d4 ♘f6 2 c4 g6 3 ♘c3 ♗g7 4 e4 d6 5 f3 0-0 6 ♗e3 a6 7 ♗d3 c5 8 dc dc 9 ♗xc5 ♘c6 10 ♘ge2?! ♘d7! 11 ♗f2 ♘de5 12 ♘c1 ♗h6! 13 ♘d5?! (13 ♗e2) 13 ... e6 14 ♗b6 ♕g5! 15 0-0! ed! 16 f4 (16 cd!?) 16 ... ♕h4 17 fe d4! 18 ♘e2 ♗e3+ 19 ♔h1 ♘xe5 20 ♗c7 (20 ♗xd4 ♘g4 21 h3 ♗xd4) 20 ... ♕e7 21 ♗xe5 ♕xe5 and Black went on to convert his substantial advantage into a win.

With White, 1 d4 became the standard opening for the young player, and the Exchange Variation of the Grünfeld was joined by the out-of-fashion Petrosian Variation (4 a3) of the Queen's Indian. The latter opening not only enjoyed a revival due to Kasparov's advocacy, but can now be said to be the main line of the Queen's Indian Defence. Even though the World Champion has switched his attention to the Hybrid and Nimzo–Indian lines, he has not entirely abandoned his former love. For example:

Kasparov – van der Wiel, Amsterdam 1988: 1 d4 ♘f6 2 c4 e6 3 ♘f3 b6 4 a3 ♗a6 5 ♕c2 ♗b7 6 ♘c3 c5 7 e4 cxd4 8 ♘xd4 ♗c5 9 ♘b3 ♘c6 10 ♗g5 (The most topical continuation.) 10 ... a6 11 0-0-0 ♕c7 12 ♔b1 0-0-0 13 ♕d2 d6 (At the time this game was played, Black was considered to have a fully playable position.) 14 f3! h6 15 ♗f4 ♘e5 (15 ... g5? 16 ♘xc5 gxf4 17 ♘xb7 ♔xb7 18 ♕xf4++ Kristiansen.) 16 h4 ♔b8 17 h5 ♖d7 18 ♖c1 ♖c8 19 ♗e2 ♔a7 20 ♖hd1 ♖dd8 21 g4 ♘g8 22 ♗g3 ♘e7 23 f4 ♘5c6 24 ♗f3 ♖b8 25 ♗h4 ♖d7 26 ♘b5+! axb5 27 cxb5 ♘a5 (Or 27 ... ♘d8 28 ♖xc5! bxc5 29 ♘xc5, △ ♘xd7, ♕xa5 Kristiansen.) 28 ♘xa5 bxa5 29 ♖xc5 dxc5 30 ♕xd7 ♕xf4 31 ♖d6 1-0. On 31 ..., ♖c8 32 ♖a6+ ♔b8 33 ♗xe7++; 31 ..., ♔a8 32 ♕c7 ♖c8 33 ♖a6+++.

Challenging the crown

The ascent to the Olympus of the chess world (to use the standard Russian metaphor) is often accompanied by innovations in the opening. Kasparov brought the Tarrasch Defence back from obscurity just at the time when its leading advocates, most notably John Nunn, were about to abandon it. In addition, he took the Catalan (an opening played extensively by Margeir Petursson, who was also a Tarrasch exponent) and brought it back into the

Grandmaster ranks. These two openings had suffered from neglect for some time, as evidenced by the fact that no important literature on either opening had appeared since the 1960's. The authors wrote *Play the Tarrasch* in 1983, the same year co-author Schiller published his monograph on the Catalan. Kasparov had access to both manuscripts at the time he was preparing these openings, but had decided to examine the lines before receiving the material. We mention this only because some of our critics have accused us of making a living off of Kasparov's openings, a charge they are free to level at this book, if they wish! But a serious point is that the World Champion has always shown a willingness to examine material from all sources, from Grandmaster down to amateur games. He understands that creative ideas appear in a wide variety of chess contexts, not merely in top level play.

World Champion Kasparov

Unfortunately, the political problems which plagued the chess world in the mid 1980's have prevented Kasparov from participating in large numbers of tournaments. He has spent most of his time either preparing for or playing against his arch-rival Anatoly Karpov, and his choice of openings on other occasions must be viewed in that light. He was not about to expose his match preparation in minor tournaments and training matches, and often seemed to choose lines just for fun, for example his use of the Meran Defence against Tony Miles.

His faith in the Grünfeld Defence is indisputable, and he has always considered the 'Spanish Inquisition' one of the highest forms of chess art. They are likely to remain staples of his repertoire. Recent experimentation with the Najdorf may bring that variation into his primary repertoire. Kasparov's penchant for complicated positions has seen the King's Indian return recently, particularly against lower ranked opposition. The Réti, which brought him success in the critical 24th game of the 4th match against Karpov, will probably be reserved for similar situations in which a small amount of annoying pressure is required. Interestingly, Tal adopted the same opening for a critical last round game in the 1988 National Open in Chicago, and the opening may become a favourite weapon in these sorts of cases.

Some final advice: What to do when things go wrong

Of course, it would be incorrect to suggest that Kasparov's preparation is always correct. In the opening of this game Kasparov recovers from an experiment gone awry. He found himself in a critical position as a result of his fifth move – a dubious try. Then he took extraordinary measures to improve his position. He decided to seek active counterplay with a heavy dose of tactics. As a result he almost managed to equalize the game. This attitude carried over into the endgame, where Kasparov sacrificed his weak pawn in order to make the rest of his pieces active. In spite of considerable simplifications Black achieved sufficient counterplay, forcing Karpov to return his surplus material.

Karpov–Kasparov
Brussels 1987

1	d4	♘f6
2	c4	g6
3	g3	c5
4	♘f3	cd
5	♘×d4	♕c7?! *(1)*

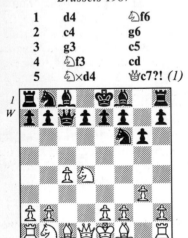

It is hardly likely that Kasparov will ever repeat this dubious and rather strange move. Black places his queen in a very unsafe position and lacks control over the critical

d5 square. True, he does attack the pawn at c4, but White can afford to ignore the threat and reply 6 ♘c3! If 6 ... ♕×c4 then 7 e4 ♕c7 8 ♖c1 and Black gets into trouble. Kasparov, a clever psychological player, probably knew that Karpov would not accept the proffered gift.

| 6 | b3 |

This is not as principled, but a good enough move.

| 6 | ... | ♗g7 |
| 7 | ♗g2 | d5! |

Black seizes the first opportunity to create complications, because after the trivial 7 ... a6 8 ♘c3 d6 9 ♗b2 Black would be facing an uphill climb in the endgame.

| 8 | cd | ♘×d5 |
| 9 | 0-0! *(2)* |

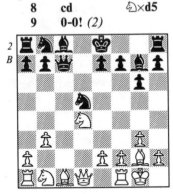

Now what should Black do? His poorly placed queen hampers normal development or further counterplay. If, for example, 9 ... ♕b6, trying to exploit the pin of the ♘d4, then 10 ♗b2 ♘c6 11 ♗×d5 ♘×d4 12 e3! ♘f3+ 13 ♕×f3 ♗×b2 14 ♕×f7+ ♔d8 15 ♖d1 ♔c7

(15 ... ♗×a1 16 ♗e6+ ♔c7 17 ♕f4+ ♕d6 18 ♖×d6 ed 19 ♘a3! ±±) 16 ♘c3! ♗×c3 (16 ... ♗×a1 17 ♕f4+) 17 ♖ac1 wins.

Also in White's favour is 9 ... ♘c6 10 ♘×c6 ♗×a1 11 ♕×d5 or 9 ...♕e5 10 ♗b2 0-0 11 ♘d2. Kasparov finds a wonderful opportunity to keep the game balanced.

9 ... ♕d7!?

Black withdraws his queen from the danger zone and takes control of the important b5 and d5 squares. The ♗c8 will become free later. Despite the 'ugly' nature of the move, Kasparov finds the true value.

10 ♗b2 0-0
11 ♕c1!

Some commentators criticised this move and suggested 11 ♕d2, although after 11 ... ♖d8 12 ♖d1 ♕e8! 13 ♘a3 ♘a6 and Black holds on. With the text, White is freeing d1 for his rook and protects the ♗b2 as well. This is a very logical plan.

11 ... ♖d8
12 ♖d1 ♘c6!
13 ♘×c6 ♕×c6
14 ♕×c6 bc
15 ♗×g7 ♔×g7 *(3)*

The curtain rises on the second act, an endgame with a weak backward pawn at c6. In addition, the ♘d5 is pinned and White's bishop is now much stronger than Black's. How can he create serious counterplay?

16 ♖c1

White could not play 16 e4

since 16 ... ♗g4! 17 f3 ♘e3! 18 ♖×d8 ♖×d8 19 ♘c3 ♖d2 gives Black a strong counterattack. It is only one tactical nuance of Kasparov's dynamic plan in this seemingly quiet position.

16 ... ♗g4!

A passive defence of the weak pawn with 16 ... ♗b7 is counter-indicated for Black. Kasparov sacrifices the pawn for genuine counterplay.

17 ♔f1 a5!
18 h3

The pawn on c6 is doomed, but the immediate 18 ♖×c6? would fail to 18 ... ♘b4! 19 ♖c1 ♖ac8 20 ♘c3 (20 ♖×c8?? ♖d1 mate) 20 ... ♖d2! 21 h3 (if 21 f3 then 21 ... ♗e6!) 21 ... ♘c2 22 ♘e4 ♘×a1 23 ♖×a1 ♖×a2! and it is White who has to save the game.

18 ... ♗e6
19 ♘c3

Karpov shows his customary caution. The pawn at c6 is still inedible due to 19 ♖×c6 ♘b4 (or 19 ... a4).

19 ... ♘×c3
20 ♖×c3 ♖d2

21 ♖×c6

At last!

21 ... ♖ad8

22 ♖cc1 ♖b2! *(4)*

Black's well-placed rook is full compensation for his missing pawn. It is curious that only in the endgame was Black able to improve his position, which deteriorated quickly as a result of his poor choice at move 5.

23	♖cb1	♖dd2
24	♖×b2	♖×b2
25	♔e1	♗f5
26	♔d1	g5
27	♗d5	♔f6
28	♗c4	e6
29	g4	♗g6
30	a4	♔e5!

White found himself in zugzwang, and quickly dropped a couple of pawns. Black's choice of active counterplay proved to be a most effective strategy.

1 Queen's Gambit

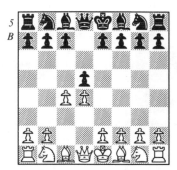

This venerable opening has seen many waves of fashion for play on both sides. It can lead to the wild complications of the Semi-Slav or to the quiet positional play of the Orthodox Variation. Kasparov has enjoyed both sides of the opening, and we will deal with two systems, the Tartakower Variation and the Tarrasch Defence in Chapter 12.

Here we will discuss the following variations:

Variation I: The Petrosian System 2 ... e6 3 ♘c3 ♘f6 4 ♗g5 ♗e7 5 ♘f3 0-0 6 e3 h6 7 ♗×f6 ♗×f6

Variation II: The Botvinnik System 2 ... e6 3 ♘c3 ♘f6 4 ♗g5 c6 5 ♘f3 dc 6 e4 b5

Variation III: The Geller Gambit 2 ... dc 3 ♘f3 ♘f6 4 ♘c3 c6 5 e4

Variation I:
The Petrosian System

The authors found the pamphlet *Developments in the Orthodox Queen's Gambit 1984–1987* by Julian Way most helpful in compiling the relevant games for this chapter. All analysis is our own, unless otherwise indicated.

1	d4	♘f6
2	c4	e6
3	♘c3	d5
4	♗g5	♗e7
5	♘f3	h6
6	♗×f6	♗×f6
7	e3	

Recently the World Champion has chosen another variation. *Kasparov–Timman, Amsterdam 1988:* 1 d4 ♘f6 2 c4 e6 3 ♘f3 d5 4 ♘c3 ♗e7 5 ♗g5 h6 6 ♗×f6 ♗×f6 7 ♕b3 c6 8 e3 0-0 9 ♖d1 ♕b6 10 ♕c2 dc 11 ♗×c4 c5 12 ♘e4 ♗e7 13 dc ♗×c5 14 0-0 ♗e7 15 ♗e2 ♗d7 16 ♘e5 ♖c8 17 ♕d3 ♗e8 18 ♘c4 ♕c7 19 ♘ed6 ♖d8 20 ♘×e8 ♖×e8 21 ♗f3 ♖d8 22 ♕b3 ♘c6 23 g3 ♗f6 24 ♔g2 ♖ab8 25 ♖×d8+ ♖×d8 ½-½.

7	...	0-0 *(6)*
8	♖c1	c6

This is by far the most common move, although a number of alternatives have been tried:

(a) 8 ... a6 is also seen, but after 9 a3 Black has nothing better than 9 ... c6 anyway, and now 10 ♗d3 (10 c5!? should also bring White a better position.) 10 ... ♘d7 11 0-0 makes the inclusion of the a-pawn moves better for White unless Black does something like 11 ... b5, but then after 12 cd cd 13 ♘e2! White is better, for example 13 ... ♗b7 14 ♗b1 ♖e8 15 ♕d3, Karpov–Short, Brussels SWIFT 1987 which saw White obtain a small advantage.

(b) 8 ... b6 is an interesting option, but it seems that Black is really mixing systems here, for example Gulko–Shamkovich, New York Open 1987: 9 ♗d3 dc!? 10 ♗e4 (if 10 ♗×c4, then Black plays 10 ... ♗b7 △ ♘d7 and c5) 10 ... c6 11 ♘d2 ♗a6 12 ♕f3 b5 13 a3 ♘d7 (13 ... ♕b6!? was an option, △ ♖c8 and ♘d7) 14 ♗×c6 ♖b8 15 0-0 ∞.

White can also play the thematic 9 cd ed 10 ♗d3, although after 10 ... ♗b7 11 0-0 Black might adopt Neishtadt's idea 11 ... ♖e8!? or 11 ... ♘d7 △ 12 ... c5.

(c) Former World Champion Boris Spassky has seen both sides of 8 ... ♘c6. But his experience as Black encouraged him to prefer the White side, as demonstrated by his 1968 USSR encounter with Zhukhovitsky: 9 ♗e2 dc 10 ♗×c4 e5 11 d5 ♘e7 12 ♘e4 ♗f5 (12 ... ♘f5 was seen in Portisch–Campora, Amsterdam 1984, but 13 ♕c2!? ♘d6 14 ♗d3 is a strong idea from Belyavsky in *ECO*.) 13 ♘×f6+ gf 14 ♘h4 ♗h7 15 0-0 and Black is suffocating. Perhaps Black can revive Spassky's idea with 11 ... ♘a5!? 12 ♗e2 e4 e.g. 13 ♘×e4 ♗×b2 ∞ or 13 ♘d2 ♗×c3 14 ♖×c3 ♕×d5 ∞.

(d) 8 ... ♗e7 returns a tempo a bit too early, as demonstrated in Petrosian–Hübner, m/4 1971: 9 a3 c6 10 ♗d3 ♘d7 11 0-0 b6 12 ♕e2 ♗b7 13 ♖fd1 ♕b8 14 cd ed 15 ♗f5±.

(e) 8 ... ♖e8 9 ♗e2 dc 10 ♗×c4 ♘d7 11 0-0 c5 12 ♘e4 cd 13 ed ±, Furman–Bukhman, USSR Ch. 1965.

9 ♗d3   ♘d7
10 0-0   dc

(a) Black is not forced to capture here. 10 ... ♕e7!? is possible, leading to unclear complications, e.g. 11 a3 ♖d8 12 ♖e1 g6 13 c5 e5 14 e4 ed 15 ed, where instead of 15 ... ♕×e1+, which failed to 16 ♕×e1+ dc 17 ♖×c3! ♗×c3 18 ♕×c3 cd 19 h4 in Rashkovsky–M. Gurevich, USSR Ch. 1987, Black can play 15 ... ♕×c5 ∞, Belyavsky suggests 11 ♖e1 ♖d8 12 ♕b3 dc 13

♕xc4 ± in *ECO*.

(b) Black tried the retreat 10 ... ♗e7 in Petursson-Large, Hastings, 1986/87, but after 11 ♕e2!? a6 12 e4 dc 13 ♗xc4 b5 14 ♗b3 c5 15 ♖fd1 ♕b6 16 e5 ♗b7 17 d5 c4 18 ♗c2 ed 19 ♘xd5 ♗xd5 20 ♖xd5 White was slightly better. Somewhat less logical, but also good is 12 ♗b1 f5 13 a3 ♗d6 14 ♗d3 ♕e7 15 ♔h1 ♔h8 16 ♘d2 ♘f6 17 f4 ♗d7 18 ♘f3±, Epishin-Kuporosov, Tallinn 1986.

(c) After 10 ... b6 11 e4 White has a traditional advantage, Agzamov-Vaganian, USSR 1982.

11 ♗xc4 e5

11 ... c5 12 ♕e2 a6 13 ♖fd1 cd 14 ♘xd4 ♕e7 15 ♘e4 ♗e5 16 ♘f3?! ♗b8 17 ♕d2 b5 18 ♗e2 ♘f6! brought Black equality in Kasparov-Karpov, London m/12 1986. But after the match the World Champion improved with 16 ♕h5!, which is much better for White: Kasparov-H. Olafsson, Dubai Ol. 1986 went 16 ... ♖d8 17 ♗f1 ♗b8 18 ♕a5! b6 19 ♕c3 ♗b7 20 ♘c6 ♗xc6 21 ♕xc6±.

11 ... b6?! was demolished in Karpov-Spassky, Lucerne 1985: 12 e4! ♗b7 13 e5 ♗e7 14 ♕e2 b5 15 ♗d3 c5 16 ♘xb5 cd 17 ♗e4 ♗xe4 18 ♕xe4.

12 h3! (7)

This is Kasparov's innovation, which revitalized the line.

12 ... ed
13 ed ♘b6

13 ... c5 is one alternative and now:

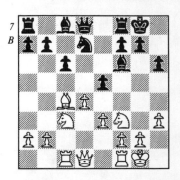

(a) Timman has recently tried 14 ♘e4 but after 14 ... cd 15 ♖e1 (15 ♘xf6+ ♘xf6 16 ♕b3 ♕b6! = Kasparov.) 15 ... ♘b6 16 ♗b3 ♗d7 17 ♘xf6+ ♕xf6 18 ♕xd4 ♕xd4 19 ♘xd4 Black had full equality in Timman-Korchnoi, Amsterdam 1987, with 19 ... ♖fc8, while Black was also fine after the other rook move 19 ... ♖ac8 in Dohosian-Pigusov, USSR 1986.

(b) 14 ♗b3 is best. Kasparov-Karpov, London m/10 1986, saw 14 ... cd 15 ♘d5 b6 16 ♘xd4 ♗xd4 17 ♕xd4±.

13 ... ♖e8 has also been seen. Browne-Abramović, New York Open 1987 continued 14 ♕b3 ♖f8 (14 ... ♖e7 15 d5 ♘b6 16 dc ♘xc4 17 ♕xc4 bc 18 ♖fd1 ♕a5 19 ♘d4 ♗xd4, Yrjölä-Jonsson, Reykjavik 1986, would lead to an advantage for White after 20 ♕xd4.) 15 ♕c2 ♘b6 16 ♗b3 ♗xd4 17 ♖cd1 c5 18 ♘b5 ♗d7 19 ♘bxd4 cd 20 ♖xd4 ♕f6=, but White can strive for the initiative with 19 ♘fxd4!? cd 20 ♘d6 ♗c6 21 ♖xd4±.

14 ♗b3 (8) ♗f5

Again Black has explored a number of paths:

(a) 14 ... ♗g5 was tried in Ribli-Short, Dortmund 1986 but after 15 ♖c2 ♗f5 16 ♖e2 ♗f4 17 ♖fe1 the doubled rooks secured a strong advantage which was demonstrated after 17 ... ♘d7 18 d5! ♘c5 19 ♗c2 ±.

(b) 14 ... ♖e8 is another possiblity which was tried in Kasparov-Karpov, Moscow m/23 1985. After 15 ♖e1 ♗f5 (15 ... ♖×e1+ 16 ♕×e1 ♗f5 17 ♘e4 ♕e7 18 ♘c5 ± Epishin-Faibisovich, USSR 1986. A recent try was 16 ... ♗d7 but White was still able to exploit his advantage: 17 ♕e4 ♕e7 18 ♕f4 ♖e8 19 ♖e1 ♗e6 20 ♗×e6 f×e6 21 ♕g4 ♘d5 22 ♘×d5 c×d5 23 g3 ♕f7 24 h4 ♗d8 25 h5 ♖f8 26 ♔g2 ♖e8 27 ♖e3 ♗b6 28 a4 ♖e7 29 ♘h4 ♕f6 30 ♖f3 1-0, Speelman-Benko, Europa Cup 1987) 16 ♖×e8+ ♕×e8 17 ♕d2 ♕d7 18 ♖e1 ♖d8 19 ♕f4 ♘d5 20 ♘×d5 c×d5 21 ♘e5 ♗×e5 22 ♖×e5 White held a small but persistent advantage. Perhaps the other capture, 22 ♕×e5, is even more promising (Tal-Grigorian,

Yerevan 1986).

(c) 14 ... a5 is likely to transpose below after 15 a3 ♗f5 16 ♖e1.

15 ♖e1 a5

Here there are a number of alternatives:

(a) 15 ... ♗g5 is met by 16 ♖a1!, for example, Kasparov-Short, Brussels 1986: 16 ... ♘d7 17 d5! ♖c8 (17 ... ♘c5 18 ♗c2 ♗×c2 19 ♕×c2 cd 20 ♖ad1 would only have been slightly better for White according to Kasparov.) 18 ♘d4 ♗g6 19 ♘e6! fe 20 de ♔h7 21 ♕×d7 ♕b6 22 e7 ♖fe8 23 ♕g4 ♕c5 24 ♘e4 ♕×e7 25 ♗c2! ♖f8 26 g3 ♕d8 27 ♖ad1 ♕a5 28 h4 ♗e7 29 ♘c3! ♗×c2 30 ♖×e7 ♖g8 31 ♖dd7 ♗f5 32 ♖×g7+ ♔h8 33 ♕d4 1-0. 17 ... ♘c5 is relatively better, but Black is still worse.

(b) 15 ... ♕d7 robs the ♘b6 of its natural development. After 16 ♕d2 a5 17 a3 a4 (or 17 ... ♖fe8 18 ♖e3 a4 19 ♗a2 ♗e6 20 ♗×e6 ♖×e6 21 ♘e4 ♗e7 22 ♘c5 ♗×c5 23 ♖×e6 ♕×e6 24 dc ♘d5 25 ♖e1 ♕f5 26 ♖e5 ♕g6 27 g3 ½-½ Ljubojević-Andersson, Wijk aan Zee 1987.) 18 ♗a2 ♖fe8 19 ♕f4 Black nevertheless managed to equalize with 19 ... ♗e6! 20 ♗×e6 ♖×e6 21 ♖×e6 ♕×e6 22 ♕c7 ♕b3! in Rashkovsky-Belyavsky, USSR Ch. 1986. 16 ♘e5 is more promising, for example 16 ... ♗×e5 17 de ♕×d1 (17 ... ♖fe8 18 ♕f3 ♗g6 19 ♖cd1 ♕f5 20 ♕e3 h5 21 ♖d4 c5 22 ♖f4 ♕c8 23 ♘b5 ♗e7 24 ♘d6 ♕c6 25 ♕g3 ♖d8 26 ♕×g6 1-0 S. Ivanov-Krivov, Jaroslavl Teams

1986.) 18 買cxd1 買fd8 19 g4 兔d3 20 e6!? fe 兔×e6+ ± Andersson-Belyavsky, Reggio Emilia 1986/87.

(c) 15 ... 營d6 16 營e2 買ad8 17 買cd1 h5 18 ②e5 兔×e5 19 d×e5 營g6 20 營e3 was better for White in Dlugy-Ornstein, New York 1987.

(d) 15 ... 買e8 is a solid move. After 16 買×e8+ 營×e8 17 營d2 營d7 18 買e1 and now:

(d1) 18 ... a5 19 營f4 g5 (19 ... a4 20 兔×f7+±) 20 ②e4 兔g7 21 營c1 兔×e4 22 買×e4 a4 23 兔c2 買e8 24 營e1 買×e4 25 營×e4 營e6 16 營×e6 fe 27 含f1 both 27 ... 含f7 G. Garcia-Geller, Sochi 1986, and 27 ... 兔f8 28 含e2 a3! M. Gurevich-Belyavsky, USSR Ch. 1987, seem adequate for Black.

(d2) 18 ... 買d8 19 營f4 ②d5 20 ②×d5 cd 21 ②e5 transposes to note (b) to Black's 14th move.

(d3) 18 ... 買e8 is to be avoided, however, because of 19 買×e8+ 營×e8 20 營f4! with a strong attack, according to Gligoric.

16   a3 *(9)*

An interesting alternative is 16 ②e5, for example 16 ... a4 17 ②×a4

②×a4 18 兔×a4 兔e6 19 兔c2 買e8 20 營d3 g6 (Hjartarson-H. Olafsson, Reykjavik 1987).

16   ...   買e8

16 ... 營d7 is inferior: 17 ②e5 兔×e5 18 買×e5! ±, e.g. 18 ... 買fe8 19 營e2 買ad8 20 買e1 買×e5 21 營×e5 a4 22 營c5! ± Karpov-Belyavsky, CSKA v. Trud, European Team Championship 1986. Belyavsky suggests 18 ... 兔g6!?

17   買×e8+   營×e8
18   營d2   營d7

18 ... ②d7!? 19 營f4!? was seen in Kasparov-Karpov, Leningrad m/22 1986. After 19 ... 兔g6 20 h4 營d8 21 ②a4! h5 22 買e1 b5 23 ②c3 營b8 24 營e3 White held a slight advantage, but 22 ... 營b8!? might be better.

19   買e1   買e8

This is an improvement on 19 ... a4 20 兔a2 買d8 21 營f4 兔g6 22 ②e5! 兔×e5 23 營×e5 ∓ Epishin-Pigusov, Sevastopol 1986.

20   買×e8+   營×e8 *(10)*

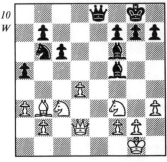

21   營f4   兔e6
22   兔×e6   營×e6
23   營c7

The alternative is 23 營b8+ but

Black seems to equalize on 23 ... ♕c8 24 ♕a7 ♘c4 25 b3 ♘xa3 M. Gurevich–van der Sterren, Baku 1986, or 25 ♕c5 ♕e6 Ftačnik–H. Olafsson, New York Open 1987.

23 ... ♘c4
24 ♕xb7 ♗xd4
25 ♕b8+

25 ♘xd4 is met by 25 ... ♕e1+ 26 ♔h2 ♕e5+ 27 g3 ♕xd4 28 ♕c8+ ♔h7 29 ♕f5+ ½-½ Chernin–M. Gurevich, USSR Ch. 1987.

25 ... ♔h7
26 ♘xd4 ♕e1+
27 ♔h2 ♕xf2
28 ♕c8

and a draw was agreed in H. Olafsson–van der Sterren, Wijk aan Zee 1987.

Variation II:
The Botvinnik System:

1 d4 d5
2 c4 c6
3 ♘f3 ♘f6
4 ♘c3 e6
5 ♗g5 dc
6 e4 b5
7 e5 h6
8 ♗h4 g5 *(11)*

This position has been analyzed for years without a definitive conclusion being reached. Kasparov scored two impressive back-to-back victories in the 1981 USSR Ch. which seemed to bury the line for Black. A couple of years later I (ES) asked him if he thought the line was pretty much out of commission, and he expressed the

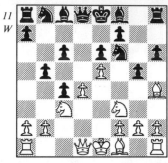

opinion that although he was doing well as White, there was still plenty of uncharted territory to be explored. The 1980s have seen a new wave of explosions in the accepted theory, and the general opinion is still that the variation is unclear. Practical experience, however, has clearly favoured the player of the White pieces.

9 ♘xg5! hg

9 ... ♘d5 is now considered to strongly favour White after 10 ♘xf7! ♔xh4 11 ♘xh8 ♗b4 12 ♖c1! ♕e4+ 13 ♗e2 ♘f4 14 a3 ♘xg2+ 15 ♔f1 ♘e3+ 16 fe ♕xh1+ 17 ♔f2 ♕xh2+ 18 ♔e1 ♗e7 19 ♔d2 ± Timman–Ljubojević, Buenos Aires 1980.

10 ♗xg5 ♘bd7
11 ef ♗b7
12 g3 *(12)* ♕b6

12 ... c5 remains a viable alternative: 13 d5 ♗h6 14 ♗xh6 ♖xh6 15 ♗g2 b4 16 ♘e4 ♘xf6 17 ♘xc5 ♗xd5 18 ♗xd5 ♕xd5 19 ♕xd5 ♘xd5 20 ♖c1 ♖c8 21 ♖xc4 ♘b6 22 ♖c1 led to an equal position in Azmaiparashvili–Dolmatov, USSR Ch. 1986.

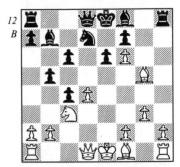

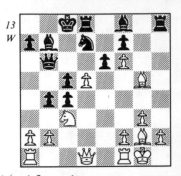

12 ... ♖g8, once a popular line, has disappeared in view of 13 h4 c5 14 d5 ♕b6 15 ♗g2 0-0-0 16 0-0 b4 17 ♘a4 ± Chandler–Westerinen, Wiesbaden 1981.

13 ♗g2   c5

13 ... 0-0-0 14 0-0 ♘e5! is a playable alternative, for example 15 de ♖×d1 16 ♖a×d1 b4 17 ♘e4 ♕a5 18 ♗f4 ♖h5 19 ♖d4 c5 20 ♖c4 and now instead of 20 ... ♗a6? 21 ♖×c5 ♗×c5 22 ♖c1 ± Ermolinsky–Machulsky, USSR 1982, Black should have played 20 ... ♗d5 21 ♖c2 c4 22 ♘d2 c3 with an unclear position according to Machulsky. 15 ♕e2!? might be met by 15 ... ♘d3 16 ♗c3 c5 17 ♗×b7+ ♕×b7 18 dc ♗×c5, since 19 ♗×c5? ♖×h2! wins for Black.

14 d5   0-0-0

Black can try 14 ... b4 15 0-0 bc, where 16 de ♘e5 is unclear, but 15 ... 0-0-0 simply transposes below.

15 0-0   b4 *(13)*

This is the starting point for most of the contemporary analysis of the Botvinnik line.

16 ♘a4   ♕b5

The two alternatives have van-ished from the scene:

(a) 16 ... ♕a6 17 a3! b3 18 ♘c3 ♘b6 19 ♕g4 ♘×d5 20 ♗×d5 ♗×d5 21 ♘×d5 ♖×d5 22 ♖ad1 ♖d3 23 ♕e4! ± Razuvayev–Vaiser, USSR 1981.

(b) 16 ... ♕d6 17 de ♕×e6 18 ♖e1 ♕f5 19 ♗×b7+ ♔×b7 20 ♗f4 ♕×f6 21 ♖e8! ± Agzamov–Timoshchenko, USSR 1982.

17 a3   ed

17 ... ♘b8 was the subject of considerable debate in 1981. In the USSR Ch., both Timoshchenko and Dorfman (later to become Kasparov's seconds) prepared new ideas, and each had a chance to display his wares against Kasparov – in consecutive rounds no less! The move 17 ... ♘b8 had been introduced a few rounds earlier in the game Anikayev–Sveshnikov, which continued 18 ab cb 19 ♗e3! ♗×d5 20 ♗×d5 ♖×d5 21 ♕e2 ♘c6 22 ♖fc1 *(14)*

In this critical position Black has tried a number of moves:

(a) Here Sveshnikov played 22 ... ♔b7 and found himself in difficulty after 23 ♖×c4 ♘a5 24 b3!

14
B

(b) 22 ... c3 is another try, but Rashkovsky–Timoshchenko saw 23 ♕×b5 ♖×b5 24 ♘×c3!! bc 25 ♖×c3 ♔d7 26 ♖a6 ♘d8 27 ♖×a7+ ♔e8 28 ♖c8 ♗d6 where White could have played 29 h4! ♖b8 30 ♖×b8 ♗×b8 31 ♖e7+ ♔f8 32 b4 ±, while Novikov–Ivanchuk, USSR 1983, continued 26 ... ♘e5 27 ♖×a7+ ♔d6 28 ♗f4 ♔d5 29 ♗×e5 ♔×e5 30 ♖×f7 ±

(c) The latest attempt is 22 ... ♘e5 but after 23 ♗×a7 ♗h6 24 ♘b6+ ♔c7 25 ♖e1 ♘d3 26 ♘d5+ ♕×d5 27 ♗e3 ♘×e1 28 ♕×e1 ♗×e3 29 ♕×e3 White had a clear advantage in Salov–Shabalov, Leningrad 1983. Less effective is the path chosen by Kasparov against Tal in the 1983 USSR Spartakiad: 23 b3 c3 24 ♘×c3 bc 25 ♖×c3+ ♔b8 26 ♕c2!? ♗d6 27 ♗×a7+ ♔b7 28 b4 ♘c6 (Black could have played for the draw with 28 ... ♖d3!) 29 ♗e3 ♗e5 with an unclear position.

(d) Our tale concerns 22 ... ♘a5 23 b3 c3! (23 ... ♘×b3 24 ♖×c4+ ♔d7 25 ♘c3! bc 26 ♖×a7+ ♔d8 27 ♖×c3! ±) 24 ♘×c3 bc 25 ♖×c3+

♔d7 26 ♕c2 ♗d6 27 ♖c1 ♕b7 *(15)* 28 b4! ♕×b4! 29 ♖b1 ♕g4.

15
W

We are still not out of the theoretical jungle. Both of Kasparov's games reached this position and he played 30 ♗×a7!! and now the first game, Kasparov–Timoshchenko, concluded 30 ... e5 31 ♕a2! ♖d1+ 32 ♖×d1 ♕×d1+ 33 ♔g2 ♕h5 34 ♕a4+ ♔e6 35 h4! ♕e2 36 ♕×a5 ♖a8 37 ♕a4! ♔×f6 38 ♕d7 ♔g7 39 ♖f3 ♕c4 40 ♕×d6 ♖×a7 41 ♕×e5+ ♔h7 42 ♖f5 ♕c6+ 43 ♔h2 1-0. At the end of the game, the position after 30 ♗×a7 was hotly disputed, with Sveshnikov claiming that 30 ...♗e5 would have given Black a good game. Kasparov was frustrated by his inability to 'defeat' Sveshnikov in the post-mortem and worked until the wee hours of the morning satisfying himself that the line was still good for White. His hard work paid off the next day when the position quickly reappeared on the board in Kasparov–Dorfmann, adopting Sveshnikov's move: 30 ... ♗e5 31 ♖c5! (This was the move that had

escaped the notice of the kibitzers
at the post-mortem!) 31 ... 鼉×c5
(31 ... 鼉a8 32 鼉×a5! 鼉×a5 33
鼉b7+ 當e8 34 鼉e7+ 當f8 35 營h7
±±) 32 奧×c5! 公c6 33 營d3+ 當c8
34 鼉d1 公b8 (34 ... 鼉d8 35 營a6+)
35 鼉c1! 營a4 36 奧d6+ 公c6 37
奧×e5 鼉d8 38 營b1! 鼉d5 39 營b8+
當d7 40 營c7+ 當e8 41 營×c6+
營×c6 42 鼉×c6 鼉×e5 43 鼉c8+ 1-0.
These two games have
discouraged Black from playing 17
... 公b8.

| 18 | ab | cb |
| 19 | 營g4 | |

White can also play 19 奧e3,
with an unclear position arising on
19 ... 公c5 20 公×c5 奧×c5 20 營g4
當b8 Kharitonov–Dorfman, USSR
1982, but we feel that the immediate pin is stronger.

19	...	d4
20	奧×b7+	當×b7
21	營e4+	營c6
24	營×d4	奧d6
23	鼉fe1	鼉de8
24	鼉×e8	鼉×e8
25	奧e3	奧b8

This position was reached in
Zarubin–Andrianov, USSR 1982.
The position is still quite complicated and the chances are
roughly level. Further developments can be expected.

Variation III:
The Tolush Gambit

| 1 | d4 | d5 |
| 2 | c4 | c6 |

This can also be reached via the
Queen's Gambit Accepted: 2 ... dc

3 公f3 公f6 4 公c3 c6.

3	公f3	公f6
4	公c3	dc
5	e4 *(16)*	

This gambit continuation has a
long history. It earned respect as a
serious weapon in the hands of
Soviet players in the early post-
war years. The first critical encounter was Tolush–Smyslov,
USSR Ch. 1947. Efim Geller was
the leading proponent of the line
for many years, scoring many impressive victories including a gem
of a win against Unzicker (the
complete game is included
below). Gary Kasparov was
responsible for the great renais-
sance in interest in this gambit
continuation in the early 1980s.
The state of the theory was both
described and considerably en-
hanced by the American theoretician IM John Watson in his 1985
book *4 公c3 Gambit in the Queen's
Gambit Accepted & Slav*. The 1987
edition of *ECO* contains no
improvements and merely cites a
few of his ideas and a couple of
more recent games. In this section

we critically examine both the existing theory and Watson's contributions.

5   ...   b5

Black must accept the gambit, as to decline will allow White to achieve an ideal centre and a great lead in development without any balancing considerations for Black.

6   e5   ♘d5
7   a4!

White must increase the pressure at every turn or he will fail to reap sufficient rewards for his investment. By this move White prepares to exchange at b5, opening up the long diagonal which will be exploited by his queen and light-squared bishop.

7   ...   e6 *(17)*

There are a host of alternatives, but they do not lead to a playable game for Black.

(a) 7 ... b4? 8 ♘e4 weakens the ♗c4 and increases White's control of the centre. After 8 ... e6 9 ♗xc4 ♘d7 10 0-0 ♗b7 11 ♘fg5 ♘7b6 12 ♗d3 a5 13 ♕h5 ♕d7 14 ♘c5 White was much better in Bondarevsky-Kalantar, USSR 1947.

(b) 7 ... ♗b7? 8 e6! forces 8 ... f6 (8 ... fe 9 ♘g5 ±) and then White clamps down on the light squares with 9 g3 ♕d6 10 ♗h3 ♘a6 11 0-0 ± Najdorf–Ojanen, Helsinki 1952.

(c) 7 ... ♗e6 is best met by Taimanov's 8 ♘g5! ♘xc3 9 bc ♗d5 (9 ... ♕d7 10 ab cb 11 ♘xe6 ♕xe6 12 ♕f3 ♘c6 13 ♖a6 ♖c8 14 ♗e2 ±) 10 e6! fe 11 ♗f4 or Watson's 11

♕g4.

(d) 7 ... ♘xc3 8 bc h6 (8 ... ♗e6 9 ♘g5 see above (c)) 9 g3 ♗e6 10 ♗g2 ♗d5 11 ♗a3! e6 12 ♗xf8 ♔xf8 13 0-0 △ ♘h4, f4-f5 − Watson.

(e) 7 ... h6 is a new move which led to an unclear position in Ermolinsky–Kupreichik, Kuibyshev 1986: 8 ab ♘xc3 9 bc cb 10 ♗a3 (10 ♗e2!? − *ECO*) 10 ... ♗e6 11 ♗e2 ♘c6 12 0-0 ♗d5 13 ♘d2 a5 14 ♗f3 ♖b8 (14 ... e6 is a playable alternative) 15 e6! g6 16 ♗e4 (16 ♖e1!? − *ECO*) 16 ... ♗xe4 17 ♘xe4 ♕d5 18 ef+ ♔xf7 19 ♖e1 ♔g7 20 ♘c5 b4 21 ♘e6+ ♔h7 22 ♗b2 ♗g7 23 ♕g4 ♖b5.

(f) 7 ... ♗f5 8 ab ♘b4! (8 ... ♘xc3? 9 bc cb 10 ♘g5! (△ ♕f3) 10 ... e6 11 g4! ♗g6 12 ♗g2 ♘d7 13 f4! ♗e7 14 ♕f3 0-0 15 h4 ♗d3 16 f5! ± Inkiov–Padevsky, Pamporovo 1982) 9 ♗xc4 ♘c2+ 10 ♔e2 ♘xa1 11 ♕a4 gives White full compensation, according to Lilienthal. Although White has a large material deficit, he has a strong attack, as shown by Watson. It would be impolite, to say the least, to replicate all of his analysis here, as none of it has been played, but his main lines run:

(f1) 11 ... ♗d7 12 e6 fe 13 ♘e5 cb 14 ♗xb5 a6! 15 ♗xd7+ ♘xd7 16 ♖d1! ♘b3! 17 ♗e3!? or 17 ♕xb3 ♘xe5 18 de.

(f2) 11 ... ♘d7 12 ♕xa1! ♘b6 13 ♗b3 cb 14 ♘xb5 and if 14 ... e6? 15 ♗a4! or 14 ... a6 15 ♘c3 e6 16 ♖d1! followed by d5.

initiative.) 23 ♗×c6! ♖×c6 24 d5! ♕×d5 25 ♕b8+ ♕d8 26 ♕b5. It is worth mentioning that *ECO* fails to note 14 ♘e4, despite liberally quoting Watson in the coverage of the line.

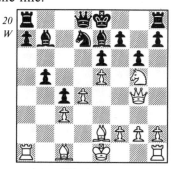

14   ♖b1!

Watson's discovery, motivated by the fact that 14 ♗f3, the normal move, may have difficulty against Geller's 14 ... ♕c8! The most recent example is Rogers–Kostić, Kraljevo 1984: 15 h4 (another Geller suggestion) 15 ... h5 16 ♕f4 ♗×g5 17 hg ♗×f3 18 ♕×f3 ♘b6 19 ♖h4 ♖g8 20 d5 ♘×d5 21 ♗a3 ♕a6 22 ♖f4 ♖g7, and White does not have sufficient compensation for his material. 16 ♕g3!? is also possible, although 16 ... a5 seems an adequate reply.

The game Geller–Unzicker, Stockholm IZ 1952 saw 14 ... ♕c7, originally suggested by Flohr. 15 ♘e4 ♘b6 16 ♗h6 ♖g8?! 17 ♗g5 ♗×e4 18 ♗×e4 ♘d5 19 ♗×d5 ed 20 ♗×e7 ♕×e7 21 0-0 ♔f8 22 ♖fb1 a6 23 ♕f3! ♕e6?! (23 ... ♔g7 ±) 24 ♕f6! ♕c8 25 f4 ♕b7 26 ♖a5 ♔e8 27 ♖ba1 b4 28 cb ♕×b4 29 ♖×d5

♕b7 30 e6 1-0.

14   ...   ♗c6

14 ... ♗×g5 15 ♗×g5 ♕a5 16 0-0 ♗d5 17 ♗f3! ♘b6!? 18 ♕f4 ± Watson–Orton, San Jose 1984. But the simple 14 ... a6 deserves attention. e.g. 15 ♗×c4 ♕c8 16 ♗b3 ♕×c3+ 17 ♗d2 ♕d3 ∓, or 16 ♗×e6 fe 17 ♕×e6 ♖f8 ∞.

15   ♗f3   ♕c8
16   0-0 *(21)*

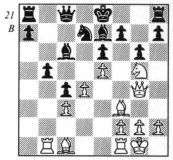

This is the critical position to which Watson devotes two full pages of analysis in his book.

16   ...   a6

This seems to be the best of the lot:

(a) 16 ... ♘b6? 17 ♘e4 ♗×e4 18 ♗×e4 ± Watson.

(b) 16 ... h5?! 17 ♕h3 ♘b6 18 ♘e4 ♘d5 19 ♗g5! Watson.

(c) 16 ... a5 17 ♖e1 0-0!?, but not 17 ... ♘b6? 18 ♘e4! Watson.

(d) 16 ... 0-0 17 ♖e1 a5 18 d5! ed was seen in Watson–Bohn, Rohnert Park 1985. Here 18 ♘×f7!? would have been the best try (Watson)

17   ♖e1

Control of e4 is the most

important factor and the source of White's compensation. The rook on the e-file assists in this cause and also sets up the central break d4-d5 at a later point.

17   ...   0-0

17 ... ♘b6 18 ♗×c6 ♕×c6 19 ♘e4 gives White sufficient compensation for his pawn.

18   d5

Watson also gives 18 ♕h3!? as an interesting alternative.

18   ...   ed

18 ... ♗×d5 19 ♗×d5 ed gains control of e4 for Black, but allows 20 ♘×f7!? ♘c5! 21 e6 ♘e4 22 ♗h6 'with attack' (Watson)

19   ♘×f7!   ♖×f7

19 ... ♘c5 20 e6 is good for White, because of the weak dark squares on the Black kingside.

20   e6

White has more than sufficient compensation for his pawn, for example 20 ... ♖g7 21 ed ♗×d7 22 ♗×d5+ ♔h8 23 ♕d4 ♗c5 24 ♕h4 ♖a7 25 ♗h6 (Watson)

2   The Catalan

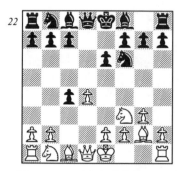

Kasparov adopted this opening for his match against Korchnoi during a period where Icelandic IM (now GM) Margeir Petursson was its leading exponent and when the literature on the opening included only an old book by Neishtadt and a small monograph in English by co-author Schiller. He retained the opening for occasional use against Karpov. Current recommended literature includes books by Neishtadt (1986), Moiseyev & Ravinsky (1984) and Schiller (1986, 1988).

Before the Korchnoi match he had used the opening only once as White − against Andersson at Nikšic 1983 − and even then he claims that he was quite sure of the defensive system Andersson would choose. It was an interesting choice, since Korchnoi was a known expert in handling the White side of the opening, and it would certainly come as a surprise. But perhaps there was an additional appeal, in that Kasparov had only recently abandoned the King's Indian as Black and might have felt some comfort in fianchettoing his bishop.

Kasparov adopted the Catalan in his marathon 1984–5 match against Karpov, and later in the 1985 match against Ulf Andersson, he brought new life to the Catalan by adopting a new move order.

We examine four variations:

Variation I: 5 ... c5
Variation II: 5 ... ♗d7
Variation III: 5 ... ♗e7 6 0-0
Variation IV: 5 ... ♗e7 6 ♕c2

Variation I:

1	d4	♘f6
2	c4	e6
3	g3	d5
4	♗g2	dc
5	♘f3	c5

In the 9th game of the match against Korchnoi, Black played 5 ... ♘bd7 6 0-0 ♖b8?!, but after 7 a4 b6 8 ♘fd2! White had already secured an advantage.

| 6 | 0-0 | ♘c6 |

In Kasparov's first Catalan

Kasparov–Korchnoi, (m/5) 1983, his opponent tried 6 ... ♘bd7, but after 7 ♘a3 ♘b6 8 ♘xc4 ♘xc4 9 ♕a4+ ♗d7 10 ♕xc4 b5 11 ♕c2 ♖c8 12 dc ♗xc5 13 ♕b3 0-0 14 ♘e5 ♕b6 15 ♗g5 ♖fd8 16 ♕f3 ♗e7 !? ♘xd7 ♖xd7 Kasparov could have obtained a significant advantage with 18 ♖fc1!, instead of 18 ♖ac1 as played in the game.

7 ♕a4

In the 1985 match against Andersson, Kasparov obtained a small advantage with 7 ♘e5 ♗d7 8 ♘a3 and now:

(a) 8 ... cd 9 ♘axc4 ♖c8 10 ♕b3 ♘xe5 11 ♘xe5 Kasparov–Andersson (m/1) 1985.

(b) 8 ... ♘d5 9 ♘axc4 cd 10 ♘xc6 ♗xc6 11 ♕xd4 ♘b4 12 ♗xc6+ ♗xc6 13 ♕c3!, Kasparov–Andersson (m/3) 1985.

7 ... cd!? (23)

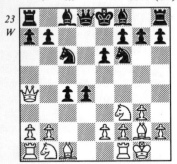

Kasparov has no fear of the wild complications introduced by this move. 7 ... ♗d7 is a calmer alternative.

8 ♘xd4! ♕xd4

Black has no choice. After 8 ... ♗d7 9 ♘xc6:

(a) 9 ... ♗xc6? 10 ♗xc6+ bc 11 ♕xc6+ ♘d7 12 ♕xc4 ♘b6 13 ♕c6+ ++ Toran–Miagmasuren, Lugano Ol 1968.

(b) 9 ... ♕b6 10 ♘d2 ♗xc6 11 ♗xc6+ bc 12 ♘xc4 ♕b5 13 ♕c2 ♗e7 14 b3 ± Cobo–Vasquez, Skopje Ol 1972.

9 ♗xc6+ ♗d7

Not 9 ... bc?! 10 ♕xc6+ ♕d7 11 ♕xa8 ♗c5 11 ♘c3 ± Christiansen–Lhagva, Lucerne Ol 1982.

10 ♖d1 ♕xd1+

Black is virtually forced to give up his queen, since 10 ... ♗xc6 11 ♕xc6+ bc 12 ♖xd4 does not give Black sufficient compensation for his material:

(a) 12 ... c5 13 ♖xc4 and now:

(a1) 13 ... ♗d6 14 ♘d2 ♔d7 15 b3 ± Kavalek–Radulov, Montilla 1974.

(a2) 13 ... 0-0-0 14 ♘c3 ♘d5 15 ♘e4 ♘b6 16 ♖c2 ♖d1+ 17 ♔g2 f6 18 ♘xc5 ♗xc5 19 ♖xc5+ ♔b7 20 b3 ± Szymczak–Franzen, Poland 1979.

(b) 12 ... ♘d5 13 ♖xc4 ♔d7 14 b3 ♗d6 15 ♗b2 f6 16 ♘d2 a5 17 ♘e4 ♗e7 18 ♗d4 ± Vuković–Nikolov, Mezdra 1984.

(c) 12 ... ♖d8 13 ♖xc4 ♖d1+ 14 ♔g2 ♔d7 15 ♘c3 ± Pomar–Palacios, Malaga 1965.

11 ♕xd1 ♗xc6 (24)

Black has ♖, ♗ and ♙ for his queen, but the game is just beginning!

12 ♘d2

12 ♕c2 can be adequately met by 12 ... h5!

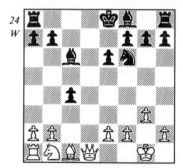

The text, an idea of Tukmakov later worked on by Gutman, is the most popular move, and is favoured by Kasparov. There are two common replies:

A   12 ... b5
B   12 ... c3

A

12   **...**   **b5**
13   **a4** *(25)*

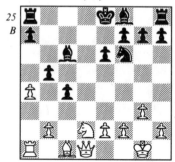

13   **...**   **♗e7**

13 ... a6 14 ab ♗×b5 ±, but not 14 ... ab 15 ♖×a8+ ♗×a8 16 ♘×c4 ±.

14   **ab**   **♗×b5**
15   **♘×c4**   **0-0**

Not 15 ... ♗×c4? 16 ♕a4+.

16   **b3**   **♖fd8**
17   **♕c2** ±

Kasparov–Andersson, Niksić 1983. White's small advantage is not easy to exploit. Indeed, Kasparov failed to do so and wound up with a half-point for his efforts: 17 ... ♖dc8 18 ♗a3 ♗×a3 19 ♖×a3 h6 20 ♕c3 ♗×c4 21 bc ♖c7 22 ♕d4 ♖ac8 23 ♖a4 ♖d7 24 ♕a1 ♖dc7 25 ♕a2 ♘e4 26 ♖×a7 ♖×c4 27 ♕b2 ♘f6 28 ♕b7 ♖f8 29 f3 ♖d4 30 ♕e7 ♖dd8 31 ♔f2 ♖a8 32 e4 ♖×a7 33 ♕×a7 e5 ½–½.

B

12   **c3!?** *(26)*

This is the primary alternative.

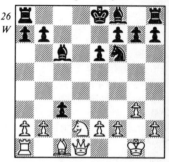

Black gives up the pawn without a fight, and loses time into the bargain. But there is a definite advantage to this move — it breaks up the White queenside pawns and creates a useful target for Black's operations.

13   **bc**

Is this obvious move necessary? Neishtadt (1986) points out that after 13 ♘f3 ♖d8 14 ♕b3 cb 15 ♗×b2 White stands better.

13   **...**   **0-0-0**

13 ... ♖d8 14 ♕b3 ♗c5 15 ♘f3 ♘e4 16 ♘d4 ♗d5 17 ♕b5+ ♖d7 18

♗e3 ± Neishtadt (1986).

    14   ♕b3   ♗c5
    15   ♘f3!

This new move improves on 15 h3 which gave White a microscopic advantage in Gutman-Kraidman, Ramat Hasharon 1980.

    15   ...   ♘e4
    16   ♘d4   ♖×d4

It seems that there is nothing better. Helgi Olafsson gives

    (a) 16 ... ♗d5 17 ♕c2 e5 18 ♗e3! ±.

    (b) 16 ... ♗×d4 17 cd ♖×d4 18 ♗b2 or 18 ♗e3 ±.

    (c) 16 ... e5 17 ♘×c6 ♗×f2+ 18 ♔g2 bc 19 ♕a4 ++.

    17   cd   ♗×d4
    18   ♖b1   ♗×f2+
    19   ♔f1   h5

19 ... ♖d8 20 ♕c2! ♖d5 21 ♖b3 ±.

    20   ♗e3 ±

Hjartarson–Hardarson, Neskaupsstadt 1984 saw further 20 ... h4 21 g4 ♗g3 22 ♖c1 ♗×h2 23 ♖×c6+ bc 24 ♕a4 ++.

Variation II:

    1   d4   ♘f6
    2   c4   e6
    3   g3   d5
    4   ♗g2   dc
    5   ♘f3   ♗d7 *(27)*

Black's fifth move was introduced in the 7th game of the Kasparov-Korchnoi Candidates match, London 1983. In the press room Miguel Najdorf immediately asserted that he had played it sometime in the middle of the present century.

    6   ♕c2   c5

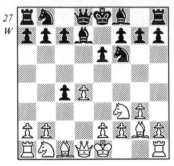

Parma considered this position unclear in *New in Chess*.

6 ... ♗c6 is also possible, and transposes to more familiar lines where White obtains only a minimal advantage.

    7   0-0

7 ♕×c4 ♗c6 8 dc ♘bd7 9 ♗g5 ♗d5 10 ♕b5 was equal in Sosonko-Karpov, Wijk aan Zee 1988, while 8 0-0 ♘bd7 transposes below.

An interesting alternative is 7 ♘e5, e.g. 7 ... ♘c6 8 ♘×c6 ♗×c6 9 ♗×c6+ bc 10 dc ♗×c5 11 0-0 ♕d4 12 ♘c3 ∞, Vaganian–Portisch, St. John (m/6) 1988.

    7   ...   ♗c6
    8   ♕×c4

This position also arises from the move order 4 ... dc 5 ♘f3 c5 6 ♕a4+ ♗d7 7 ♕×a4 ♗c6 8 0-0.

    8   ...   ♘bd7

8 ... ♗d5 9 ♕d3 ♗e4 10 ♕d1 ♘c6 11 dc ♗×c5 12 ♘c3 ± Neishtadt (1986). Kasparov remarks that Black can already be satisfied with his position.

    9   ♗g5   ♖c8

Neishtadt (1986) recommends

9 ... cd (actually Kasparov's suggestion) 10 ♘×d4 ♗×g2 11 ♔×g2 ♗e7 12 ♖d1 0-0 13 ♘c3 ♖c8 14 ♕a4 ♕b6, as in Opočensky–Prukha, CSSR 1945, where 'White can hardly count on an advantage'.

10 ♗×f6 *(28)*

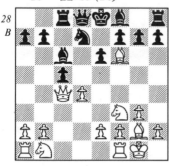

10 ... ♘×f6

Kasparov considers this dubious. There are two other ways to recapture:

(a) 10 ... ♕×f6 11 ♘c3 is better for White, for example 11 ... ♗e7 12 e4 0-0 13 d5 ±.

(b) 10 ... gf! 11 dc (Spiridonov) 11 ... ♗×c5 12 ♕h4 is unclear, but 11 ♘c3 b5 12 ♕d3 c4 13 ♕c2 b4 is no more clear, Inkiov–Pinter, Zagreb IZ 1987.

11 dc ♗×f3

11 ... b5 12 cb ♗×f3 13 ♕a4+! Neishtadt (1986).

Gligoric and Krogius suggest 11 ... ♕d5 12 ♕×d5 ♘×d5 13 ♘e5 ♗×c5 14 ♘×c6 bc (14 ... ♖×c6? 15 ♘c3), but Neishtadt (1986) points out that White is better in the endgame after 15 ♘d2.

12 ♗×f3 ♗×c5 *(29)*

Keene's comment in this pos-

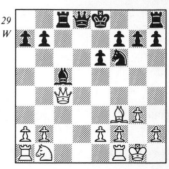

ition is appropriate: 'Strategically, Black has accomplished everything which he should, in theory, strive for in the Catalan. First of all, he has liquidated the central pawns, then he has achieved near parity in development and finally he has established an opposite bishop situation, which normally facilitates a drawn outcome. The only problem he faces is the slight exposure of his b7 pawn to White's kings's bishop operating along the a8–h1 diagonal'. Kasparov lost no time in exploiting his single resource.

13 ♕b5+ ♕d7
14 ♘c3 ♕×b5

14 ... 0-0 15 ♕×b7 ♕×b7 16 ♗×b7 ♖b8 17 ♗a6! △ 17 ... ♖×b2 18 ♘a4 ♖c2 19 ♗d3 Kasparov.

15 ♘×b5 ♔e7
16 b4!! ♗×b4
17 ♘×a7 ±

Korchnoi now should have settled for an uncomfortable position after 17 ... ♖a8 18 ♖fb1 ♖×a7 19 ♖×b4 ♖b8 20 a4, but instead chose 17 ... ♖c7, and after 18 ♖fc1 ♖d7 19 ♖ab1 ♗d2 20 ♖c2 ♖hd8

21 ♗×b7 Black's rooks were falling all over each other (Kasparov).

Against Karpov, Kasparov finally had an opportunity to explore the main lines of the opening.

Variation III

1	d4	♘f6
2	c4	e6
3	g3	d5
4	♗g2	dc
5	♘f3	♗e7
6	0-0	0-0
7	♕c2	a6
8	♕×c4	b5
9	♕c2	♗b7
10	♗d2	♗e4

Four years later Karpov tried 10 ... ♘c6?!, but after 11 e3 ♘b4 12 ♗×b4 ♗×b4 13 a3 ♗d6 14 ♘bd2 ♖c8 15 b4! White was clearly better (Belyavsky–Karpov, Brussels 1988).

11	♕c1	♗b7

Black invites a repetition of the position after 12 ♕c2 ♗e4 13 ♕c1 ♗b7 etc. Alternatively, he can try 11 ... ♘bd7, e.g. 12 ♗a5 ♖c8 with unclear complications in Belyavsky–Vaganian, Brussels 1988 or 11 ... ♘c6 12 ♗e3 ♘b4 12 ♘bd2 Korchnoi–Kasparov, London (m/4) 1983 where White might be able to obtain a small advantage with 14 ♘b3!?

12	♗e3	

Probably best, although 12 a3!? is worth trying.

12	...	♘d5

12 ... ♘bd7 13 ♘bd2 a5 14 ♘b3 a4 15 ♘c5 ±.

13	♘c3	♘d7

13 ... ♘×e3 14 ♕×e3 leaves White with control of the central files.

14	♖d1	

14 ♘×d5 ♗×d5 15 ♘e1 (Yusupov). After 15 ... ♗×g2 White can choose between the quiet 16 ♔×g2 c5 = and 16 ♘×g2 ♖c8 17 ♕c6 ♘b6 which is unclear.

14	...	♖c8
15	♘e5	

Dorfman's suggested improvement on 15 ♘×d5 ♗×d5 16 ♘e1 c6! 17 ♘d3 ♕b6 = Kasparov–Karpov (m/8), 1984.

15	...	♘×c3

If 15 ... ♘×e3 16 ♗×b7 ♘×d1 17 ♘c6 ♘×c3 18 ♕×c3 ♕e8 19 ♗×c8 ♘c5 20 ♘×e7 ♕×e7 21 ♕×c5 White is much better (Shamkovich).

16	♕×c3	♗×g2
17	♘×d7!	

If 17 ♔×g2, then 17 ... ♘×e5 18 de ♕e8 brings equality.

17	...	♕×d7
18	♔×g2 ±	

Analysis by Josef Dorfman.

Variation IV

1	d4	♘f6
2	c4	e6
3	g3	d5
4	♗g2	♗e7
5	♘f3	0-0
6	♕c2 *(30)*	

This system enjoyed a surge in popularity in 1985–1986.

A   6 ... dc

B   6 ... ♘c6

7 0-0 &b4
8 &d1 (31)

8 &b3!? dc 9 &×c4 &d5 10 &×c7 &d6! 11 &c3 &×a2 12 &d2 ∞, Sveshnikov-Klovans, Pinsk 1986.

C 6 ... b6
D 6 ... c5

6 ... &bd7 7 0-0 transposes to the Closed System of the Catalan.

A

6	...	dc
7	&×c4	a6
8	&f4!	

This is the only plan which will secure an advantage for White.

8	...	&d5
9	&c3	b5

9 ... &×f4 10 gf &d6 11 e3 &d7 12 0-0 &b6 13 &b3 f5 14 &ac1 c6 15 &a4 &×a4 16 &×a4 &d7 17 &b3 &e7 18 &e5 ±, Adamski-Velimirović, Bela Crkva 1984.

10	&d3	&×f4

10 ... &b7 11 &×d5 &×d5 12 0-0 &d7 13 &fd1 c5 14 e4 &b7 15 d5 ed 16 ed &f6 17 &c2 &e8 18 h4 h6 19 &d2 ±, Dorfman-Bönsch, GDR 1984.

11	gf	&a7

11 ... &b7 12 &e4 &d7 13 &fg5!? g6 14 h4–Ribli.

12	&e4! ±	

Analysis by Zoltan Ribli.

B

6	...	&c6

8 ... dc 9 &a3! ±, Gavrikov-Speelman, London 1985. The players agreed a draw here.

9	a3	&a6
10	cd	&×d5
11	&c3	&ac7
12	&×d5	&×d5
13	dc	&×c5
14	e4	

14 &e5!? is suggested by Vilala.

14	...	&b6
15	&c2 ±	

Vera-Vilala, Cuban Ch. 1985.

C

6	...	b6
7	cd	ed
8	&a3	

A reasonable alternative is 8 &c3 &b7 9 &e5 ±.

Now if Black plays 8 ... &b7, then after 9 0-0 White stands better. Black should therefore try to put pressure on the centre immediately.

| 8 | ... | c5 |
| 9 | 0-0 | ♘c6! *(32)* |

Black should again avoid the simple 9 ... ♗b7, as after 10 ♖d1! White is better, according to Razuvayev.

10 ♗f4

Razuvayev suggests two alternatives, 10 ♖d1 and 10 ♗e3.

10	...	♗b7
11	dc	bc
12	♘e5	♘×e5
13	♗×e5 =	

Razuvayev-Vaganian, Sochi 1986.

D

| 6 | ... | c5 |
| 7 | 0-0 | cd |

7 ... ♘c6!? 8 cd (8 dc d4!? ∞) 8 ... ♘×d4 9 ♘×d4 cd 10 de ♗×e6! 11 ♗×b7 ♖b8 12 ♗g2 ♕b6 ⩱ Kengis.

8 ♘×d4 ♘c6

(a) Not good is 8 ... ♘a6 9 cd ♘×d5 10 ♖d1 ♘db4 11 ♕b3 ♕b6 12 ♗e3 ♘c5 13 ♕c4 ♘d5 14 ♘f5! ef 15 ♗×d5 ±, Kurajica-Groszpeter, Oberwart 1984.

(b) 8 ... ♕b6 is an interesting alternative, for example 9 ♖d1 ♘c6 (9 ... ♗c5!?) 10 ♘×c6 bc 11

♘c3 ♕a6 12 ♘a4 ♖b8 13 b3 and now:

(b1) 13 ... e5 14 ♗g5 dc 15 ♘b2 ⩱ Gulko-Georgadze, Tashkent 1984.

(b2) 13 ... dc 14 ♗f4 ♖b4 15 ♗d2 cb 16 ab ♖d4 ∞ Georgadze.

| 9 | ♘×c6 | bc |
| 10 | b3 *(33)* | |

This position has been heavily discussed lately.

10 ... a5

There are several alternatives:

(a) 10 ... e5 11 ♗b2 ♗d6 was seen in Dautov-Pigusov, USSR 1986. Now Dautov gives 12 ♘c3!? ♗b7 13 ♖fd1 ♖c8 14 e3 ♕e7 15 cd cd 16 ♕e2 e4 ±.

(b) 10 ... ♗b7 11 ♗b2 ♕a5 12 ♘c3 ♖fd8 13 e3 intending ♖fd1 – Ribli. This is better than 13 ♘a4 ♘d7 14 ♖fe1 ♖ac8 15 e3 ♘b6 = Korchnoi-Lengyel, Havana Ol. 1966.

(c) 10 ... ♗b4 is the latest word, from Tukmakov-Belyavsky, USSR Ch. 1987: 11 ♗b2 ♕e7 12 a3 ♗d6 13 ♘c3 ♗b7 14 ♖fd1 ♖ac8 14 e4 dc 16 bc e5 17 ♘a4 ♖cd8 18 ♖d3 ♗c7 19 ♖ad1 ½- ½.

11 ♗b2

The bishop does not have to be developed in this direction. Kurajca–van der Sterren, Thessaloniki Ol, 1984 saw instead 11 ♘c3 ♗a6 12 ♘a4 ♖c8 13 ♖d1 ♕c7 14 ♗e3 c5 15 cd ♘xd5 16 ♗xd5! ed 17 ♖ac1 ♖fe8 18 ♕d2 ♕a7 19 ♕xd5 ±

11 ... ♗a6

11 ... a4!? is interesting, for example 12 ♘d2 a3 13 ♗d4 dc! 14 e3 cb 15 ♘xb3 ⩱ Kengis.

12 ♘d2 ♘d7
13 ♖fd1 ♖c8
14 ♘f3 ♗f6
15 ♖ac1

15 ... ♕e7?! 16 ♗xf6 ±, H. Olafsson–Geller, Reykjavik 1986. After the game Geller, who was involved in a lot of heavy theory in this event, suggested 15 ... ♗xb2 16 ♕xb2 ♕b6. Word spread quickly, and in Kengis–Klovan, USSR 1987 this variation was put to the test.

15 ... ♗xb2
16 ♕xb2 ♕b6
17 e4 ♘c5

17 ... ♗xc4 18 ♖xc4 dc 19 ♖xd7 ♖fd8 20 ♖xd8+ ♖xd8 21 ♕c2 ± Kengis.

18 ♕d4! dc

White now should have played 19 bc, with good prospects, instead of 19 ♘e5?!

Kasparov seems to have set aside the Catalan for the time being, but it may be that he feels it is not the appropriate weapon against Karpov. As the return to the three-year cycle gives him more time to play in tournaments, we may see its return.

3 Hybrid Nimzo-Queen's Indian

34
B

Kasparov adopted this opening for his 1985 KRO match against Timman in Hilversum.

1	d4	♘f6
2	c4	e6
3	♘f3	b6
4	♘c3	♗b4

If Black chooses 4 ... ♗b7 then he is back in the main lines of the Queen's Indian Defence, but is unable to exercise the same number of options. For example, if 5 a3, then the Petrosian System cannot be sidestepped as in the case of 4 a3, where 4 ... a6 and 4 ... c5 are available.

But White need not enter the theoretical frying pan with 5 a3. He can instead opt for less charted waters, for example Korchnoi's 5 ♗f4, which has not had sufficient tests. Two examples:

(a) 5 ... ♗b4 6 ♕b3! a5?! (6 ... c5 is stronger.) 7 e3 ♘e4 (7 ... d6 8 ♗e2 ♘e4 9 0-0 ♗xc3 10 bc has been played, but Black will have to improve on 10 ... g5 11 ♗xg5! ♘xg5 12 ♕b5+ ♘d7 13 ♕xg5 ♕xg5 14 ♘xg5 ♗xg2 15 ♔xg2 ± Korchnoi–Tarjan, Lone Pine 1981.) 8 ♗d3 ♘xc3?! (8 ... ♗xc3+ 9 bc d6 is recommended by Ribli and Kallai, although it is by no means clear that their suggested plan of 10 ... 0-0, 11 ... ♘bd7 and 12 ... f5 will bring about full equality.) 9 bc ♗e7 10 e4! ± Korchnoi–Hübner, (m/10), Merano 1980/81.

(b) 5 ... ♗e7 (A bit passive, but possibly more accurate.) 6 ♕c2!? ♘h5? (Black overreacts to the threat of e2–e4. The bishop retreats to a reasonably useful post while the knight is left dangling.) 7 ♗d2 d5 8 cd ed 9 g3 0-0 10 ♗g2 ♘f6 11 0-0 and White was clearly better, since as in some lines of the Catalan the ♗b7 is blocked in by its own pawn, which has no way of releasing the diagonal. This means that the d5–pawn will be under pressure for a long time. If Black advances ... c7–c5, then White can also develop pressure along the c-file.

5	♗g5	♗b7
6	e3	h6

Black is committing himself to an expansion of the kingside which will weaken the area surrounding his king. In return, he will achieve a powerful outpost for his knight at e4. A lively game is virtually guaranteed!

In the United States, 6 ... ♗×c3+ 7 bc d6 has been seen, trying to avoid the weakening effect of the kingside pawn advances.

7   ♗h4 *(35)*

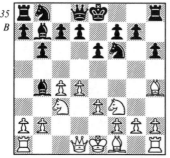

Here we examine two lines:
  I 7 ... ♗×c3
  II 7 ... g5!

I

| 7 | ... | ♗×c3+ |
| 8 | bc | d6 |

This is an alternative which pits the classical central control on White's part against the hypermodern flexibility of Black's pieces. It was seen in the 18th Game of Kasparov–Karpov III which we follow here.

9   ♘d2   g5

9 ... e5 10 f3 ♕e7 11 e4 ♘bd7 12 ♗d3 ♘f8 13 c5 ±, Tal–Hecht, Varna Ol 1962, or 9 ... ♘bd7 10 a4!?

a5 11 ♖b1 0-0 12 ♗d3 ♕e8 (12 ... ♗×g2?! 13 ♖g1 gives White a strong attack.) 13 0-0 e5 14 e4 ± Toshkov–Kosten, Yurmala 1987.

10   ♗g3 *(36)*

10   ...   ♕e7!?

10 ... ♘bd7 is a more logical plan which brought Black at least equality in Miles–Sokolov, Bugojno 1987, after 11 h4 ♖g8 12 hg hg 13 ♕c2 ♕e7 14 e4 0-0-0 15 ♗e2 e5. Better is 11 f3 ♘h5 12 ♗f2 f5 13 ♗d3 ♕f6 14 ♕a4! ♕g7 15 0-0-0 0-0 16 h3 ± Miles–Seirawan, Sarajevo 1987.

11   a4

The promising sacrifical line 11 h4 ♖g8 12 hg hg 13 ♗e2!? ♗×g2 14 ♖h6! g4 15 ♗h4 was successful for White in Bareyev–Dolmatov, USSR Ch. 1987.

11   ...   a5

11 ... ♘c6 12 ♘b3 ♘e4 13 ♗d3 ♘×g3 14 hg is better for White, according to Kasparov.

12	h4	♖g8
13	hg	hg
14	♕b3!	♘a6
15	♖b1!	♔f8
16	♕d1	

White already holds a clear advantage.

16	...	♗c6
17	♖h2	♚g7
18	c5!	bc
19	♗b5	♘b8
20	dc	d5
21	♗e5	♚f8
22	♖h6	♘e8

Here Kasparov erred with ...

23   ♕h5?

23 c4! would have been quite strong. Kasparov gives the line 23 ... ♗×b5 24 cb ♘d7 25 ♗b2 ♘×c5 26 ♕c2 where White's positional superiority is far more convincing than Black's pawn. The opening battle is now over, and we present the rest of the game in abbreviated form.

23 ... f6 24 ♖h7 ♘g7?

Karpov should have settled for 24 ... ♖g7 25 ♕h6 ♗×b5 26 ab ♘d7, with a probable draw.

25 ♕f3 ♚f7 26 ♕h5+ ♚f8 27 ♕f3 ♚f7 28 ♖h6 ♘e8 29 e4 g4 30 ♕f4 ♗×b5 31 ♖×b5 ♘d7 32 ♗×c7 ♘×c5 33 ♕e3 ♘×e4?

33 ... ♘×c7 34 ♖×c5 ±.

34 ♘×e4 de 35 ♗×a5 f5 36 ♗b4 ♕d7 37 ♕d4! ♖a7 38 ♖h7+?

Time trouble. 38 ♕e5! would have been devasting.

38 ... ♘g7 39 a5?? ♚g6?

39 ... ♕×b5! ∓.

40 ♕×d7 ♖×d7 41 ♖h4 ♖gd8 42 c4 ♖d1+ 43 ♚e2 ♖c1!? 44 a6?? ♖c2+! 45 ♚e1 ♖a2 46 ♖b6 ♖d3! 47 c5 ♖a1+ 48 ♚e2 ♖a2+ 49 ♚e1 g3 50 fg ♖×g3 51 ♚f1 ♖g×g2 52 ♗e1 ♖gc2 53 c6 ♖a1 54 ♖h3 f4 55

♖b4 ♚f5?! 56 ♖b5+ e5 57 ♖a5 ♖d1?

57 ... ♖ac1! would have secured victory.

58   a7??

A horrible oversight! 58 c7! would have saved the game.

58   ...   e3

0-1

One of the worst played games of the many Kasparov-Karpov encounters, but one which illustrates the complexity of the positions arising from this line.

II

7   ...   g5!

7 ... c5?! 8 ♗d3 cd 9 ed ♗×f3 10 ♕×f3 ♘c6 11 ♕e3 ♗e7 12 ♗g3 ♘b4 13 ♗b1 ♘h5 14 0-0 0-0 15 a3 ♘c6 16 ♖d1 was better for White in Tukmakov-Salov, USSR Ch. 1987.

8   ♗g3 *(37)*

From this position we examine games from the Kasparov-Timman match held in Hilversum, 1985.

8   ...   ♘e4

Kasparov-Timman (m/2):

This saw a new and typically

Kasparovian gambit line:

9	**♘d2**	**♘×c3**

9 ... ♘×g3 10 hg ♗f8 was tried in Kasparov–Miles, Dubai Ol. 1986. After 11 f4 ♗g7 12 ♕a4 ♕e7 13 0-0-0 White held a small but well-defined advantage.

10	**bc**	**♗×c3**
11	**♖c1**	

The authors feel that 11 ♖b1!? deserves serious attention, since it prevents the bishop from drawing back to b4. But the position after 11 ... d6 12 ♕c2 ♗×d2+ 13 ♕×d2 ♘d7 is very messy and holds dangers for both sides.

11	**...**	**♗b4**
12	**h4**	**gh**

This is a risky plan. 12 ... ♖g8 13 hg hg 14 ♕c2 is an alternative.

13	**♖×h4**	**♗d6**
14	**♕g4**	**♗×g3**

14 ... ♕e7 15 c5 ♗×g3 16 ♕×g3 ♘c6 ∞ Plaskett–Short, Brighton 1984.

15	**♕×g3**	**♘c6**

15 ... ♘a6 would be met by 16 c5 with a strong attack, according to Adorjan.

16	**d5**	**♘e7**
17	**♗d3**	**d6**
18	**♕g7**	**♖g8**
19	**♕h7**	**♖f8**

Not 19 ... ed 20 cd ♗×d5 21 ♘e4 ♗×e4 22 ♖×e4 winning for White.

20	**♘e4**	**♘f5**
21	**♖h3**	**♕e7**
22	**g4**	**♘h4**
23	**♕g7**	**0-0-0**
24	**♘f6**	**ed**
25	**cd**	**♔b8**

26	**♖×h4**	**♗×d5**
27	**g5**	

White has a won position and finished up with 27 ... ♗×a2 28 gh d5 29 h7 ♕a3 20 ♖d1 ♖h8 31 ♘g8 ♗b3 32 ♖a1 ♕c5 33 ♕×h8 d4 34 ♖×d4 ♕c3+ 35 ♔e2.

Kasparov–Timman (m/4)

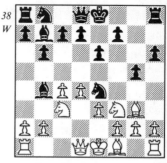

38
W

9	**♕c2**

This is the more conservative route, reinforcing the centre and relying on the solidity of the pawn structure.

9	**...**	**♗×c3+**

9 ... d6 10 ♗d3 ♗×c3+ 11 bc transposes.

9 ... f5 10 ♗d3 ♗×c3+ 11 bc is better for White:

(a) 11 ... ♘×g3 12 hg ♘c6 13 d5 ♘a5 14 g4! ± Keene–Burger, New York 1981.

(b) 11 ... d6 12 d5! ed 13 cd ♗×d5 14 ♘d4 ♕f6 15 f3 which has seen two impressive wins for White, separated by two decades:

(b1) 15 ... ♘×g3 16 hg ♘d7 17 ♗×f5 ♘c5 (17 ... 0-0-0 18 ♕a4! is good for White after either 18 ... ♕e5 19 ♔f2 a5 20 g4 ♖he8 21

🗒ae1 ♗b7 22 🗒×h6 or 18 ... a5 19 ♔f2 h5 20 🗒ab1 h4 21 e4 ♗b7 22 gh gh 23 ♘e6.) 18 ♘b5 ♕g7 19 ♗g6+ ♔d7 20 ♗f5+ ♗e6 21 ♗×e6+ ♘×e6 22 ♘d4 ♘c5 (Slightly better was 22 ... ♘×d4 23 ed c5, although after 24 0-0-0 White would still have a clear advantage.) 23 ♕f5+ ♔e7 24 ♕d5 ♕f6 25 0-0-0 🗒af8 26 e4 ♕f7 (26 ... h5 27 e5! ±) 27 ♘f5+ ♔d7 28 ♕×f7+ 🗒×f7 29 🗒×h6 🗒×h6 30 ♘×h6 and White went on to win (Tal–Dückstein, Zürich 1959).

(b2) 15 ... ♘c5 16 ♗×f5 ♘bd7 17 ♘b5 0-0-0 18 🗒d1!! ♗e6 19 ♗e4 ♔b8 20 🗒×d6! ♘e5 21 🗒×d8+ 🗒×d8 22 0-0 ♗d7 23 ♘d4 ♗a4? 25 ♗×e5 1-0 (Ribli–Seirawan, Malta Ol. 1980).

10   bc   d6

10 ... ♘×g3 11 hg ♘c6 was the standard continuation until 12 🗒h5! provided a clear advantage in Ionescu–Kengis, Timisoara 1987.

11   ♗d3   f5

11 ... ♘×g3 12 hg! ♘d7 (12 ... ♕f6 13 ♗e4! ±) 13 ♗e4 ♗×e4 14 ♕×e4 ♘f6 15 ♕d3 g4 16 ♘d2 ♕e7 17 a4 a5 18 🗒b1 ± Christiansen–de Firmian, USA 1985.

12   d5 (39)

An interesting alternative is 12 c5!? Black should reply 12 ... dc 13 ♘e5 with an unclear position in which White has full compensation, but not 12 ... bc 13 ♕b3 after which it is very difficult for Black, for example 13 ... ♕c8 14 ♗×e4! fe 15 ♘d2 cd 16 cd ♗d5

17 ♕c2 ♕b7 (17 ... ♘c6 18 0-0 ♕a6 19 ♘×e4 ♗×e4 20 ♕×e4 ± Bareyev–Salov, USSR Ch. 1987.) 18 0-0 h5 (18 ... 0-0?! 19 f3 ± Basin–Agzamov, Pitsunda 1985, or 18 ... ♘d7 19 🗒fc1 ± Agzamov–Bibilashvili, Pitsunda 1985.) 19 h4 g4 20 f3! ± Kapengut and I. Botvinnik.

39
B

12   ...   ♘c5

Other paths have been explored, and new ones sought,

(a) 12 ... ed 13 cd ♗×d5 14 ♘d4 transposes to Ribli–Seirawan, above.

(b) 12 ... ♘d7 13 ♗×e4 fe 14 ♕×e4 ♕f6 15 0-0 0-0-0 has been suggested by Kharitonov as an improvement on 15 ... ♘c5 16 ♕d4 ± Kharitonov–Vaiser, USSR 1984. But Kharitonov supplies his own remedy: 16 ♕×e6 ♕×e6 17 de ♘c5 18 ♘d2 ♘×e6 19 f3 where White stands better.

(c) 12 ... ♕f6 was introduced in Salov–Timman, St. John (m) 1988: 13 ♗×e4 fe 14 ♕×e4 (14 ♘d4 ed) 14 ... ♕×c3+ 15 ♔e2 ♕b2+ 16 ♘d2 ♕f6 17 h4 g4 18 h5 (18 ♕×g4 ed) 18 ... ♘d7 19 ♗h4 ♕f5 20 ♕×e6+

♕xe6 21 de ♘c5 22 e7 ♔d7 (22 ... ♗xg2? 23 ♖hg1 ♗h3 24 e4 intending 25 ♔e3, ♖g3.) 23 f3 ♖ag8 24 e4 gf+ 25 gf ♖g2+ 26 ♔e3 ♖hg8 27 ♖af1 ♘e6 28 ♖f2 ♖xf2 29 ♔xf2 ♘f4 (29 ... ♘g5 30 ♘f1) 30 ♗f6 ♗c6 31 ♘b3 ♔e8 32 ♘d4 ♗d7 33 ♘b5 ♔f7 34 ♗h4 ♖g2+ 35 ♔e3 ♘e6 36 ♘c3 c5 37 ♘e2 ♗a4 38 ♘c3 ♗c6 39 ♘e2 ♗a4 40 ♘c3 ♗c6 41 ♘b5 ♗xb5 42 cb ♘d4 43 ♗f6 ♖xa2 44 ♗xd4 ♖a3+ 45 ♔f4 cd 46 ♖g1 ♔xe7 47 ♖g7+ ♔e6 48 ♖g6+ ♔e7 49 ♖xh6 ♖b3 50 ♖h7+ ♔e6 51 ♖h6+ ♔e7 52 ♖h7+ ♔e6 53 ♖xa7 ♖xb5 54 h6 ♖h5 55 h7 ♖h3 56 ♖b7 ♖h1 57 ♖g7 ♔f6 58 ♖b7 ♔e6 59 ♖xb6 ♖xh7 60 ♖b5 ♖h1 61 ♖d5 ♖d1 62 ♖h5 ♖d3 ½-½.

13   h4

13 de would be met by 13 ... ♘xd3+ 14 ♕xd3 ♕f6 15 ♕d4 ♖f8 with unclear complications.

13   ...   g4

13 ... ♘xg3 14 fg is significantly better for White.

14	**♘d4**	**♕f6**
15	**0-0** *(40)*	

15	**...**	**♘ba6**

15 ... ♘xd3 16 ♕xd3 e5 has also

been seen with some regularity, but both Kasparov and Tony Miles have been quite effective in dealing with it. 17 ♘xf5 is the strongest move, and on 17 ... ♗c8, then, with the brilliant 18 f4!! (Kasparov–Timman, Hilversum (m/6) 1985 saw 18 ♘d4 ed 19 cd ♕f5! 20 e4 ♕g6 21 ♕c3 0-0 22 ♖fe1 ♘d7 23 e5 ♗b7 24 ♖e3, but now with 24 ... ♖ae8! 25 ♖ae1 de 26 de ♘c5 27 e6 ♖e7 the situation would be unclear, not much better for Black, as some authorities have claimed. White plays 28 ♗e5!, e.g. 28 ... ♘xe6 29 ♗g3 or 29 de where Black would have to avoid 29 ... ♕xe6? because of 30 ♗d6, and adopt 29 ... ♖xe6 30 ♗xc7 ⩲⩲), White breaks through to score the point:

(a) 18 ... ♗xf5 19 e4 ♕h5 20 fe de 21 c5 ♔d8 22 d6 ♕e8 23 dc+ ♔xc7 24 ♕d5 ♘c6 25 ♖f7+ ♗d7 26 ♖af1 ♖d8 27 ♖1f6 ♔c8 28 cb ab 29 ♕b5! 1-0 Miles–Belyavsky, Tilburg 1986.

(b) 18 ... ♗xf5 19 e4 ♗h7 20 fe ♕g7 21 ed cd 22 ♗xd6 ♘d7 (Nunn).

(c) 18 ... gf 19 ♖xf3 ♗f5 20 ♖xf5 ♕g7 21 ♗xe5! de 22 d6 ♘c6 23 ♕d5 ♕d7 24 ♖xe5+ ♘xe5 25 ♕xe5 ♔f7 26 ♖f1+ ♔g8 27 ♖f6! cd 28 ♕g3+ ♕g7 29 ♖g6 ♖h7 30 ♕xd6 ± is but one line of John Nunn's extensive analysis of this position in *New In Chess Yearbook 6*.

16	**♘xe6**	**♘xe6**
17	**♗xf5**	**♘g7**

18	♗g6+	♔d7
19	f3	♖af8
20	fg	♕e7
21	e4	♔c8
22	♕d2	♔b8

Miles–Timman, Tilburg 1986 saw instead 22 ... ♘c5 23 ♖×f8+ ♖×f8 24 ♕×h6 ♕f6 25 ♗f5 ♘×f5 26 ♕×f6 ♖×f6 27 e×f5 ♗a6 28 ♗f2 ♗×c4 29 ♗d4 ♖f7 30 f6 and now instead of 30 ... ♖h7? 31 ♗×c5!, the best move was 30 ... ♘d7, after which the chances would have been equal.

23   ♖×f8

23 ♕d4 was suggested by Timman in his notes to the game, and was seen in van der Linde-Duistermaat, Utrecht 1986: 23 ... ♘e8 24 e5! de 25 ♗×e5! (improving on Kasparov's 25 ♕×e5) 25 ... ♖hg8 26 h5 ♘d6 27 ♖×f8 ♖×f8 28 ♗g7 ♖g8 29 ♗×h6±.

23	...	♖×f8
24	♕×h6	♗c8
25	♖e1	

Kasparov claimed that 25 g5 leads to a substantial advantage for White but Timman gives 25 ... ♘c5 26 ♖f1 ♖×f1+ 27 ♔×f1 ♗a6 28 ♔g1 ♗×c4 intending 29 ...

♘×e4 30 ♗×e4 ♕×e4 31 ♕×g7 ♗×d5 and Black wins.

25	...	♗×g4
26	c5	

According to Timman, 26 e5 is better, for example 26 ... de 27 ♗×e5 ♘f5 28 ♗×f5 ♖×f5 29 d6 ♕d7 30 dc+ ♔b7 31 c5 with counterplay.

26	...	♕f6!
27	cd	♗h5
28	e5	

If 28 dc+, then Black would reply 28 ... ♔b7.

28	...	♕×g6
29	♕×g6	♗×g6
30	e6	♘c5
31	d7	♘×d7
32	ed	♖d8
33	♖e6	

Here Timman erred with 33 ... ♗h5 and the game eventually ended in a draw. He should have played 33 ... ♗f5, where his analysis runs 34 ♖f6 ♗×d7 (34 ... ♖×d7 35 ♗e5) 35 ♖f7 ♘f5 36 ♗f4 ♔c8 37 h5 ♖h8 38 g4 ♘h6! 39 ♗×h6 ♖×h6 40 ♖g7 ♗×g4! 41 ♖×g4 ♖×h5 42 c4 ♖f5 with an endgame that Black should win.

4   Modern Benoni

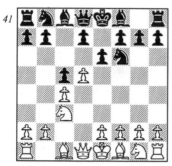

Kasparov, once an advocate of this opening for Black, has been devastating against it with White. Watson (1985) is a good survey of the theory.

1	d4	♘f6
2	c4	c5
3	d5	e6
4	♘c3	ed
5	cd	d6
6	e4	g6
7	f4	♗g7

White is preparing to blast open the centre so Black must not be tardy with his development, e.g.

(a) 7 ... a6? 8 e5! ♘fd7 9 ♘f3 ♗g7 10 ♘e4! d×e5 11 ♘d6+ ♔f8 12 ♗e2 (Kapengut) or 12 ♘g5 ef 13 ♘d×f7 ♕e7+ 14 ♗e2 intending 15 ♗×f4! ± Sishkin–Volovich, USSR 1960.

(b) 7 ... ♕e7 8 ♘f3 ♘bd7 (8 ... ♗g4 9 h3 ♗×f3 10 ♕×f3 ♗g7 11 ♗d3 ± Panno–Aitken, Munich Ol.

1958.) 9 e5! de 10 fe ♘×e5 11 ♗b5+ ♘ed7+ 12 ♔f2 ♘g4+ 13 ♔g3 ♘e5 14 ♘×e5 ♕×e5+ 15 ♗f4 ± Shamkovich–Zhelandinov, USSR 1959.

8   ♗b5+!

Here Black usually chooses between:

I   8 ... ♘fd7
II   8 ... ♘bd7

8 ... ♗d7 9 e5 ♘h5 10 ♘f3 0-0 runs into trouble on Watson's 11 ♗e2 or 11 ♗×d7 ♘×d7 (11 ... ♕×d7 12 0-0 ±) 12 g4 ♘×f4 13 ♗×f4 de (Garcia–Rossetto, Buenos Aires 1959) and now 14 ♗e3 (Watson) is clearly better for White.

I

8	...	♘fd7
9	a4 *(43)*	0-0

This sensible move is practically forced:

(a) 9 ... a6 10 ♗e2! ♕h4+ 11 g3

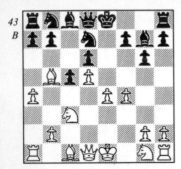

*43
B*

♕d8 12 ♘f3 0-0 13 0-0 ♖e8 14 ♕c2! ± Cebalo–Lobron, Reggio Emilia 1985/86, and although perhaps Black is safe after 14 ... ♘f6, e.g. 15 ♘d2 ♗h3, 15 f5! gf 16 ef ♘g4 17 ♘g5 leaves White with an advantage.

(b) 9 ... ♘a6 10 ♘f3 ♘c7 (10 ... ♘b4? led to a quick kill in Kasparov–Nunn, Lucerne Ol. 1982: 11 0-0 a6 12 ♗×d7+ ♗×d7 13 f5! ± 13 ... 0-0 14 ♗g5 f6 15 ♗f4 gf 16 ♗×d6 ♗×a4 17 ♖×a4 ♕×d6 18 ♘h4 fe 19 ♘f5 ♕d7 20 ♘×e4 ♔h8 21 ♘×c5 1-0) 11 0-0 (11 ♗e2! may be a significantly stronger move) and now:

(b1) 11 ... ♘×b5 12 ab 0-0 13 ♗d2 ♘b6 is level, according to Kapengut.

(b2) 11 ... a6 12 ♗×d7+ ♗×d7 13 f5! 0-0 14 ♗g5 ♗f6 (14 ... f6 15 ♗f4 ±) 15 ♕d2! ♘e8 16 ♕f4 ♕e7 17 ♕h4! ± Baumbach–Danner, corr. 1985.

(b3) 11 ... 0-0 12 ♗d3 ♖b8 13 ♗e3 a6 14 ♗f2 b5 (14 ... ♘f6 15 ♗h4 ♕d7 16 ♕d2 b5 17 ab ab 18 ♗×f6 ♗×f6 19 e5 ♗g7 20 ♘e4 de 21 d6 ± ± Vaganian–Hausner, Athens 1971) 15 ab ab 16 ♖e1 (16 ♗h4!? ♗f6 17 ♗g3 intending e5 – Schranz.) 16 ... b4 17 ♘a4 ♘b6 18 ♘×b6 ♖×b6 19 ♕b3 ♗a6 20 e5 ±± Zerlinsky–Lipiridi, corr. 1985.

(c) 9 ... ♕h4+ 10 g3 ♕e7 11 ♘f3 0-0 12 0-0 ♘a6 13 e5! de (13 ... ♘b4 14 ♖e1 a6 15 ♗f1 de 16 d6 ♕e8 17 fe b6 18 e6 fe 19 ♗c4 was Tal–Velimirović, Moscow IZ 1982, where 19 ... ♗b7! 20 ♖×e6 ♕f7 21 ♖e4 ♕×c4 22 ♖×c4 ♗×f3 23 ♕b3 ♔h8 would have led to unclear complications according to Keene. So perhaps White should simply play 18 ♗g5 with a comfortable advantage.) 14 d6 ♕d8 15 ♘d5 ± Kouatly–Hulak, Toluca IZ 1982.

10   ♘f3 *(44)*

*44
B*

10   ...   ♘a6

Again there are a number of alternatives, but with precise play White comes out way ahead:

(a) 10 ... b6 11 0-0 ♗a6 12 ♗×a6 ♘×a6 13 f5! gives White a strong attack, Hollis–Hammar, corr. 1977/78. If 13 ... ♘e5, then 14 ♘×e5 ♗×e5 15 ♕f3 intending 16 ♗h6.

(b) 10 ... ♘f6 11 0-0 ♗g4 is met by 12 e5! ♘h5 (12 ... de 13 fe ♘fd7 14 e6! fe 15 de ♗xe6 16 ♘g5 ±) 13 ♕e1! a6 14 ♗c4 ± Dobosz-Streitberg, Prague 1981.

(c) 10 ... ♖e8 11 0-0 a6 12 ♗d3 ± *ECO*.

(d) 10 ... a6 11 ♗e2 (11 ♗c4!? comes into consideration.) and now:

(d1) 11 ... ♘f6?! 12 0-0 ♗g4 13 e5! ♗xf3 14 ♗xf3 de 15 fe ♘fd7 16 e6! ± Semkov-Popov, Bulgarian Ch. 1980/81. A striking example is 12 ... ♕c7 13 e5! ♘e8 14 e6! fe 15 ♗c4 ♕e7 16 de ♘c7 17 f5! ♘c8 18 ♗g5 ♗f6 19 ♘e4! ♗xg5 20 ♘fxg5 gf 21 ♘xd6 ± Kasparov-Kuijpers, Dortmund 1980.

(d2) 11 ... ♕c7 is dubious as well as White has a clear advantage after 12 0-0 c4 13 ♘d2 b5 14 ab ♘b6 15 ♔h1 (Li Zunian-Sax, Biel IZ 1985). But 13 ♗e3! ♘c5 14 e5 is even stronger.

(d3) 11 ... ♖e8 12 0-0 ♘f8 13 ♗e3!? is unclear, e.g. Petursson-Stefansson, Icelandic Ch. 1987: 13 ... ♗g4 14 ♕d2 ♘bd7 15 ♗d3 ♖c8 16 ♔h1 where instead of 16 ... ♕a5? 17 ♘g5 ±, Black could have created interesting complications with 16 ... c4 17 ♗c2 ♗xf3 18 ♖xf3 ♘c5. Better is 13 e5! ♘bd7 14 ♘g5 de 15 f5 ♘f6 16 fg hg 17 ♗e3 ♘8h7 18 ♘xh7 ♘xh7 19 ♗xc5 ± Barbero-Szalanczi, Bundesliga 1987.

(d4) 11 ... a5 12 0-0 ♘a6 13 ♘b5 ♘f6 14 e5 de 15 fe ♘xd5 16 ♗g5 ♕d7 ∞ Kouatly-Sax, Budapest 1982.

11   0-0   ♘b4

Kapengut suggested 11 ... ♘c7!? here but after 12 ♗c4 (12 ♗d3 is a viable alternative, e.g. 12 ... a6 13 ♖e1 ♖e8?! ♗e3! ± Federau-Tringov, Berlin Open 1985.) and now:

(a) 12 ... ♖e8 13 ♖e1 ♘b6 14 ♗b3 White stands better, according to Kasparov.

(b) 12 ... a6 13 ♖e1 ♖b8 (13 ... b5 14 ab ± Horstmann-Soos, Lugano 1984.) 14 e5 b5 15 e6 (Watson's 15 ♗a2 is also good.) 15 ... bc 16 e7 ♕e8 17 f5!! ♔h8 18 ef(♕)+ ♕xf8 19 fg hg 20 ♘g5 ± Cherepkov-Mochalov, USSR 1983.

(c) 12 ... ♘b6 13 ♗a2 ♗g4 14 h3 ♗xf3 15 ♕xf3 ♘a6 16 a5 ♘d7 17 ♗c4 ♘b4 18 ♘b5 ♕f6 19 ♕b3 a6?! 20 ♘c7! ♖ac8 21 ♘e6 ♖fe8 and in Pergericht-Grünfeld, Brussels 1986 White broke through with 22 f5! fe 23 fe ♕d8 24 ♗g5.

12   ♖e1   a6

12 ... ♖e8 (12 ... ♘f6 13 h3 ± Watson.) 13 h3 a6 14 ♗c4 ♗d4+ 15 ♘xd4 cd 16 ♘a2! ♘xa2 17 ♖xa2 ♕h4 18 b3! worked to White's advantage in Meyer-Einarsson, Reykjavik 1984.

13   ♗f1 *(45)*

The bishop must retreat all the way home, to avoid being further harrassed by the black knights.

13   ...   ♖e8

13 ... ♘f6 14 h3 ♖e8 15 ♗c4! ♘d7 (15 ... b6 16 ♕b3 ♖a7 17 e5 ♘d7 18 ♘e4 de 19 ♘d6 ♖f8 20 ♘xf7! ♔xf7 21 d6+ ♔e8 22 ♗xa6!

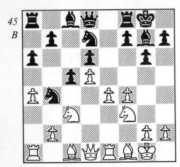

± Pevenka–Jandovsky, corr. 1984.)
16 ♗e3 ♘b6 17 ♗f1 ♗d7 18 ♗f2
♖c8 19 g4 c4 20 a5 ♘a8 21 e5 gives
White a dominating position
(Horvath–Bönsch, Kezthely 1980).

14   h3   ♖b8

Alternatives are not sufficient:
(a) 14 ... ♕c7 15 ♕b3 f5 16 ♗d2
♘f8 17 e5 was crushing in
Nyepomayaschy–Agapov, Leningrad 1980.

(b) 14 ... b6 15 ♗e3 ♗b7 16 ♗f2
♖c8 (Ree–Hulak, Wijk aan Zee
1983) 17 ♕b3 ± Ilić.

(c) 14 ... ♘f6 15 ♗c4 transposes
to Horvath–Bönsch, above.

15	**♗e3**	**b6**
16	**♕d2**	**♗b7**
17	**♗f2**	**♕e7**
18	**♗c4**	**♕f8**
19	**♗g3**	**♗h6**
20	**♕f2**	

This position is clearly better
for White (Enevoldsen–Filipowicz,
Siegen Ol. 1970)

II

8   ...   ♘bd7 *(46)*

Kasparov (BCO 2) proclaims
this line pretty much dead after:

9   e5   de

10	**fe**	**♘h5**
11	**e6**	**♕h4+**

11 ... fe 12 de 0-0 13 ♘f3 ♗d4 14
♗e3 or 14 ♗g5!

12   g3

Co-author Shamkovich pro-
poses 12 ♕d2!, e.g. 12 ... fe 13 de
♕g5+ 14 ♔c2 ♕f5+ 15 ♕d3 ♕×e6
16 ♘f3 with a decisive attack, since
16 ... 0-0 is met by 17 ♗c4, and
otherwise 17 ♖e1 is coming:

12	**...**	**♘×g3**
13	**hg**	**♕×h1**

It is possible, however, that
recent developments may re-
habilitate the line:

14   ♗e3

Another alternative is 14 ed+
♗×d7 15 ♗×d7+ (15 ♕e2+!? ♔f8
16 ♗e3 ♖e8 favours Black) 15 ...
♔×d7 16 ♕g4+ f5 (Not 16 ... ♔d8?!
17 ♗g5+ f6 18 0-0-0! ±± Plaskett–
Norwood, Chester 1983.) 17 ♕a4+
♔c8 18 ♗e3 ♗×c3+ (18 ... ♗h6?!
19 ♗×c5 ♕g2 20 ♕c4! with better
chances for White; Burgess–J.
Anderson, London 1985) 19 bc
♕×d5 20 ♖d1 ♕c6 (Riemersma–
Bezemer, Hilversum 1986) 21
♕×c6!? bc 22 ♘f3 ∞ Norwood.

14 ...   ♗×c3+!

14 ... 0-0 15 ed ♗×d7 16 ♘×d7 ♖ae8 17 ♗×e8 ♖×e8 18 ♕e2! ♗d4 19 0-0-0! ♖×e3 was played in Littlewood–Norwood, London Docklands 1985, and now 20 ♕c2! would have secured a significant advantage.

15	bc	♕e4
16	♕f3	♕×f3
17	♘×f3	fe
18	de	0-0
19	ed	♗xd7
20	♗×d7	♖×f3

This position was supposed to be clearly better for White, according to Norwood, but 21 ♗×c5 ♖×g3 22 ♗e6+ ♔g7 23 ♗d4+ ♔f8 24 ♔d2 b6 brought Black equality in G. Nikolić–Lindemann, Harkany 1987. So White should play ...

21	♗f4!	♖×c3

21 ... g5 22 ♔e2! ♖×c3 23 ♗e6+ ♔f8 24 ♗d6+ ♔e8 25 ♔d2 leads to a similar advantage as that presented below.

22	♗e6+	♔f8
23	♗d6+	♔e8
24	♔d2	♖f3
25	♖e1	♖f2+

Or 25 ... ♔d8 26 ♗d5 ♖f2+ 27 ♔c3 ♔d7 28 ♗×c5 ♖h2 29 ♖e7+ ♔d8 30 ♗×b7 ♖b8 31 ♖g7 ♖×a2 32 ♗d6 ++.

26	♔c3	♖f3+
27	♔c4	♔d8
28	♗×c5	

White has a winning position — analysis by co-author Shamkovich.

5   King's Indian

47

Kasparov was an advocate for the Black side of this opening for some time in the early stages of his career, and seems to be rediscovering it now. This may have something to do with the fact that Anatoly Karpov is one of the leading exponents of the White side of the opening! As Karpov no longer employs the defence as Black, we have had little opportunity to see how Kasparov reacts to it these days. Nevertheless, his brave gambiteering interpretation of most of the common systems is of great interest to modern chess players, being part of a long creative tradition which has featured such players as Boleslavsky, Bronstein, Geller, Stein and Fischer. We recommend that you study his brilliant handling of this opening in games against Vaiser

(Moscow 1981), Kavalek (Bugojno 1982), Belyavsky (m/8 1983) and Tukmakov (USSR Ch. 1981), all of which are annotated in detail by Kasparov in *The Test of Time*.

1	d4	♘f6
2	c4	g6
3	♘c3	♗g7
4	e4	d6
5	♘f3	0-0
6	♗e2	e5

Other moves are not considered to be sufficient for equality:

(a) 6 ... ♗g4 7 ♗e3 ♘fd7!? 8 ♘g1! ±, e.g. Kasparov–Vukic, Banja Luka 1979: 8 ... ♗xe2 9 ♘gxe2 e5 10 0-0 a5 11 ♕d2 ♘c6 12 f3 ed 13 ♘xd4 ♘c5 14 ♖ad1 ♘e6 15 ♘db5! ♖e8 16 ♕c1 ♕b8 17 ♗h6 ♗h8 18 ♘d5 ♘b4 19 a3 ♘a6 20 f4 c6 21 f5 cd 22 fe ♖xe6 23 ed ♖e7 24 ♗f4 ♖d7 25 ♘xd6 ♕d8 26 ♘b5 ♘c5 27 ♕e3 b6 28 b4 ab 29 ab ♘a6 30 ♗g5 ♕b8 31 d6 ♘xb4 32 ♗e7 ♕b7 33 ♖xf7 ♔xf7 34 ♖f1+ ♗f6 35 ♗xf6 1-0.

(b) 6 ... ♘c6 7 d5 ♘b8 8 ♗g5 h6 9 ♗e3 c5 10 ♘d2! ♘a6 11 0-0 ♗d7 12 f4 ± Najdorf–Cordovil, Siegen Ol. 1970.

(c) 6 ... c5 7 d5 e6 8 0-0 ♖e8 9 ♗f4! ed 10 ed ♘e4 11 ♘xe4 ♖xe4 12 ♕d2 ± Sosonko–Keene, Hastings 1975/76.

7 ♗e3

It is this fairly conservative treatment which has brought Kasparov significant success as White. White postpones castling in favour of rapid development, with an eye toward an early queenside battle.

Black has no fewer than eight defensive tries:

I 7 ... ♘c6
II 7 ... ♘g4
III 7 ... ♘bd7
IV 7 ... ed
V 7 ... c6
VI 7 ... ♕e7
VII 7 ... ♕e8
VIII 7 ... h6!?

I

| 7 | ... | ♘c6 (48) |

48
W

| 8 | d5 | ♘e7 |
| 9 | ♘d2 | c5 |

9 ... ♘d7 10 b4 f5 11 f3 and now:
(a) 11 ... f4 12 ♗f2 a5 (12 ... g5 13 c5 ♘f6 14 ♘c4 ♘e8 15 cd cd 16 ♘b5 b6 17 a4 ± Gligorić–Nagendra, Lucerne Ol. 1982) 13 a3! g5 14 c5 ♘f6 15 cd cd 16 ♘c4 ab 17 ab ♖×a1 18 ♕×a1 ♘e8 19 ♕a5! was decisive in Wirthensohn–Valiente, Lucerne

Ol. 1982.
(b) 11 ... a5 12 ba ♖×a5 13 ♘b3 ♖a8 14 c5 ± Magerramov–Lechtynsky, Baku 1980.
(c) 11 ... ♘f6 12 c5 h5 13 h3 ♔h8 14 ♘c4 ♘e8 15 ♕d2 ♗d7 16 0-0-0 ♘g8 17 ♔b1· ♕b8 ∞ Stone–Gurevich, World Open 1987.

| 10 | g4 | ♘e8 |

10 ... ♘g4 runs into 11 ♗×g4 f5 12 h3!? fg 13 hg a6 14 a4 ♗d7 15 f3 ± Polugayevsky–Rodriguez, Toluca IZ 1982.

| 11 | g5 | ♗h3 |

11 ... f5 creates serious kingside weaknesses: 12 gf ♘×f6 13 h4 a6 14 h5 ± Petkevich–A. Petrosian, USSR 1974.

12	♖g1	a6
13	a4	♖b8
14	♗g4!	♗×g4
15	♕×g4	b6
16	♖b1	

White has a much better game (Portisch–Andersson, Siegen Ol. 1970).

II

| 7 | ... | ♘g4 (49) |

49
W

If any move were to directly refute White's plans it might be this one, since it attacks the strong ♗e3. But White can attack the Black queen with tempo, and this leaves the ♘g4 looking a bit silly. Nevertheless, this is a popular option for Black these days.

8 ♗g5! · f6
9 ♗h4 ♘c6

If Black continues the assault with 9 ... g5 then after 10 ♗g3 ♘h6 either 11 h3 or Geller's interesting idea 11 c5!? intending 11 ... g4 12 ♘h4 is sufficient to guarantee an advantage for White.

9 ... c6 10 ♕c2 ♘d7 11 ♖d1 ♕e7 12 0-0 h5!? 13 h3 ♘h6 seems inadequate for equality after 14 c5!? dc 15 de ♘xe5 16 ♘xe5 ♕xe5 17 ♗c4+ ♔h8 18 ♗g3 ± Bialas-Werner, Germany 1987.

9 ... ♘d7 is a more reasonable plan. After 10 0-0 ♘h6 11 ♕c2, 11 ... g5 is playable, for example 12 ♗g3 g4 13 ♘h4!? 14 ♘b5 f5 ∞ Garcia Palermo-Klundt, Germany 1987.

10 d5 ♘e7
11 ♘d2 ♘h6

11 ... h5 allows White to take charge on the queenside with 12 0-0 ♘h6 13 f3 c5 14 ♖b1! f5 15 b4 b6 16 bc bc 17 ♕a4 ± Grefe-Quinteros, Lone Pine 1976.

12 f3 g5

12 ... c5 13 ♖b1 f5 14 0-0 ♘f7 15 b4 b6 16 bc bc 17 a4 also gives White a strong queenside initiative (Spassov-Doncev, Bulgarian Ch. 1981).

13 ♗f2 f5
14 0-0 ♘g6

14 ... c5 (via transposition) was seen in Ki. Georgiev-Damljanović, Vršac 1987: 15 a3 g4 16 fg ♘xg4 17 ♗xg4! fg 18 b4! b6 19 ♗h4 ±.

15 c5 ♘f4
16 cd cd
17 ♔h1

White stands better (Podgaets-Legky, USSR 1981). Although the Black pawns seem to be advancing toward the White monarch, White can exchange on f5 and then use e4 as a base of operation for his knights.

III

7 ... ♘bd7 (50)

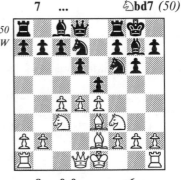

8 0-0 c6

As might be expected there are a large number of alternatives. We cannot go into great detail in a book of this size, but refer the reader to Keene *et al.* (Forthcoming).

(a) 8 ... ed 9 ♘xd4 ♖e8 10 f3 c6 11 ♘c2 ♘b6 12 ♕d2 ♗e6 13 b3 d5 14 ed cd 15 c5 ± Cobo-Hulbrandsen, Siegen Ol. 1970.

(b) 8 .... ♕e7 9 de de 10 ♘d5 ♕d8 (10 ... ♘xd5 11 cd would also leave White in control) 11 ♕c2 ♘g4 12 ♗g5 f6 13 ♗d2 c6 14 ♘e3 f5 15 ef ♘xe3 16 ♗xe3 gf 17 c5 is better for White, but Antunac suggests 14 ... ♘c5.

(c) 8 ... ♖e8 appears sensible, but it is hard for Black to achieve equality after 9 d5! e.g. 9 ... ♘g4 10 ♗g5 f6 11 ♗h4 h5 (11 ... ♘f8 12 ♘d2 ♘h6 13 f3 ♘f7 14 b4 ♗h6 15 ♗f2!? f5 16 c5 ♘d7 17 c6!? is given by Gligorić.) 12 ♘d2 ♘h6 13 f3 ♘f7 14 b4 ♗h6 15 ♘b3 c5 16 dc bc 17 b5 ♗b7 18 a4 a5 19 ♕d3 c5 20 ♘d5 ± Reshevsky-Kavalek, Netanya 1971.

(d) 8 ... a5 is a premature flank action which is countered in the centre with 9 de de 10 ♕c2 ♘g4 11 ♗d2 c6 12 ♘a4 h6 13 h3 ♘gf6 14 ♗e3 ± Uhlmann-Knaak, Leipzig 1980.

(e) 8 ... ♘g4 9 ♗g5 f6 10 ♗d2! is probably the best path to the advantage, e.g. 10 ... c6 11 b4 f5 12 d5 f4 13 ♗c1! c5 14 ♘b5 ♘df6 15 ♘g5 ± Uhlmann-Knaak, Leipzig 1977 or 10 ... ♘h6 11 b4 ♘f7 12 ♕b3 c6 13 ♖ad1 ♕e7 14 ♗e3 f5 15 de de 16 ef gf 17 ♖fe1 ♔h8 18 ♗f1 ± Miles-Ciocaltea, Montilla 1978.

9   d5   cd

It seems that this is the best available move, in light of:

(a) 9 ... ♘g4 10 ♗g5 f6 11 ♗d2! ♕e7 12 ♘e1 f5 13 ef gf 14 ♗xg4 fg 15 ♘e4 is better for White, according to Tseitlin.

(b) 9 ... c5 10 ♘e1 ♘e8 11 ♘d3 a6 12 a4 ♕e7 13 ♕d2 ♘c7 14 a5 f5 15 f3 f4 16 ♗f2 ♗f6 17 b4 cb 18 ♘a4

gave White a tremendous game in Polugayevsky-Nunn, Toluca IZ 1982.

10   cd   ♘g4
11   ♗g5   f6
12   ♗d2 *(51)*

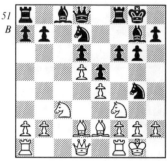

51
B

12   ...   ♘c5

Also inadequate is 12 ... ♘h6 13 ♖c1 a6 14 a4 ♘f7 15 ♕c2 ♗h6 16 b4 ± Vogt-Kaspaer, Leipzig 1982.

13   b4   ♘a6
14   a3

White's spatial advantage on the queenside, combined with the lack of Black counterplay on the kingside, gives the first player much better chances (Yusupov-Gavrikov, Yerevan 1982)

IV

7   ...   ed
8   ♘xd4 *(52)*

The surrender of the centre is rarely a good idea so early in the opening.

8   ...   ♖e8
9   f3   c6
10   ♗f2

10 0-0 d5 11 cd ♘xd5 12 ♘xd5 cd was roughly level in Damljanović-Byrne, New York

Open 1987.

10 ♕d2 d5! 11 ed cd 12 0-0 ♘c6 13 ♘×c6 bc provided equality in Portisch–Bouaziz, Szirak IZ 1987.

| 10 | ... | | d5 |

If Black does not aim for this central counterplay he will sit by idly while his opponent continues to improve his position.

11	ed		cd
12	0-0		♘c6
13	c5!		

White stands better, for example 13 ... ♘h5 14 ♕d2 ♗e5 15 g3 ♘g7 16 ♖fe1 ♘e6 17 ♘×e6 ♗×e6 18 f4 ♗×c3 19 bc ± Hort–Gligorić, Tilburg 1977.

V

| 7 | ... | | c6 *(53)* |

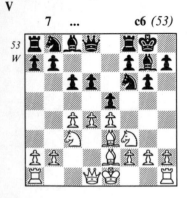

| 8 | d5! | | |

Once again this central advance is the correct response to the move ... c6.

8	...		cd
9	cd		♘g4
10	♗g5		f6
11	♗d2!		♘h6
12	0-0		♘f7
13	♘e1		f5
14	♘d3		

White is better, for example 14 ... ♘d7 15 ♖c1 ♘f6 16 f3 ♗d7 17 ♕b3 ± I. Adamski–J. Adamski, Poland 1981.

VI

| 7 | ... | | ♕e7 *(54)* |

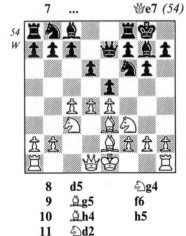

8	d5		♘g4
9	♗g5		f6
10	♗h4		h5
11	♘d2		

11 h3 is not as good. Kasparov–Chiburdanidze, Baku 1980: 11 ... ♘h6 12 ♘d2 c5 and Black could be satisfied with the results of the opening. Kasparov won the middlegame battle, however: 13 ♘f1 ♘f7 14 g4 hg 15 ♗×g4 g5 16 ♗×c8 ♖×c8 17 ♘e3! gh 18 ♘f5 ♕d8 19 ♕g4 ♘g5 20 ♘×h4 ♖c7 21

♘f5 a6 22 h4 ♘h7 23 ♖g1 ♕f8 24
♔e2 ♖a7 25 a4 b6 26 ♕h5 ♔h8 27
♖g6 ♖d7 28 ♖ag1 ♖ab7 29 ♕g4
♖bc7 30 ♖g2 ♖b7 31 ♔f1 ♖a7 32
♔g1 ♖f7 33 ♘e2 ♕c8 34 f4 b5 35
ab ab 36 cb ♖ab7 37 h5 ♘f8 38
♕h3! ♘×g6 39 hg+ ♔g8 40 gf+
♔f8 1-0.

11	...	c5
12	dc	bc
13	b4	♗e6
14	0-0	♘d7
15	♘b3	g5!

In Kasparov-Morrison, Graz
World Youth Team Championship 1981 15 ... ♘×h2? led to rapid
disaster: 16 ♔×h2 g5 17 ♘a5! ♘b8
18 ♗g3 h4 19 ♗g4 ♗×g4 20 ♕×g4
hg 21 fg a6 22 ♘d1! d5 23 ♘e3 ♖a7
24 cd ♕×b4 25 ♕e6+ ♖af7 26
♘ac4 ♕e7 27 ♘f5 1-0.

| 16 | ♗g3 | f5 |
| 17 | ef | ♗×f5 |

Chances are roughly level, but
the position holds plenty of possibilities for White.

VII

| 7 | ... | ♕e8 *(55)* |

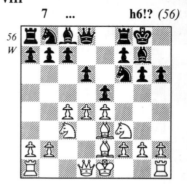

| 8 | de | ♘g4 |
| 9 | ♗g5 | h6 |

10	♗d2	♘×e5
11	♘d5	♘×f3+
12	♗×f3	♕d8
13	♗c3	♗×c3
14	♘×c3	

White stands better (Ivkov-
Byrne, Bugojno 1978).

VIII

| 7 | ... | h6!? *(56)* |

This is a new and popular variation.

| 8 | d5 | |

The point of Black's strategy is
revealed if White goes pawn-
hunting: 8 de ♘g4! 9 ed ♘×e3 10 fe
♗×c3+! 11 bc cd 12 0-0 ♘c6 and
Black has plenty of compensation
for the pawn (Glek-Khalifman,
Leningrad 1985). 9 ♗f4 may be a
bit better, e.g. 9 ... ♘×e5 10 ♕d2
♔h7 11 ♘d4 (11 0-0 ♘bc6 =
Renet-van der Wiel, Budel Z 1987)
11 ... c5?! 12 ♘c2 ♗e6 13 ♘e3
♘bc6 14 0-0 and White was
slightly better in Douven-
Riemersma, Amsterdam 1987.

White has tried 8 h3, to keep the
knight off g4, but he has been get-
ting beaten up lately.

| 8 | ... | ♘g4 |

Here Kasparov-Short, London (m/1) 1987 saw 14 b4?! ba 15 ba ℤab8 16 ℤfb1 c5! 17 ♕c1 ℤfc8 18 ♕e3 cd 19 ♕×d4 ♕c5 20 ℤb5 ♕×d4 21 ♘×d4 and now Goodman suggests 21 ... dc 22 ♘×e6 ♔f7.

Instead, Goodman's 14 ♘c2 should still leave White with a small advantage.

II Leningrad

2	...	g6
3	g3	♘f6

3 ... ♗g7 4 ♗g2 d6 5 ♘f3 ♘h6 is favoured by IM Michael Basman. White should neither castle, which practically removes his option of attacking on the kingside with h4 and h5, nor adopt the 'recommended' 6 h4, which is premature until Black castles. Instead, he should play 6 ♘c3 0-0 7 h4 with a strong attack. Black cannot delay castling for too long: 6 ... c6 7 ♕c2 ♕c7 8 b3 ♘a6 9 ♗b2 0-0 10 h4! ±.

4	♗g2	♗g7
5	♘f3	0-0
6	0-0	d6
7	♘c3	(59)

On 7 ... c5, 8 dc dc 9 ♕×d8 ℤ×d8 10 ♗f4 or 10 ♘b5 ♘a6 11 ♗f4 looks strong.

| 7 | ... | ♕e8 |

(a) 7 ... ♘c6 8 d5 and now:

(a1) 8 ... ♘e5 9 ♘×e5 de 10 e4 f4 (10 ... e6 11 ef ef *(11 ... gf!? was suggested by Botvinnik.)* 12 ♗e3 e4 13 ♗d4 ℤe8 14 ℤe1 b6 15 f3 ± Collins-Sherwin, New York 1952

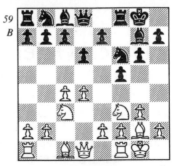

or 10 ... fe 11 ♘×e4 ♘×e4 12 ♗×e4 and now: 12 ... ♗f5 13 ♕e2 ♕d7 14 ♗g5 ℤf7 15 ℤae1 Menchik-Seitz, England 1930 or 12 ... ♗h3 13 ℤe1 ♕d7 14 ♗e3 ♗f5 15 ♕c2 Radulov-Kolarov, Varna 1968.) 11 b4 g5 12 ℤe1 a6 13 ♗b2 ♕e8 14 ℤc1 ♘g4 15 ℤc2 ± Farago-Poutiainen, Budapest 1975.

(a2) 8 ... ♘a5 9 ♕d3 c5 (9 ... e5 10 de ♗×e6 11 b3 ♘c6 12 ♗b2 ♘e4 13 ℤac1 ℤe8 14 ℤfd1 ♗f7 15 e3 g5 16 h4 h6 ± Scheeren-Chernin, Amsterdam 1980) 10 b3 a6 (10 ... ♘e4 11 ♗b2 a6 12 ♘d2 b5 13 ♘d×e4 fe 14 ♗×e4 bc 15 bc ℤb8 ± Udovcić-Matulović, Yugoslavia 1960.) 11 ♗b2 ℤb8 12 ℤae1 b5 13 ♗a1 bc 14 bc ℤb4 15 ♘d2 ♘g4 16 a3 ℤb8 17 ♕c2 ♗d7 18 e3 ♘e5 19 ♘e2 ± Nikolac-Bertok, Yugoslavia 1969.

(b) 7 ... c6 8 d5!:

(b1) 8 ... ♕e8 9 ℤb1 ♘a6 10 b3 ♗d7 11 ♗b2 and Mikhalchishin-Lerner, USSR 1983, saw 11 ... ♘c5?! 12 b4 ♘a6 13 a3 ♘c7 14 ♕d2 ♔h8 (14 ... ℤd8 intending ... e5 was a bit stronger) 15 ℤfe1 ♕f7 16 e4 fe 17 ♘g5 ♕g8 18 ♘c×e4 ♘g4

19 ♘xd6!! cd (19 ... ♖xf2 20 ♕xf2 ♘xf2 21 ♘df7+ ±) ♖e7+ ±.

(b2) 8 ... ♕c7 is an important line, since it can also arise from the move order 2 ... ♘f6 3 g3 d6 4 ♗g2 c6 5 ♘f3 ♕c7 6 d5 g6 7 ♘c3 ♗g7 8 0-0 0-0. White should play 9 ♘d4 ± (Gaprindashvili–Gurieli, USSR 1980).

(b3) 8 ... e5 9 de (The automatic reply, although Tukmakov's 9 dc!? deserves tests.) 9 ... ♗xe6 10 ♕d3 ♘a6 (10 ... h6 11 ♗f4 d5 12 ♖ad1 ♘a6 13 cd ± Amado–Tempone, Buenos Aires 1983, or 10 ... ♘bd7 11 ♗f4 ♘b6 12 b3 ♘e4 13 ♘d4 ± Kasparov.) 11 ♗f4 ♘e4 (11 ... ♘e8

12 ♘g5 ♕d7 13 b3 ± Yusupov or 11 ... ♕b6 12 ♘g5 ♖fe8? 13 ♗xd6! ± Hulak–Gazic, Montpellier 1985) 12 ♘xe4 fe 13 ♕xe4 ♘c5 14 ♕e3 ♗xc4 15 ♖ad1 ♖e8 16 ♕c1 ♗xe2 17 ♖xd6 ♕a5 18 ♗d2 ± Yusupov–Barbero, Mendoza 1985.

After 7 ... ♕e8, Kasparov (*BCO2*) gives 8 ♘d5 ♘xd5 9 cd ♕b5 10 ♘e1 (10 ♕b3 ♕xb3 11 ab cb 12 ♗g5 ♖e8 ∞ Zhukovitsky–M. Tseitlin, USSR 1986) 10 ... ♘a6 11 e3 ♗d7 12 ♘d3 c5 13 dc6 ♗xc6 14 ♗xc6 bc 15 ♕b3+ ♖f7 16 ♕xb5 cb 17 ♗d2 e5 = Balashov–Malanyuk, USSR Ch. 1986.

7 Grünfeld
(Modern Exchange Variation)

60

Even a little bit of thought will suffice to demonstrate that no matter how one structures one's repertoire there must be at least one position which one must play for both sides. Perhaps the most prominent overlap in Kasparov's repertoire is the Grünfeld, which he has had to face frequently as White ever since taking up 1 d4, and which he now also plays as Black. Now if it were a simple matter for White to obtain an advantage against the Grünfeld, Kasparov would hardly make the defence his primary weapon with Black. So it is not surprising that we are no more successful in establishing an edge for White than Kasparov's opponents! But the lines in this chapter lead to rich, if balanced play and are by no means drawish. They remain extremely

popular at all levels of play.

In Chapter 8 we examine the Grünfeld from Black's point of view, but here we examine the system which Kasparov has used very successfully to defeat Natsis at the 1980 Malta Olympiad. Although he has recently adopted a fianchetto approach, his most impressive victories have come in the Modern Exchange Variation.

1	d4	♘f6
2	c4	g6
3	♘c3	d5
4	♘f3	♗g7
5	cd	♘×d5
6	e4	♘×c3
7	bc	c5

If Black plays an immediate 7 ... 0-0, then 8 ♗e2 c5 9 0-0 ♗g4 10 ♗e3 e6 11 ♖b1 achieves a position which holds even more promise than the text, for example 11 ... ♕c7 12 ♕b3 b6 13 ♖fd1 ♘d7 14 h3 ♗×f3 15 ♗×f3 ± Chekhov-Tomaszewski, Moscow 1986.

8 ♖b1!? (61)

This move was introduced by co-author Shamkovich in his game against Gheorghiu, played in Cleveland 1975, a fact not mentioned by Adorjan in his recent book on the Grünfeld.

8 ... 0-0

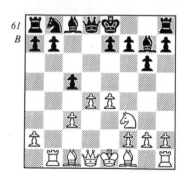

61
B

The alternatives have dropped from sight:

(a) 8 ... ♕a5 9 ♖b5! ♕xa2? allows White to establish a strong attacking position with 10 ♖xc5, for example 10 ... 0-0 11 ♗c4 ♕a1 12 ♗xf7+! ♔xf7 13 ♘g5+! (Our suggestion, which we feel is stronger than 13 ♕b3+, as suggested by many pundits.) 13 ... ♔g8 14 ♖xc8! ♖xc8 (14 ... ♕b1 15 ♖xf8+ ♗xf8 16 0-0 is also hopeless for Black.) 15 ♕b3+ with mate to follow.

If instead of taking the a-pawn, Black tries 9 ... ♕xc3+, then 10 ♗d2 ♕a3 11 ♕c2! c4 12 ♗xc4 is much better for White (Gaprindashvili–Khadilkar, Lucerne Ol. 1982).

(b) 8 ... ♘c6 9 d5 ♗xc3+ 10 ♗d2 ♗xd2+ 11 ♕xd2 ♘d4 12 ♘xd4 cd 13 ♕xd4 ♕a5+ 14 ♕d2 ♕xd2+ 15 ♔xd2 gave White his customary endgame advantage in Ksieski–Szitkey, Trnava 1986.

(c) 8 ... cd 9 cd ♕a5+ 10 ♕d2 ♕xd2+ 11 ♗xd2 0-0 12 ♗c4 e6 13 d5! also secures a significant endgame advantage for White, for example 13 ... ♖e8 14 0-0 b6 15 ♖bc1 ♗a6 16 de ♗xc4 17 ♖xc4 ± van der Sterren–Sokolovsky, Dortmund 1986.

(d) 8 ... a6 9 ♗e2 ♕a5 10 0-0 is a perfectly sound gambit, e.g. 10 ... ♕xa2 11 ♗g5 ♕a5 12 d5! h6 13 ♗e3 ♘d7 (13 ... ♗xc3 14 ♘d2!) 14 c4 ♕c7 15 ♘d2 where White is clearly better. (Petursson–Gutman, Biel IZ 1985).

(e) 8 ... ♗g4 9 ♕a4!+ ♗d7 10 ♗b5 0-0 11 0-0 ♘c6 12 d5 a6 13 ♗xc6 bc 14 dc ♗e8 15 ♗f4 ± Rashkovsky–Veingold, USSR 1981. On 9 ... ♘d7, Rashkovsky gives 10 ♘e5 ♗xe5 11 de 0-0 12 h3 ♗e6 13 f4 ♘b6 15 ♕c2 ♗c4 15 ♗xc4 ♘xc4 16 0-0 ±. We find 16 ♖xb7!? ♘b6 17 ♗e3 to be a good alternative.

9 ♗e2

I	9 ... cd
II	9 ... ♕a5
III	9 ... b6
IV	9 ... ♘c6
V	9 ... ♗g4

No longer seen is 9 ... ♕c7 10 0-0 ♗g4 11 d5 a6 12 c4 b5 13 cb ab 14 ♕c2 c4 15 ♖b5 ± Yusupov–Kouatly, Toluca IZ 1982.

9 ... ♘d7 10 0-0 ♘f6 11 ♗d3 leaves White holding the initiative (Danner–Wittman, Caorle 1985).

I

	9	**...**	**cd**
	10	**cd**	**♕a5+**

The best move, according to both Kasparov and Karpov.

11 ♕d2

The pawn sacrifice 11 ♗d2!?

♛×a2 is still unclear, but in our opinion it is probably not quite correct.The critical position arises after 12 0-0 *(62)*

62
B

(a) 12 ... b6 13 ♕c1 ♕e6 14 ♗c4 ♕d7 (14 ... ♕×e4 15 ♖e1 ♕b7 16 ♗b4 ♗e6 17 ♖×e6! fe 18 ♘g5 ♔h8 19 ♘×e6?! ♘d7 ∞ Gelfand–Dorfman, Minsk 1986, but 16 ♗h6!? and 19 ♖b3 are two possible improvements for White.) 15 ♘e5 ♗×e5 16 de ♗a6! 17 ♗h6 ♗×c4 18 ♗×f8 ♕e6 19 ♕h6 ♕×e5 20 ♖fc1 b5 21 ♖×b5! ♗×b5 22 ♗g7! f6 23 ♗h8!! ♔f7 24 ♕×h7+ ♔e6 25 ♕g8+ ♔d6 26 ♕d8+ ♔e6 27 ♕g8+ ♔d6 28 ♕d8+ ½–½, Petursson–Ftacnik, Tallinn 1981.

(b) 12 ... ♕e6 13 ♕c2 ♕d7 14 d5 b6 15 ♕a2 (15 ♗b5!? ♕d6 16 ♖fc1!?) 15 ... ♕d8?! (15 ... ♗b7! intending ... ♖fc8) 16 ♗e3 ♘d7 17 ♘d4 ♗b7 and now instead of 18 ♘c6?! (Conquest–Korchnoi, Lugano 1986), White could have obtained a superior position with 18 ♖fc1! ♘c5 19 f3.

(c) 12 ... ♘d7?! 13 ♗b4 ♕e6 14 ♕c2 ♘b6 15 ♗b5 ♗d7 16 d5 ♕g4 17 h3 ♕f4 18 ♗×d7 ♘×d7 19 ♗×e7

♖fe8 20 d6 ± R. Short–Moraza, Dubai Ol. 1986.

11   ...   ♕×d2+
12   ♗×d2 *(63)*

63
B

12   ...   e6!
Also playable is 12 ... b6 13 0-0 (13 ♖c1 ♗b7 14 ♗d3 ♘a6 15 ♔e2 ♖fc8 16 a4 ♘c7 17 ♗e3 e6 with roughly level chances; de Boer–Mikhalchishin, Cascais 1986) 13 ... ♗b7 (13 ... ♖d8 14 ♖bc1 ♗a6 15 ♗×a6 ♘×a6 16 ♖c4! ± Samo-Lputian, Geneva 1986) 14 d5 ♗a6 15 ♗×a6 ♘×a6 16 ♗e3 with about equal chances, according to Karpov. Schmidt-Bañas, Trnava 1986, continued 16 ... ♖fe8 17 ♘d4 ♗×d4 18 ♗×d4 e6 19 de ♖×e6 20 f3 ♖d8 21 ♗e3 ♖d3 22 ♖b3! ♖ed6 23 ♖c1 ♔g7 24 ♔f2 ♘c5 25 ♗×c5 bc 26 ♖×c5 with a better endgame, so clearly there is still reason for White to adopt this line.

13   0-0   b6
Black has already achieved equality. But that does not mean that the whole line must be abandoned.

14   ♖fd1
Perhaps 14 ♖fc1 is a better try.

Our only example involves mismatched players, so it is not surprising that White obtained an edge in Gaprindashvili–Erenska, Dubai Ol 1986 after 14 ... ♗a6 15 ♗×a6 ♘×a6 16 ♖c4 ♖fc8 17 ♖bc1 ♖c4 h6 19 h4 ♖d8 20 a4 ♔h7 21 ♗f4 ♗f6 22 g3. Further tests were awaited.

14	...	♗b7
15	d5	ed
16	ed	♘d7
17	♗b4	♖fc8
18	♗e7	

Gufeld suggested 18 ♘d4, but after 18 ... ♘f6! Black has a strong position, for example:

(a) 19 ♘c6 ♘×d5.

(b) 19 ♘b5 ♗×d5.

(c) 19 d6 ♗e4! 20 ♖bc1 ♘d5 21 ♖×c8 ♖×c8 22 f3 ♘e3! ∓.

18	...	♗f6!
19	d6	♔g7

In this unclear position Black's chances are to be preferred. We now follow Karpov–Kasparov (m/13) 1987.

20	♖e1

According to Karpov this was a dubious move, and either 20 ♗b5 or 20 ♘d4 would have led to equality. Gligorić prefers the latter course.

20	...	♖c5
21	♗b5	♗c6
22	♗×c6	

Karpov suggests that at this point he had nothing better than 22 ♗×f6+ ♘×f6 23 ♘d4, but he felt that it was a bit drawish and did not wish to bring the game to a close so soon.

22	...	♖×c6
23	♖ad1	♗c3
24	♖e3	f6

The game continued 25 g4 g5 26 h4 h6 27 hg hg 28 ♘d4 ♗×d4 29 ♖×d4 ♖h8 30 ♖e1 ♖c2 31 a4 a5 32 f4 ♔g6 33 fg ♔×g5 34 ♖f1 ♔g6 35 ♖f2 ♖hc8 36 ♖df4 ♖×f2 and a draw was agreed. Note that 37 ♔×f2 ♔g5? 38 ♖×f6! ♔×f6 39 d7 would have won for White, but Karpov no doubt realised that his opponent was unlikely to fall into that trap!

II

9	...	♕a5 (64)

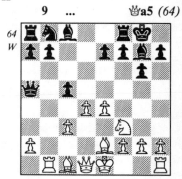

10	0-0

10 ♖b5 ♕×c3+ 11 ♗d2 ♕a3 12 ♖×c5 with an unclear position was seen in the seminal game Shamkovich–Gheorghiu, Cleveland 1975. Recently this line has scored well, with White choosing 12 ♖a5, for example 12 ... ♕b2 13 ♖×c5 ♕×a2 14 0-0 ♕e6 15 ♗c4! ± Delmas–Gorlinger, corr. 1984, or 13 ... ♘c6 14 d5 ♘d4 15 ♘×d4 ♗×d4 16 ♖c4 ♗g7 17 0-0 b6 18 ♖c2 ♕d4 19 ♗c3! ± Danner–

Schmidt, Wroclaw 1985.

10 ... ♕×a2

An alternative path is 10 ... ♕×c3 11 ♗d2 (11 d5 ♕a5 12 ♗g5 ♖e8 13 ♕c1 a6 14 ♖d1 ♘d7 gives Black adequate counterplay; Raetsky-Konopa, USSR 1985.) 11 ...♕a3 12 ♕c2 ♗d7 13 ♖×b7 (A more ambitious path is 13 dc ♗c6 14 ♗b5 ♘a6 15 ♖fc1 ♘c7 with unclear complications in Belyavsky-Tukmakov, USSR Ch. 1983) 13 ... ♗c6 13 ♖b3 ♗a4 15 ♖×a3 ♗×c2 16 dc ♗×e4 with roughly even chances in Miniböck-Konopka, Eger 1985.

11 ♗g5

11 d5!? deserves consideration.

11 ... ♕e6

12 e5?!

More promising is 12 ♖e1!?, since 12 ... ♕×e4 is met by 13 ♗b5 ± although 12 ... b6 13 d5 leads to an unclear position where White has a strong initiative in compensation for his material.

12 ... ♖d8

13 ♕a4 h6

13 ... ♕c6 14 ♕b3 ♗e6 15 c4!! is better for White, for example 15 ... cd 16 ♗×e7 ♖d7?! 17 ♗d6 ♕e4 18 ♗d3 ♕f4 19 ♖e1 ± Ubilava-Georgadze, USSR 1984, or 17 ... ♕c8 18 ♘g5 ♗f5 19 c5! ♘c6 20 ♗c4 ± Ehlvest-Stohl, Leningrad 1984.

14	d5	♕g4
15	♕×g4	♗×g4
16	♗×e7	♖×d5
17	h3	♖d7
18	♗×c5	♗f5

19	♖bd1	♖×d1
20	♖×d1	♘c6
21	♗d6	

½-½ Yonov-Zernitsky, USSR 1985.

III

9 ... b6 (65)

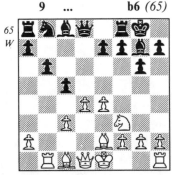

10 0-0 ♗b7

The immediate 10 ... cd is met by 11 cd and now 11 ... ♗b7 12 ♕d3 transposes below, but 11 ... e6 allows White to seize the initiative with 12 ♗g5 ♕d6 13 ♕d2 ♗b7 14 ♕e3, Lputian-Lalić, Sarajevo 1985.

11 ♕d3 cd

11 ... ♗a6 12 ♕e3 ♕c8 13 d5 ♗×e2 14 ♕×e2 is slightly better for White, as the Black queen seems misplaced. An interesting example is Whitehead-Fernandez, New York 1987, which saw 14 ... c4!? 15 ♖b4 ♘d7 16 ♖×c4 ♕a6 17 ♖e1 ♘c5 18 ♗g5 ♖fe8 19 e5 ♖ad8 20 ♖d4 ♕×e2 21 ♖×e2 f6 with some, but probably not enough, compensation for the pawn.

11 ... ♕d7 12 ♗g5 h6 13 ♗f4 f5 14 ♘e5! ♗×e5 15 ♗×e5 clearly favours White (Kengis-

Tseshkovsky, Minsk 1985).

12 cd ♗a6

12 ... e6 13 ♗g5 ♕d6 14 ♕e3 ♖c8 15 ♖fd1 was clearly better for White in Lputian-Lalič, Sarajevo 1985.

13 ♕e3 ♕d7
14 ♗×a6 ♘xa6
15 ♕a3 ♕b7
16 ♗e3 e6
17 h4

This led to a complicated position with chances for both sides in Cvitan-Gavrikov, Vršac 1985.

IV

9 ... ♘c6 (66)

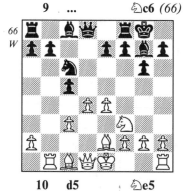

10 d5 ♘e5

10 ... ♗×c3+ 11 ♗d2 ♗×d2+ 12 ♕×d2 and now:

(a) 12 ... ♘a5 13 h4 is currently held to favour White:

(a1) 13 ... ♗g4 14 h5 ♗×f3 (14 ... ♗×h5? 15 ♕h6 intending 16 ♘g5, 16 g4 ±±) 15 gf e5 (15 ... b6 16 ♕h6 ♕d6 17 hg ♕×g6 18 ♕h2! ♔h8 19 ♔d2 ♕g7 20 e5! ±± or 16 ... g5 17 ♕×g5+ ♔h8 18 ♖g1 ♖g8 19 ♕×g8+ ♔×g8 20 ♖×g8+ ♖×g8 21 f4 ±) 16 hg! fg 17 d6! ± Novikov-Danailov, Poznan 1985.

(a2) 13 ... f6 14 h5 gh 15 ♘g5 fg 16 ♕×g5+ ♔h8 17 ♕×h5 ♖f7 18 ♕×f7 ♕g8 19 ♕×e7 b6 20 ♗d3 c4 21 ♗c2 ♕g7 22 ♕d8+ ♕g8 23 ♕f6+ ♕g7 24 e5 1-0 Frank-Sildmets, 6th US corr. Ch.

(b) 12 ... ♘d4?! 13 ♘×d4 c×d4 14 ♕×d4 is clearly better for White:

(b1) 14 ... ♕a5+ 15 ♕d2 ♕×d2+ 16 ♔×d2 ♖d8 17 ♔e3 gave White a dominating endgame advantage in Kasparov-Natsis, Malta Ol. 1980.

(b2) 14 ... e6 15 d6! ♕a5+ 16 ♕d2 ♕×d2+ 17 ♔×d2 e5 18 ♔e3 and again the endgame was much better for White (Popescu-Stefanov, corr. 1983).

11 ♘×e5 ♗×e5
12 ♕d2 e6

An interesting option is 12 ... b6 13 f4 ♗g7 14 0-0 e6 15 d6 ♗b7 16 ♗f3 e5 17 c4 ef! 18 ♕×f4 ♗d4+ 19 ♔h1 f6 20 ♗b2 ♗×b2 21 ♖×b2 with a complex middlegame (Olafsson-Ftačnik, Esbjerg 1985).

13 f4 ♗g7
14 c4 ed

14 ... ♖e8 15 e5! is better for White, for example 15 ... f6 16 d6 fe 17 ♗b2 ef 18 ♗×g7 ♔×g7 19 0-0 ♖f8! (19 ... e5 20 d7! ♕×d7 21 ♕×d7 ♗×d7 22 ♖×b7 ♖ad8 23 ♗g4! ♖e7 24 ♖d1 ±) 20 ♖×f4 ♖×f4 21 ♕×f4 ♕f6 Tal-Vaganian, USSR Ch. 1984, and now White should have played 22 ♕e4! e.g. 22 ... ♖b8 23 ♖f1! ♕d4+ 24 ♕×d4 cd 25 ♖b1! ♗d7 26 ♗f3 b6 27 c5 ♖c8 28 c6! ♗×c6 29 ♖c1 ♗d7 30 ♖×c8

♗xc8 31 ♗c6 intending 32 d7 (Gligorić). Instead, the game ended in a draw after 22 ♕e3 b6 23 ♕e4.

15	cd	♗d4
16	♗b2	♕b6!
17	♗d3	c4!
18	♗xc4	♖e8

... and it is not clear who stands better (H. Olafsson–Helmers, Gjovik 1985).

V

9	...	♗g4 *(67)*

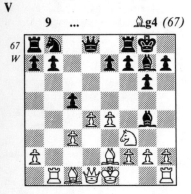

67
W

10	0-0	♗xf3
11	♗xf3	cd
12	cd	♗xd4

12 ... ♕xd4 led to a slight advantage for White in Lerner–Vatnikov, USSR 1983, after 13 ♖xb7 ♘c6 14 ♗e3 ♕xd1 15 ♖xd1 ♖fc8 16 ♗e2.

13	♖xb7	♘c6
14	♕a4	♕d6
15	♗a3	

According to Gligorić, White might pursue 15 ♖b5 here.

15	...	♗c5

... with a balanced game in Rubinetti–Sax, Lucerne Ol. 1982.

Although White cannot find an easy advantage against the Grünfeld (that's why Kasparov plays it as Black!), these lines provide interesting dynamic play.

Grünfeld Defence (Black)

Kasparov adopted this opening for his 1986 match against Karpov. When it was first seen there was pandemonium in the press room.

1	d4	♘f6
2	c4	g6
3	♘c3	d5 *(68)*

The opening became the centre of a theoretical debate in the third and fourth matches.

In spite of failures in the first part of match III, Kasparov maintained his faith in the opening and it carried him to victory in both matches. Altogether, the matches saw 19 Grünfelds, applying a variety of systems. Kasparov also used the opening with success in games against Hübner, Seirawan and others. As in the case of the Tarrasch Defence, Kasparov's advocacy of the opening brought many other players' attention to it.

Because of the wide range of variations in which Kasparov has made significant contributions, we shall examine a number of lines.

I	White fianchettoes
II	White plays ♗c1-f4
III	Russian Systems with ♕d1-b3
IV	Classical Exchange Variation
V	White plays ♗c1-g5
VI	White plays ♕d1-a4+

I

1	d4	♘f6
2	c4	g6
3	♘f3	♗g7
4	g3	c6
5	♗g2	

A recent example of the immediate central capture (after 4 ... d5 instead of 4 ... c6) is 5 cd ♘xd5 6 ♗g2 ♘b6 7 ♘c3 ♘c6 8 e3 0-0 9 0-0 ♖e8 10 ♖e1 e5 11 d5 ♘a5 12 e4 c6 13 ♗g5 f6 14 ♗e3 ♘ac4!? 15 dc ♘xe3 16 ♕xd8 ♖xd8 17 cb ♗xb7 18 ♖xe3 ♗h6 19 ♖ee1 ♘c4 20 ♖ad1 (After 20 b3 ♘a3! 21 ♖ed1 ♘c2 22 ♖ab1! ♘a3 23 ♖a1 ♘c2 with a draw, since 22 ♖xd8+ ♖xd8 23 ♖f1 ♖d3 24 ♘d5 ♗xd5 25 ed ♖xd5 gives Black a slight advantage — Kristiansen.) 20 ... ♔f8 21 h4 ♖ac8 22 ♗h3 ♖xd1 23 ♖xd1

♘xb2 24 ♖d7 ♖xc3 25 ♖xb7 ♘c4 26 ♘h2 ♘d6 27 ♖xh7 ♗g7 28 h5 gh 29 ♖xh5 ♖c1+ 30 ♔g2 ♖c2 31 ♗e6 ♘xe4 32 ♘g4 ♖d2 33 ♗b3 a5 34 ♖f5 ♘d6 35 ♖h5 ♘e4 36 ♖f5 ♘d6 37 ♖h5 ♘e4 ½-½ Karpov-Kasparov, Amsterdam 1988.

5   ...   d5 *(69)*

This is the move order that was applied in games 3 and 13 of the third Kasparov-Karpov match. In the fourth match, games 1 and 3 saw the move order 3 g3 c6 4 ♘f3 ♗g7 5 ♗g2 d5. What is the difference between the two approaches? The main point is that after 3 g3 c6 White can play 4 d5!? if he wishes, even though this is not known to bring any significant advantage after 4 ... cd 5 cd d6. With the delayed fianchetto this is not possible, since 5 d5 would have been met by 5 ... cd 6 cd ♕a5+ 7 ♘c3 ♘xd5!

6   cd   cd
7   ♘c3

On 7 0-0 0-0, 8 ♘e5 is less effective. Kasparov has played 8 ... ♗g4. After 9 ♘xg4 ♗xg4 10 ♘c3 ♘c6 it is not easy for White to obtain an advantage: 11 h3 ♗d7! 12 e3 e6 13 b3 ♕a5 14 ♗d2 ♕c7 15 ♖c1 ♖ac8 = Polugayevsky-Kasparov, Moscow 1981. Or 11 ♗xd5 ♘xd4 12 ♗xb7 ♘xe2+ 13 ♘xe2 ♕xd1 14 ♖xd1 ♗xe2 15 ♗xa8 ♗xd1 = Velićković-Henley, Tbilisi 1983. But one notes that he didn't choose to play this line against Karpov!

7   ...   0-0
8   ♘e5

This is the most accurate manoeuvre. After 8 0-0 ♘e4! 9 ♕b3 ♘c6 Black equalizes very easily and faces no problems, according to Kasparov.

8   ...   e6

This is not the first time that the variation has seen action in World Championship play. Botvinnik-Smyslov, (m/21) 1957 saw 8 ... ♗f5 9 0-0 ♘e4 10 ♘xe4 ♗xe4 11 f3 ♗f5 12 ♗e3 ♘d7 13 ♘xd7 ♕xd7 ½-½. One must keep in mind, however, that Botvinnik had just lost a critical game which had broken Botvinnik's spirit and left him too tired to try to overcome an 11½-8½ score. The next, final game of the match was drawn in just eleven moves. Geller tried 10 ♗e3 ♘xc3 11 bc ♘c6 12 ♘xc6 bc 13 ♕a4 against Fischer at Palma de Mallorca 1970, but came away empty handed after 13 ... ♕b6. Larsen notes, however, that White was not obliged to throw away first a pawn, and then a possibly tenable endgame.

9   0-0

This is better than 9 ♗g5 ♛b6!
10 ♛d2 ♘fd7 11 ♘f3 ♘c6
(Karpov-Timman, Bugojno 1986)
played before the match, where
White did not achieve any
advantage.

| 9 | ... | ♘fd7 *(70)* |

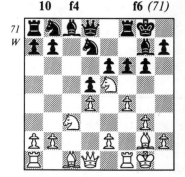

From this position experience
has been varied. Karpov-
Kasparov, (m/3) 1986 went:

| 10 | ♘f3 | ♘c6 |
| 11 | ♗f4 | ♘f6 |

A good alternative is 11
... ♛b6, seen in Akhmilovskaya-
Chiburdanidze, match 1986, which
continued 12 ♘a4 ♛a5 13 ♖c1 b5
14 ♘c5 ♘xc5 15 ♖xc5 ♗d7 with
equal chances.

12	♘e5	♗d7
13	♛d2	♘xe5
14	♗xe5	

If 14 de, then 14 ... ♘g4! 15 e4
d4! 16 ♛xd4 ♗c6 17 ♛d6 ♛b6
intending 18 ... ♖fd8 (Dlugy).

14	...	♗c6
15	♖fd1	♘d7
16	♗xg7	♔xg7
17	♖ac1	♘f6

Black has already equalized,
according to Kasparov.

18	♛f4	♛b8
19	♛xb8	♖axb8
20	f3	♖fd8
21	♔f2	

The methodical 21 e4 can be
met by 21 ... de 22 fe e5! 23 d5 ♗d7,
according to Kasparov. With the
text move White concedes equality. In the next example, Karpov
tries a more ambitious plan.

21	...	♖bc8
22	e3	♘e8
23	♖d2	♘d6

and Black had no problems.
In game 13 of the same match,
Karpov tried:

| 10 | f4 | f6 *(71)* |

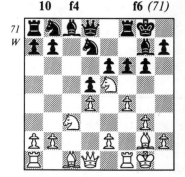

Boleslavsky recommended 10
...♘xe5 11 fe f6, and this has been
passed on uncritically in the literature. Each co-author of this book
separately found the simple 12 ef,
after which it is difficult for Black
to equalize: 12 ... ♖xf6 13 ♗f4 ± or
12 ... ♗xf6 13 ♗h6 ±. The obvious
nature of this line has no doubt
contributed to its failure to
apppear in praxis.

11 ... ♘c6 has disappeared as
a result of Kasparov-Nunn,

Brussels 1986: 12 e4! de 13 ♗e3 f5 14 ef ♖xf6 15 ♘xe4 ♖xf1+ 16 ♕xf1 (±) ♘xd4?? (16 ... ♗xd4 17 ♗xd4 ♕xd4+ 18 ♔h1 intending 19 ♖d1 or 19 ♘f6+ or 16 ... ♗d7 17 ♖ad1 h6 18 ♘c5 ♕c7 19 ♗e4.) 17 ♖d1 e5 18 ♘g5! 1-0

    11   ♘f3   ♘c6

    12   ♗e3

Keene and Goodman suggest 12 e4, an interesting move, but one which lacks punch after 12 ... de 13 ♘xe4 ♘b6.

    12   ...   ♘b6

    13   ♗f2

White prepares two strong advances: e4 and g4–g5. Black stops both.

    13   ...   f5

More exciting was 13 ... ♘c4!? followed by 14 b3 (14 ♕b3 also deserves consideration) 14 ... ♘d6! seizing control of the important e4-square. But 14 e4!? ♘xb2 15 ♕e2 ♘c4 16 ed ed 17 ♘xd5 is unclear, though perhaps in White's favour. Meanwhile, 13 ... ♗d7 is dubious on account of 14 e4! (Kasparov).

    14   ♘e5   ♗d7

    15   ♕d2   ♘c8

    16   ♕e3!   ♔h8 (72)

Not 16 ... ♘d6? 17 ♘xc6 ♗xc6 18 ♕xe6+. The text prevents this manoeuvre because Black will have the resource ... ♖f8–e8.

    17   ♖fd1

Some commentators, including Eduard Gufeld, recommended the sharp thrust 17 g4, intending 17 ... ♘xe5 (17 ... ♘8e7 g5 ±) 18 de fg

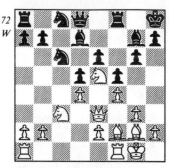

19 ♕g3 h5 20 h3!? *(73)*. The resulting position is very important for the evaluation of the entire variation starting with 13 ... f5.

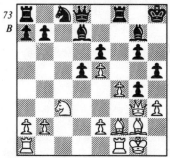

White has clear compensation for the pawn after 20 ... gh 21 ♗xh3 ♘e7 (or 21 ... ♕e8 22 e4!) 22 ♗c5 as well as after 20 ... g5 21 e3 ♘e7 22 hg h4 23 ♕h2 ♘g6 24 ♘e2 ♗b5 25 ♘d4. It is easy to understand why Kasparov declined to enter this variation in the fourth match.

After the text Kasparov not only equalized, but even seized the initiative:

    17   ...   ♘d6

    18   b3   ♖c8

    19   ♖ac1   ♗e8

    20   ♗e1   ♗f6! ∓

Karpov–Kasparov, (m/3) 1987:

10	**f4**	**♘c6** *(74)*

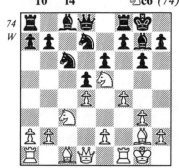

74
W

11	**♗e3**	**♘b6**

11 ... ♘dxe5 is dubious: 12 fe f6 13 ef ♖xf6 was unclear in Karpov–Chiburdanidze, Bilbao 1987: 14 ♕d2 ♗d7 15 ♔h1 ♖xf1+ 16 ♖xf1 ♕e7 17 ♖d1 with a slight advantage for White. In *Soviet Sport* 17 ♗g1 is suggested, but after 17 ... ♖d8! 18 e4 de 19 ♘xe4 ♘xd4 20 ♗xd4 ♗c6 21 ♗c5 ♖xd2 22 ♗xe7 ♖xg2! we feel that it is Black, if anyone, who holds the advantage.

12	**♗f2** *(75)*	

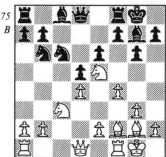

75
B

White is ready to advance in the centre. In Karpov–Kasparov, (m/1) 1987, Black entered unclear complications with 12 ... ♗d7 13

e4! ♘e7 (13 ... de 14 ♗xe4 would have given White a slight advantage due to his control of the centre) 14 ♘xd7 ♕xd7 15 e5 ♖fc8 16 ♖c1 ♗f8 17 ♗f3 (17 g4 is interesting here, for example 17 ... ♗h6 18 ♗h4 ♘c4 19 ♕e2 ♘c6 20 ♖cd1 b5 21 ♖d3 ∞, with an initiative for White.) 17 ... ♖c7! 18 b3 ♖ac8 19 ♕d2 ♘c6 20 ♕b2 a6 and Black had equalized.

12	**...**	**♘e7!**
13	**a4**	

Here 13 e4 would have been met by 13 ... de, equalizing.

13	**...**	**a5**
14	**♕b3**	**♗d7**
15	**♖fc1**	**♗c6**
16	**♘b5**	**♘bc8**
17	**e3**	**♘d6**
18	**♘xd6**	**♕xd6**
19	**♗e1**	**♖fb8**
20	**♗f1**	**f6**
21	**♘f3**	**♕d7**
22	**♕c2**	**♘f5**
23	**♗d2**	**♘d6**

Black can claim more than equality, so it seems that Kasparov has solved the problems posed by this opening system.

II

1	**d4**	**♘f6**
2	**c4**	**g6**
3	**♘c3**	**d5**
4	**♗f4**	**♗g7** *(76)*

When Karpov was first confronted by Kasparov's use of the Grünfeld Defence, he chose to adopt a fairly mild system in reply.

A   5 ♘f3
B   5 e3

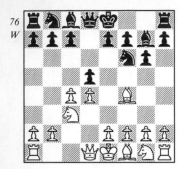

A

5   ᗺf3

This position can also arise from the move order 4 ᗺf3 ᗺg7 5 ᗺf4.

5   ...   c5!? *(77)*

This is a typical counterthrust in the Grünfeld Defence, but often Black delays it until after 5 ... 0-0 6 ᗺc1.

6   dc   ♛a5
7   ᗺc1

Theoreticians have concentrated on the line 7 cd ᗺ×d5 8 ♛×d5 ᗺ×c3+ 9 ᗺd2 *(78)* and now:

(a) 9 ... ᗺ×d2+ 10 ♛×d2 ♛×c5 11 ᗺc1 ♛f5, seen in Petrosian–Shamkovich, Moscow 1966, is no

longer appropriate because of Botvinnik and Estrin's 12 ᗺd4! ♛d7 13 ♛h6!

(b) 9 ... ᗺe6!? 10 ♛×b7 (10 ᗺ×c3 ♛×c3+ 11 ♛d2 ♛×c5! =) 10 ... ᗺ×d2+ 11 ᗺ×d2 0-0 and now:

(b1) 12 ♛×a8? is strongly countered by 12 ... ᗺd8! 13 ᗺd1 (13 b4!? ♛×b4 14 ᗺd1 ᗺ×d2 =) 13 ... ᗺd5 ∓.

(b2) 12 e4 is also possible, but Dreyev–Yepishin, Tallinn 1986, saw 12 ... ᗺc6! 13 ♛a6 ♛×c5 14 ♛b5 ♛d6 15 ᗺc4 ♛d4 16 ᗺe2 ᗺfc8 17 0-0 ᗺab8 18 ♛a4 ♛×e4 19 ᗺfe1 ᗺd4 20 ᗺf1 ♛f4 21 b3 ᗺc5 22 ♛×a7 ᗺh5 23 h3 ᗺ×h3 24 ♛×b8+ ♛×b8 25 gh ᗺf3+ 26 ♛g2 ᗺd5 0-1.

(b3) 12 b4 ♛a4 13 e4 ᗺd7 14 ♛b5 ♛a3 15 c6 ᗺf6 16 ᗺe2 ♛c3 17 ᗺd1 ᗺfd8 (17 ... ᗺ×e4 18 ♛d3 ±) 18 f3 a5! gives Black counterplay, according to Belyavsky. 13 ♛×a8!? is more principled. After 13 ... ᗺc6 14 ♛b7 ᗺd8! 15 ᗺd1 (15 ᗺc1 ♛a3) Black can go for the draw with 15 ... ᗺd7 16 ♛a8+ (16 ♛c8+ ♛g7 ∓) 16 ... ᗺd8 etc, but risky is 15 ... ᗺ×b4 16 e3 (forced) 16 ...

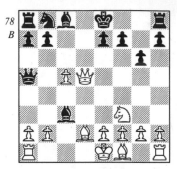

♘c2+ 17 ♔e2 ♗d5! (Co-author Shamkovich originally suggested 17 ... ♗g4+? 18 f3 ♘xe3 but Robert Ciaffone came up with 19 ♕b3!!, refuting the line. 17 ... h5 may be playable.) 18 ♕c7 or 18 ♕xe7.

Summing up, it is clear that Karpov avoided the 7 cd line out of respect for 9 ... ♗e6.

7	...	dc
8	e3	♕×c5
9	♕a4+	

Jon Tisdall gives both 9 ♘d2 ♘h5! and 9 ♘e5 ♘h5 10 ♕a4+ ♘c6! but in this latter line White could play the much stronger 10 ♕d5!, so in our opinion 9 ♘e5 is best met by 9 ... ♘c6.

9	...	♘c6

An interesting alternative is 9 ... ♗d7!? 10 ♕xc4 ♕b6 11 ♗e2 (11 ♗c7 ♕xb2 12 ♖b1 ♕a3 13 ♖xb7 0-0 and 11 ♘b5 ♘a6 12 ♗c7 ♕e6! are acceptable for Black, according to Kasparov.) 11 ... 0-0 12 0-0 and now 12 ... ♗e6! is equal, but not 12 ... ♖c8? 13 ♕xc8+! ♗xc8 14 ♘d5 ♕e6 15 ♖xc8+ ♗f8 16 ♖fc1 with a very dangerous attack (Kasparov).

10	♗×c4	0-0
11	0-0	♗d7 *(79)*
12	♕b5	

Kasparov has not mentioned Taimanov's suggestion of 12 ♘b5 intending 13 ♗×f7+), but Black can reply 12 ... ♕h5 13 ♗e2 e5! 14 ♗g3 (14 ♘fd4 ♘xd4! 15 ♗xh5 ♗×b5 ∓) 14 ... a6 15 ♘c3 ♘d4 16 ♘xd4 ♗xa4 17 ♗xh5 ♘xh5 18 ♘xa4 ♘xg3 19 hg ed ∓.

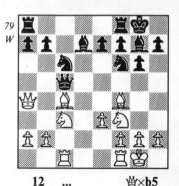

79
W

12	...	♕×b5

Karpov-Kasparov, (m/1) 1986 now went 13 ♗×b5 ♖ac8 14 ♖fd1 ♖fd8 15 h3 h6 16 ♔f1 a6 17 ♗e2 ♗e6 18 ♖×d8+ ♖×d8 19 ♘e5 ♘xe5 20 ♗xe5 ♖d2 21 b3 and a draw was agreed.

B

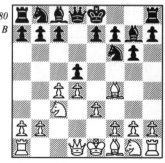

5	e3 *(80)*

80
B

5	...	c5

Here the central thrust is the normal move for Black.

6	dc	♕a5
7	♖c1	dc

This is safer than 7 ... ♘e4, as played in Karpov-Kasparov, (m/5) 1986. After 8 cd ♘xc3 9 ♕d2 ♕xa2 10 bc Kasparov chose 10 ... ♕d2+!? (Petrosian-Fischer, (m/2) 1971,

saw 10 ... ♛a5 11 ♝c4 ♘d7 12 ♘e2
(*12 ♘f3!?*) 12 ... ♘e5 13 ♝a2 ♝f5?
14 ♝xe5! ♝xe5 15 ♘d4 ±. But
Fischer could have kept the
balance with 13 ... ♛xc5 14 ♘d4
b5!) 11 ♔xd2 ♘d7 12 ♝b5 0-0 13
♝xd7 ♝xd7 14 e4 f5!? 15 e5 e6!?
(W. Schmidt-Gross, Nalechov
1984, saw 15 ... ♖ac8 16 c6?! bc 17
d6 ed 18 ed and now Black could
have obtained an advantage with
Adorjan's 18 ... ♖fe8! The
Hungarian theoretician also gives
16 d6 ♖xc5 and 16 e6 ♝a4 17 ♝e3
♝b3! as leading to an advantage
for Black, but Kasparov showed
that 16 c4 ♖xc5 17 ♝e3 actually
leaves White in charge, and we
feel that 16 ♝e3 ♝xe5 17 ♘f3 is
also promising. So while we agree
with Kasparov that the line played
in the game with 10 ... ♛xd2+ is
not refuted, nevertheless it is not
clear that Black will be able to
achieve equality. We can say, however, that 10 ... ♛xd2+ has been
rehabilitated, at least for the time
being.

8   ♝xc4

Black has nothing to fear on
8 ♛a4+ ♛xa4 9 ♘xa4 ♝d7 10
♖xc4 ♘d5!, seen in Wexler-
Foguelman, Buenos Aires 1964.

8   ...   0-0

Now 9 ♘e2 is interesting, for
example 9 ... ♛xc5 10 ♛b3 ♛a5 11
0-0 ♘c6, Kraidman-W. Schmidt,
Nice Ol. 1974, where *ECO* recommends 12 h3 with a slight
advantage to White. We feel that
10 ... ♘c6 is significantly stronger,

intending 11 ... ♘a5, for example
11 ♛b5 ♛xb5 12 ♝xb5 (12 ♘xb5
♘a5! ∓) 12 ... ♘b4 13 0-0 a6 14 ♝c4
b5 ∓.

9   ♘f3 *(81)*

9   ...   ♛xc5

There is no particular reason
why 9 ... ♘c6 cannot be played
here, delaying the capture until
the following move.

10   ♝b3

The aggressive 10 ♘b5?! allows
easy equality with 10 ... ♛b4+ 11
♘d2 ♘d5 or 11 ♔e2 ♝e6! 11 ...
♘e4, which occupied the attention
of the press room during the 1986
London match, is also a very
interesting idea.

10   ...   ♘c6
11   0-0   ♛a5

11 ... ♛h5 is an alternative
which we feel is in no way inferior
to the text. After 13 h3 ♖d8 White
can choose between 13 ♘d2 ♘e8,
correctly evaluated as even by
Boleslavsky, and 13 ♛e2 e5, which
led to an unclear position in
Ageychenko-Gik, USSR 1966.

12   h3   ♝f5 *(82)*
13   ♛e2

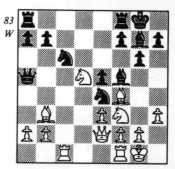

The normal move. Karpov–Kasparov, (m/9) 1986, saw instead 13 ♘d4 ♗d7! 14 ♕e2 ♘xd4! (Kasparov's improvement on 14 ... e5 played in Gulko–Tseshkovsky, Sochi 1975.) 15 ed e6! 16 ♗d2 ♕b6 17 ♖fd1 ♗c6 18 ♗e3 ♕a5 19 ♗d2 ♕b6 20 ♗e3 ♕a5 ½–½. The feeling in the press room at the time was that Black would have had the better chances had White not opted for the draw by repetition.

13 ... ♘e4
14 ♘d5

14 ♘xe4 ♗xe4 leads to equality:

(a) 15 ♖fd1 ♗xf3 16 ♕xf3 ♗xb2 17 ♖b1 ♗g7 18 ♗d5 e6 19 ♗e4 ♘e5 20 ♕e2 ♖ad8 = Hansen–Wiedenkeller, Helsinki 1986.

(b) 15 ♘g5 ♗d5 16 ♗c7 ♕xc7 17 ♗xd5 ♕e5 18 ♕b5 ♘d8 where Black's chances are no worse (Sahović–Lanka, Jurmala 1978).

(c) 15 ♘d2 ♗d5 16 ♗xd5 ♕xd5 and a draw was agreed in Hort–Uhlmann, Moscow 1971.

14 ... e5 *(83)*
15 ♖xc6!?

Tremors were felt in the analysis room when this move was played in Karpov-Kasparov (m/11) 1986. Amazingly, it seems to have been a novelty. Tisdall suggested that the effect on Kasparov was more psychological than 'chessic', but we are not so sure.

The alternative 15 ♗h2 is an abject retreat which can be dealt with by 15 ... ♗e6 16 ♖fd1 ♖ad8 17 ♕c4 ♘d6 18 ♕e2 (Moran–Wittmann, Dubai Ol. 1986) 18 ... ♘e4 = Gipslis.

15 .... ef

15 ... bc 16 ♘e7+ ♔h8 requires some analysis:

(a) 17 ♘xe5 ♗xe5 19 ♘xc6 ♕d2! ∓.

(b) 17 ♘xc6 ♕b6 18 ♘cxe5 ♗e6! leads to unclear complications, according to Kasparov.

(c) Co-author Shamkovich has proposed 17 ♗xe5!, where White has more than sufficient compensation for his exchange, for example:

(c1) 17 ... ♗xe5 18 ♘xc6 (intending 19 ♘cxe5) 18 ... ♗h2+! 19 ♘xh2 (19 ♔xh2? ♕c7+ ∓) 19 ...

♕d2! with an unclear position, e.g. 20 ♖e1 ♖ac8 (20 ... ♕xe2 21 ♖xe2 ♖ac8 22 ♘d4 ♖c1+ 23 ♘f1 ♗d7 24 ♗c2! ♖e8 25 ♘b3 ♖xf1+ 26 ♔xf1 ♗b5 27 ♘d4 ♗xe2+ 28 ♔xe2 ±) 21 ♘d4 ♕xe2 22 ♖xe2 ♖c1+ 23 ♘f1 (intending 24 g4) ±.

(c2) 17 ... f6 18 ♘xf5 fe 19 ♘xg7 ♔xg7 20 ♕c2 ♘c5 21 ♘g5!

The text is not necessarily inferior (despite Gipslis's pejorative comment in *ECO*), and allows Black to hold the balance with precise play.

16   ♖c7   ♗e6!
17   ♕e1

Gipslis (in *ECO DII*) gives this ?! and claims that 17 ♘e7+ ♔h8 18 ♖fc1 is ± even though after 18 ... ♗xb3 19 ab (19 ef?! ♗d5 ∓) 19 ... fe 20 ♕xe3 ♘d6 21 ♕f4 ♖ad8 22 ♘g5?! h6 23 ♘e6 g5! ∓ or 22 ♕h4 h6! Black is no worse in a rather unclear position. So the choice between 17 ♘e7+ and the text is more a matter of taste, and we find Karpov's choice more appealing.

An inferior alternative is 17 ♖xb7? ♘d6! 18 ♘e7+ ♔h8 19 ♘c6 ♕c5 20 ♗xe6 ♕xc6 21 ♖e7 fe 22 ef ♘f5 ∓ Szilagyi–W. Schmidt, Budapest 1986.

17   ...   ♕b5
18   ♘e7+   ♔h8
19   ♗xe6!

19 ef would fail to 19 ... ♘g3!! 20 fg ♕b6+.

19   ...   fe
20   ♕b1!   ♘g5

The game resembles a prolonged duel of the sort popular in MGM movies of the 1930s.

21   ♘h4   ♘xh3+!?

This move may be good enough to survive, but Karpov is correct when he points out that 21 ... fe! would have led to a draw after 22 ♘xg6+ hg 23 ♘xg6+ ♔g8 24 ♘e7+. That may prove to be the final word on this line.

22   ♔h2   ♕h5
23   ♘exg6+   hg
24   ♕xg6   ♕e5

The sparring continues. The game, which was awarded the brilliancy prize (paid in gold sovereigns!) for the best game of the London half of the match concluded in a draw after 25 ♖f7 ♖xf7 26 ♕xf7 ♘g5 27 ♕g6+ ♔h7 28 ♘xe5 ♘xf7 29 ♘xf7 ♔g6 30 ♘d6 fe 31 ♘c4 ef 32 ♖xf2 b5 33 ♘e3 a5 34 ♔g3 a4 35 ♖c2 ♖f8 36 ♔g4 ♗d4 37 ♖e2 ♗xe3 38 ♖xe3 ♖f2 39 b3 ♖xg2+ 40 ♔f3 ♖xa2 41 ba ½–½.

The Russian Systems

1	d4	♘f6
2	c4	g6
3	♘c3	d5
4	♘f3	♗g7
5	♕b3	

The Russian Systems have been a consistently popular reply to the Grünfeld for many years, and they are considered the main lines in the *ECO* classification. After the standard 5 ... dc 6 ♕xc4 0-0 7 e4, Black has a wide range of choices. Adorjan, in his recent book on the Grünfeld, thinks highly of 7 ... a6, but the World Champion clearly doesn't share his confidence, preferring the classical 7 ... ♗g4 and the modern 7 ... ♘a6 lines.

Karpov–Kasparov, (m/17) 1986:

5	...	dc
6	♕×c4	0-0
7	e4	♗g4
8	♗e3	♘fd7
9	♖d1	♘c6
10	♗e2	♘b6
11	♕c5	♕d6
12	e5	♕×c5

On 12 ... ♕d7?!, 13 h3 ♗×f3 14 ♗×f3 e6 15 ♘e4 gives White a clear advantage. An interesting, but flawed, option is 13 e6!?, for example 13 ... ♗×e6 (13 ... fe? 14 ♘e5!) 14 d5 ♗×c3+ (forced) 15 bc ♘×d5 16 c4 b6 17 ♕b5 (forced) ♘c3 18 ♗×d7 ♘×b5 19 cb ♗×d7 20 bc ♗×c6 ∓.

13   dc *(84)*

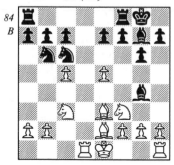

At the end of 1986 this was the critical position.

13   ...   ♘c8

13 ... ♘d7 is tempting, even though Kasparov points out 14 h3!:

(a) 14 ... ♗×f3 15 gf ♘d×e5? 16 f4 ± or 15 ... ♖fd8 16 f4 ±.

(b) 14 ... ♗e6 15 ♘g5 ♘d×e5 16 ♘×e6! (16 f4 ♘c4 17 ♗c1 ♘a3!) 16 ... fe 17 f4 ♘f7 18 ♗c4! e5 19 0-0 ef 20 ♗×f4 ♗d4+ 21 ♔h1 ♗×c3 22 bc ♔g7 23 ♖d7!

Nevertheless, in the latter line Shamkovich found 17 ... ♗h6!, a move which Kasparov missed. After 18 0-0 ♖ad8 19 ♖×d8 ♖×d8 (intending 20 ... ♘d3) 20 ♖d1 ♖×d1 21 ♘×d1 ♘d7 22 ♗c4 ♔f7 23 ♘c3 ♗g7 24 ♘e4 h6 or 24 g4 ♗d4 the chances are roughly level.

14   h3!

In Karpov–Kasparov, (m/15) 1986, where Karpov first employed 5 ♕b3 against Kasparov, 14 ♘b5 was seen, but 14 ... ♖b8! proved a strong reply, as after 15 ♘×c7 e6! the knight was forced to retreat right away, or else risk being trapped by ... a6. After 16 ♘b5 ♘8e7 Karpov had to recognize the solidity of Black's position. After considerable thought (at the London Press Centre we thought our telex link had broken down!) Karpov found 17 ♖d2! but Kasparov answered boldly with 17 ... b6!?, and after 18 cb ab 19 ♗g5! ♘f5 Karpov allowed the game to quiet down: 20 b3 h6 21 ♗f6 ♗×f3 22 ♗×f3 ♘×e5 23 ♗×e5 ♗×e5 24 0-0 ♖fd8 25 ♖fd1 ♖×d2 26 ♖×d2 ♖c8 27 g3 ♖c1+ 28 ♔g2 ♔f8 29 ♗e4 ♔e7 ½-½. With 20 ♘fd4! ♘×d4 21 ♘×d4 ♘×d4 22 ♖×d4 ♗×e2 23 ♔×e2 ♗×e5 a lot of pieces come off the board, but 'White has slight pressure' (Kasparov).

Sacrificing a pawn, White obtains strong play in the centre, especially along the d-file. Karpov does not like to sacrifice material unless it is clearly worked out in advance. The speed with which he played this game (5 minutes used for the first 14 moves) shows that it was.

14 ... &xf3
15 &xf3 &xe5

In the London Press Centre we were sure that Kasparov would not go in for 15 ... ♘xe5 16 &xb7 ♖b8 17 c6 with strong pressure. Kasparov gives 17 ... ♘c4 18 ♘d5! ♘xe3 19 fe ♘d6 20 ♘xe7+ ♔h8 21 ♖xd6! cd 22 ♔e2 &xb2 23 ♖b1 &f6 24 ♘d5 &d8 and now either 25 c7 &xc7 26 ♘xc7 f5 27 ♘a6 or 25 ♖c1.

16 &xc6

Forced, according to Karpov. Kasparov analysed 16 ♖d7 e6 17 &xc6 bc 18 f4 &g7! 19 ♖xc7 ♖e8 20 ♖xc6 ♘e7 21 ♖a6 ♖eb8 22 ♘a4 ♘d5 23 &c1 e5!

16 ... bc
17 &d4

We do not award the customary exclamation mark here. Shamkovich presents strong arguments in favour of 17 f4!?:

(a) 17 ... &xc3+ 18 bc ♖b8 19 0-0 f5?! (19 ... f6 is much better, although Black is still fighting to hold the position.) 20 ♖b1 ♖xb1 21 ♖xb1 ♖d8 22 ♖b7 ♖d7 23 ♖b8 ♖d8 24 &d4 ♔f7 25 &e5 ±.

(b) 17 ... &g7 18 0-0 ♖b8 19 ♖f2 f6 (19 ... f5 20 ♖d7 ♖b7 21 ♖fd2

and 22 &d4) 20 ♖d7 ♖b7 21 ♖fd2 ♔f7 22 g4 intending f5.

Maybe Black can hold, but it certainly isn't pleasant!

17 ... &f4

It is obvious that Black cannot afford to exchange bishops because this would allow immediate infiltration of the seventh rank by the white rook, where the pawns on the c-files must eventually fall. The bad position of the ♘c8 causes Black too many problems. In London, we analysed 17 ... &xd4 18 ♖xd4 ♖b8 19 b3 f5 (or else ♘c3–e4) 20 ♖d7 ♖b7 21 ♔e2 e6 22 ♖hd1 ♖e8 23 ♖d8+ and Black is very passive. Kasparov looked at 19 ... a5 20 ♖a4! Eventually, he concluded that after the trade of bishops, 18 ... a6 would have been relatively best, but even so Black would be uncomfortable.

18 0-0 a5??

18 ... e5! equalized in Karpov–Timman, Tilburg 1986: 19 &e3 &xe3 20 fe ♘e7 21 ♖d7 ♘f5 22 ♖xc7 ♖fc8=.

18 ... ♖e8 19 ♖fe1 ♔f8 would have been better than 18 ... a5, which was tantamount to resignation.

19 ♖fe1 a4

19 ... f6 20 ♖e6 ♖a6 21 ♘d5 is easy. Perhaps 19 ... ♖e8 should have been tried, although White is still clearly better (20 ♘e4 ♔f8 21 &c3). Karpov had only consumed 30 minutes to this point.

20 ♖e4 &h6
21 &e5 a3

22 b3

In Leningrad, the press had already given up the game as hopeless. In London, we all agreed with Jon Speelman, who said of the pawn on a3: 'This pawn either lives (which means that Black successfully sacrifices on b3 or wins the a2 pawn; then he would have adequate counterplay and would wriggle out of a serious problem) or dies. If it dies, then Black is totally lost.'

22 ... ♘a7

Kasparov decided to jettison his pawn on c7 and seeks counterplay. If 22 ... ♗g7 23 ♗×g7 ♔×g7 24 ♖d7 ♖a7 Black is totally tied down and White can go after Black's stranded pawn with ♖d7-d4-a4 etc.

23 ♖d7!

23 ♗×c7 ♗g7! gives Black chances.

23 ... ♗c1

None of the published analysis has addressed Basman and Ravikumar's suggestion of 23 ... ♖fd8!? e.g.:

(a) 24 ♖×e7 ♗f8 25 ♖×c7 ♗×c5;

(b) 24 ♖×c7 f6 25 ♗f4 ♗×f4 26 ♖×f4 ♖d3;

(c) 24 ♖ed4! ♖×d7 25 ♖×d7 ±.

This was published in the London Press Centre bulletin, but copies are rare because some British Chess Federation (BCF) officials refused to allow reprints due to their unhappiness with some of the editorial comment.

24 ♖×c7 ♗b2
25 ♘a4!

Kasparov remarks that '25 ♖×e7 would also have won.' In London, a Psion computer program gave 25 ... ♖fd8 26 ♖e2 ♘c8 27 ♖c7 ♖d3 28 ♖c2 ♗×c3 which it evaluated as much better for White. But Karpov notes that 25 ♖×e7 would have been dubious, because of 25 ... ♗×c3 26 ♗×c3 ♘b5 intending 27 ... ♖fd8-d2×a2.

25 ... ♘b5 26 ♖×c6 ♖fd8 27 ♖b6 ♖d5

A last trap: 28 ♘×b2? ♖×e5! 29 ♖×e5 ab.

28 ♗g3 ♘c3 29 ♘×c3 ♗×c3 30 c6 ♗d4 31 ♖b7 1-0

IV The Classical Exchange Variation

1	d4	♘f6
2	c4	g6
3	♘c3	d5
4	cd	♘×d5
5	e4	♘×c3
6	bc	♗g7
7	♗c4	*(85)*

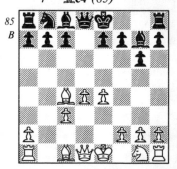

85
B

In Chapter 5 we discussed the Modern Exchange Variation, where White develops his knight at f3. Here we discuss the older variation, which Karpov used against Kasparov in the fourth match.

	7	...	c5
	8	♘e2	♘c6
	9	♗e3	0-0
	10	0-0	♗g4

This is more accurate than 10 ... cd 11 cd ♗g4.

| | 11 | f3 | ♘a5 *(86)* |

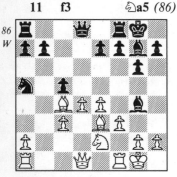

86
W

12   ♗×f7+

This was perhaps the most surprising move in Karpov–Kasparov IV, where it was introduced in the fifth game and repeated in the next three games in which Karpov had White. Karpov, whose opening preparation for this match was absolutely excellent, introduced both new moves and new ideas at a frightening pace. Modern opening theory has not taken this move very seriously, because White disrupts his own pawn structure while giving Black counterplay. It is unlikely that this judgement will change as a result of the games in this match, although it is clear that Kasparov had to work quite hard

to obtain a playable game. Grünfeld players can be grateful to the World Champion for demonstrating the correct plan for Black.

The first critical position arises after

	12	...	♖×f7
	13	fg	♖×f1+
	14	♔×f1 *(87)*	

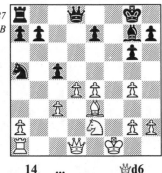

87
B

| | 14 | ... | ♕d6 |

Reacting at the board to the first use of 12 ♗×f7+ in game 5, Kasparov thought for over an hour before playing this move.

Kasparov did deviate from this plan once, in Karpov–Kasparov (m/9) 1987 14 ... cd 15 cd ♕b6!? was played. After 16 ♔g1 ♕e6 17 ♕d3 ♕×g4 18 ♖f1 ♖c8 19 h3 ♕d7 20 d5! Karpov demonstrated that the formation with pawns at d5 and e4 was superior to that with pawns at d4 and e5. Black was unable to equalize and after 20 ... ♘c4 21 ♗d4 e5 22 de ♕×e6 23 ♗×g7 ♔×g7 24 ♘f4! White held a clear advantage.

Then he returned to this principled move in the 11th game. The basic questions facing the players in this position are:

(1) Should Black be trying to regain the pawn?

(2) Should White hold on to the pawn at all costs?

(3) What positional price will be paid by White if he advances his e-pawn to e5?

(4) Is it necessary for Black to transpose to somewhat better known positions by c5×d4?

As a result of the four games played in the match, we can conclude that each question can be answered in the negative, but such questions had not been discussed before the match, and most people had forgotten about the Spassky-Korchnoi encounter in the 1955 Soviet Championship, which saw (with the inclusion of 10 ... cd 11 cd) 15 ... ♕d7 16 h3 ♕e6 17 ♕d3 ♕c4! 18 ♕d2 ♕a6 (intending 19 ... ♘b3) 19 ♕c2 ♘c4 20 ♕b3 ♔h8 21 ♔g1 ♘d2! 22 ♗×d2 ♕×e2 and Black equalized. It is not clear why Kasparov did not follow Korchnoi's plan, although he did get his queen to c4 in the 11th game. Let us now examine the Karpov–Kasparov games, beginning with game 5.

15   e5?! *(88)*

This concedes the central light squares to Black, although it is not easy to exploit this circumstance. Nevertheless, with correct play Black can take advantage of this dubious move.

15   ...   ♕d5

16	♗f2	♖f8
17	♔g1	

17 g5, as suggested by

Georgadze, comes strongly into consideration. The idea is to lock Black's bishop into the King's castle. Tisdall gives 17 ... ♕e4 18 ♘g1! ♘c4 19 ♘f3 ♘e3+ 20 ♗×e3 ♕×e3 21 ♕b3+ ♔h8 22 ♖e1 where 22 ... ♖×f3+ doesn't seem to work and 22 ... ♕×g5 is an unpalatable alternative. Correct is 17 ... ♕f7 18 ♕e1 ♕f5 19 h4 h6!, applying the same sort of strategy as in game 7. If 20 ♘g3, then 20 ... ♕g4 21 ♘e4 (or 21 ♔g1 hg) 21 ... ♕×h4 22 ♔g1 ♕g4 with counterplay.

17   ...   ♗h6!

All of Black's pieces are involved in the game.

18	h4	♕f7
19	♗g3	♗e3+
20	♔h2	♕c4
21	♖b1	b6
22	♖b2	♕d5!
23	♕d3	♘c4
24	♖b1	*(89)*

This is the critical position of a magnificent battle. Black has seized key central positions and

has more than enough compensation for his pawn. At the same time, however, he lacks any concrete attacking plan. Kasparov chose ...

24 ... b5!?

It is possible for Black to 'take the bull by the horns', as Campomanes might put it, and crush the White opposition immediately: The best method is 24 ...g5!! *(90)*.

This absolutely unexpected kingside foray was suggested by Kasparov after the game. Strangely, however, commentators have not mentioned this in published analysis to date. The rationale of the move is to seize control of the

critical f4 square in order to renew the threat of ♗f2 and ♘e3 (The immediate 24 ... ♗f2 fails to 25 ♘f4.) Here are the main variations:

(a) 25 h5 ♗f2! 26 ♗×f2 ♖×f2 27 ♖g1 ♘×e5 28 ♕g3 ♖×e2 29 de ♖×a2 30 ♖e1 ♖d2 and Black wins.

(b) White also loses on 25 hg ♗×g5 26 ♘g1 (26 ♖g1 ♕e6! and Black wins) 26 ... ♘e3 27 ♕e2 ♖f2!! or 27 ♖b2 c4! 28 ♕b1 ♖f1.

(c) 25 ♖d1 would be met by the strong reply 25 ... gh 26 ♗×h4 ♗f2 27 ♕h3 ♕e4! 28 ♗×e7 ♖f7 29 ♗f6 ♘e3 ∓ Zaitsev.

(d) Another interesting line is 25 ♔h3!? ♗f2 26 ♗×f2 (against the threat of 27 ... ♘e3) 27 ♖×f2 27 ♖g1 ♘×e5 28 ♕e3 and now Black plays 28 ... ♘×g4!! launching a punitive action against the White monarch. If 29 ♔×g4 then 29 ... ♕f5+ 30 ♔g3 (If 30 ♔h5 then 30 ... ♖f4!! wins) 30 ... ♖×e2 31 ♕×e2 ♕f4+ 32 ♔h3 ♕×h4 mate. 29 ♕×e7 also fails because of 29 ... ♘f6 30 ♘g3 (30 ♕e5 g4+ 31 ♔h2 ♕×e5 32 de5 ♘d5 33 ♖e1 ♘e3 wins) 30 ... g×h4 31 ♔×h4 ♖f4+ ends the game.

What is the final conclusion concerning the critical position of the game? In spite of Black's clear positional superiority, only one paradoxical move is capable of exploiting it, and that is 24 ... g5!! Cruder methods will not succeed. The move actually played in the game, 24 ... b5, is not nearly as strong and gives White real chances to survive after 25 ☐×b5!, permitting a forced draw after 25 ... ♞×e5 26 ☐×c5 ♞×g4+ 27 ♚h3 ♛e6! 28 ♛c4 ♞f2+ 29 ♚h2 ♞g4+ etc. If instead 25 ... ♞d2!?, then 26 ☐b1! should hold.

25 ♚h3?!

This seemed, at first glance, a cautious and reliable move, very much in keeping with Karpov's style. Now Kasparov's chances for creating any successful attack were vastly reduced. He then played the late middlegame in-exactly and fell into deep time pressure, eventually giving up the full point after the next poor move.

25 ... a6?!

Some analysts, including Kasparov, later found the very strong reply 25 ... b4!, demolishing White's pawn centre. After the virtually forced 26 cb cd we have:

(a) Jon Tisdall suggested in *Chess Life* 2/88 27 ☐d1!? ♞b2 28 ♛×e3 ♞×d1 29 ♛×d4 with the conclusion that Black faces con-siderable technical difficulties, but it is he who is playing to win. We haven't found any serious ob-stacles after 29 ... ♛×d4 30 ♞×d4 ♞f2 31 ♝×f2 ☐×f2 ∓.

(b) Tisdall is right in pointing out that 27 ♛b3 fails to 27 ... d3 28 ☐d1 d2 29 ♞c3 ♛e6 30 ♞e4 ☐d8! 31 ♞c5 ♝×c5 32 bc ☐d4! and Black is better.

(c) 27 ♞c3 ♛e6 28 ♞e4 h5! (Better than 28 ... ♞×e5 29 ♝×e5 ♛×e5 30 g3 with real chances to

hold.) 29 ♚h2 ♞×e5 ∓. It is curious that in this analysis the White king is shuttling between h2 and h3.

Against Tisdall's 25 ... ♞d2!?, White should play 26 ♞g1! (not 25 ☐×b5? ♛e6! ∓) 26 ... ♞×b1 27 ♛×e3 with an unclear position.

26	♞g1	cd
27	♞f3	☐d8
28	a4!	dc
29	♛×c3	♛e6

Better was 29 ... ♛d3! 30 ♛×d3 ☐×d3 31 ab ♞a3! ±

30 ♚h2 ba

An interesting alternative was 30 ... ♝a7!? intending ... ♞e3.

31	☐b4	♞d2
32	☐×a4	♞f1+
33	♚h3	☐d1

Kasparov was down to his last minute here.

34	♛c2	☐c1
35	♛e2	h5
36	♝e1	♛d7?

The decisive error. 36 ... ☐a1 would have given Black real draw-ing chances.

| 37 | ♛×a6 | ☐a1? |
| 38 | ♛×g6+ | 1-0 |

Now let us look at the next game, Karpov–Kasparov, (m/7) 1987 *(91)*:

16 ... ☐d8!?

Kasparov may have been afraid of Georgadze's 17 g5! in reply to 16 ... ☐f8 as played in game five.

17 ♛e1

The two players renewed their dispute of this variation at the European Options Exchange

91
B

Tournament, Amsterdam 1988. In this position, Karpov produced the innovation 17 ♕c2!?, but did not succeed after 17 ... ♕c4! 18 ♕b2 (if 18 ♕e4 ♘c6!, seizing either the d- or e-pawn) 18 ... ♗h6 19 h4 ♕f7 20 ♔g1 (if 20 g5 ♘c4 21 ♕c1 ♖f8 ∓∓) 20 ... ♖f8 21 ♘g3 (21 ♖f1? ♘c4 ∓) 21 ... ♘c4 22 ♕e2 ♕xf2+ 23 ♕xf2 ♗e3 24 ♕xe3 ♘xe3. The game is even, as 25 g5 is met by 25 ... cd 26 cd ♖f4 27 ♖c1 ♘d5 =. Karpov took the second pawn, but destroyed his pawn structure: 25 de ♖c8 26 ♖b1 ♖xc5 27 ♖xb7 ♘xg4 28 ♖b4? h5 29 ♘e4 ♖xe5 ∓ (½-½ 57). Keene suggested 28 ♖xe7 ♖xc3 29 ♘f1, but 29 ... ♖a3! should give Black even chances in the ending. Thus Kasparov succeeded again in Karpov's latest attempt to improve White's plan with ♗xf7+.

17   ...   ♕e4

White would react to 17 ... ♗h6 by playing 18 h4 followed by 19 g5. Black decided to regain his pawn, but this gives White time to regroup his pieces and seize the initiative. Since Black will not be able to deploy his bishop at h6, the plan with 16 ... ♖d8 seems faulty.

18	g5	♕f5
19	h4	♘c4
20	♔g1	♕g4
21	a4	h6!
22	♖a2!	

22 gh ♗xh6 would free the Black bishop and enable it to join in a strong attack.

22	...	hg
23	♕b1!	

Now White has a slight initiative.

23	...	gh
24	♕b3	♕e6
25	♘f4	♕f7
26	♘xg6!	♕xg6
27	♕xc4+	♔h8
28	♖b2	cd
29	cd	♕g4

The position appears to be balanced, although Tisdall maintains that after 30 ♕f7! ♖xd4 31 ♗xd4 ♕xd4+ 32 ♖f2 ♕xe5 33 ♖f5 ♕e1+ 34 ♖f1 ♕e5 Karpov, instead of playing 35 ♔h1?, could have continued 35 ♕f4! which 'would probably push Black over the brink ...'. After the move played in the game Kasparov was able to draw in 79 moves.

Game 11 saw Karpov choose to keep his centre intact and support it with his queen.

15	♔g1	♕e6
16	♕d3 *(92)*	

This is better than 16 ♘g3 cd 17 cd ♖d8 which would have given Black strong pressure for the pawn.

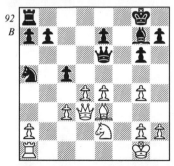

White offers the g-pawn to Black, who spurns it, preferring to exchange queens.

16 ... ♕c4!?

16 ... cd 17 cd ♕×g4 18 ♖f1! would transpose back to the 9th game of the match, an experience Kasparov would certainly not wish to repeat.

17 ♕×c4 ♘×c4
18 ♗f2

18 ♗g5 h6! 19 ♗×e7 cd? 20 cd ♖e8 21 ♖c1! ♘a5 22 ♖c7 ± was played in Seirawan–Lputian, St. John 1988. But 19 ... ♖e8! 20 ♗×c5 b6 21 ♗b4 a5 (Gligorić) was a better try.

17 ... cd
19 cd e5!
20 d5

Now Kasparov managed to bring the bishop into the game.

20 ... ♗h6
21 h4 ♗d2 *(93)*

This is a critical position for Black's imaginative bishop tour. The Black forces are very active and there is a concrete target at e4 (for example 22 a4? ♘d6 23 ♘g3 ♖c8 followed by ... ♖c4), and

White's extra pawn at g4 plays no role at all. We consider this position dynamically balanced.

22 ♖d1 ♗a5!?

The bishop may be overindulging in sightseeing. 22 ... b5 seems more logical.

23 ♖c1 b5
24 ♖c2 ♘d6
25 ♘g3 ♘c4
26 ♘f1 ♘d6
27 ♘g3 ♘c4
28 g5

Inviting a draw by repetition. Now 28 ... a6 should give Black sufficient counterplay, for example 29 ♔f1 ♖f8 30 ♔e2 ♖f4 31 h5 ♖g4 32 hg hg = (33 ♔f3 ♖f4+). In the actual game, the nervous play on both sides is not of interest to the discussion of the opening.

So what can we conclude from the theoretical battle over 12 ♗×f7+? Karpov demonstrated that the old handling of the line is not sufficient for equality, but Kasparov demonstrated that any disruption of White's pawn centre is very dangerous indeed. The best course of action for Black seems at present to be to get the queens off the board and not to worry about the extra pawn at g4.

All of this is very interesting, but is likely to remain a footnote to the main theory of the line, which we follow here, starting from diagram 86.

12   ♗d3   cd
13   cd   ♗e6 *(94)*

94
W

This is the standard position of the Classical Exchange Variation.

14   ♖c1

The long controversial exchange sacrifice 14 d5 ♗xa1 15 ♕xa1 f6 is not seen as frequently at the top level these days. The main lines run:

(a) 16 ♖b1 ♗f7 (16 ... b6, 16 ... ♔g7, and 16 ... ♗d7 are all reliable alternatives.) 17 ♗h6 ♖e8 18 ♗b5 ♕d6 (or 18 ... ♕b6+ 19 ♘d4 ♖ed8 20 ♗e3 ♕c5 21 ♘f5 ♕a3 22 ♗c1 ♕c5+ 23 ♗e3 ♕a3 24 ♗c1 ♕c5+ ½-½ van Gaalen-van der Wiel, Utrecht 1986) 19 ♗xe8 ♗xe8 20 ♕c3 b6 21 ♖c1 ♘b7 22 ♗e3 ♔f7 23 ♕d2 ♕d8 24 ♘d4 ♖c8 25 ♖f1 ♕d6 = Pinter-Přibyl, Sochi 1981.

(b) 16 ♗h6 doesn't even seem to

equalize anymore: 16 ... ♖e8 17 ♘f4 ♗f7 18 ♖e1 ♕b6 19 ♔f1 ♖ed8 20 e5 ♗xd5 21 ef ♕xf6 and Black is better, according to Boleslavsky.

(c) 16 ♕d4 ♗d7 17 ♘f4 b6 18 ♗d2 ♕c7 19 ♕b4 ♕d6 20 ♗a6 ♗c8 21 ♕b5 ♗xa6 22 ♕xa6 ♖fc8 23 ♘e6 with compensation (Toften-Martin, London 1984).

(d) 16 ♗d2 ♗d7 17 ♕e1 b6 18 ♗h6 ♖f7 19 ♕g3 e5 20 f4 ♕e7 21 h4 ♘b7 22 h5 = Vaiser-Stohl, Tallinn 1986.

14   ...   ♗xa2
15   ♕a4

15 d5 is also seen, but after 15 ... ♗b3 16 ♕e1 e6 17 ♕b4 ed 18 ♖c5 ♗c4 19 ♗xc4 ♘xc4 20 ♖xd5 ♕xd5 21 ed ♘xe3 22 ♖c1 ♘xd5 Black has full equality in this line which was originally proposed by co-author Shamkovich.

15   ...   ♗e6
16   d5   ♗d7
17   ♕b4   b6
18   f4!

18 ♗a6 (Spassky-Shamkovich, Sochi 1967, was agreed drawn here.) 18 ... ♗c8! 19 ♗xc8 ♖xc8 20 ♖xc8 ♕xc8 21 ♕xe7 ♕c2 led to an equal position in I. Sokolov-Kapetanović, Yugoslavia 1984, which was agreed drawn after 22 ♖e1 ♘c4 23 ♗f2 a5 24 d6 ♕d2 25 d7 ♘e5 26 ♘d4 ♘d3 27 ♖f1 ♘xf2! 28 d8 (♕) ♘d1! (intending 28 ... ♕e3+) 29 ♔h1 ♘f2+.

18   ...   e6

It is possible that 18 ... ♖c8!?, introduced in 1987, is a stronger move. For example:

(a) 19 ♘c3 ♘b7 20 ♗a6 ♖c7 21 e5 ♘c5 22 ♗c4 ♕b8 23 ♕a3 ♖cc8 24 ♖fd1 (Vizhmanavin–Ivanchuk, USSR 1987), and now 24 ... ♔h8! gives Black a solid position.

(b) 19 ♗a6 ♖×c1 20 ♖×c1 e6 21 d6 ♘c6 22 ♕d2 e5 23 f5 ♘b8! 24 ♗b7 gf 25 ef ♗×f5 26 ♘g3 ♗e6 27 ♘h5!? (Gligorić suggests 27 ♖c7) 26 ... ♕h4 27 ♘×g7 ♔×g7 = Dolmatov–Gavrikov, USSR Ch. 1987.

19   d6   ♘c6

19 ... e5 20 f5 ♖c8 21 ♘c3 ♗c6 22 ♘b5 ♕d7 (Or 22 ... ♗×b5 23 ♖×c8 ♕×c8 24 ♗×b5 with a big advantage for White.) 23 f6! ♗h8 24 ♗e2 ♖fd8 25 ♖cd1 ♖b8 26 h3 h5 27 ♖d2! This is stronger than 27 ♔h2, seen in Balashov–Hansen, Malmö 1987/88. White has a clear advantage in the final position.

20   ♕b3

20 ♕a3 comes into consideration.

20   ...   e5
21   f5

This position was reached in Dolmatov–Gavrikov, USSR Championship 1986. After 21 ... ♕h4! intending 22 ... ♗h6 the position is unclear, eg.:

(a) 22 f6 ♗h6;
(b) 22 g3 ♕h3;
(c) 22 ♗f2 ♕g5 23 ♘c3 ♘d4 ∞.

These last two games do not by any means constitute a refutation of Black's opening strategy, although they have presented Grünfeld practitioners with new obstacles to overcome. Kasparov

clearly preferred to steer clear of these waters, but may choose to navigate them in the future.

V

1	**d4**	**♘f6**
2	**c4**	**g6**
3	**♘c3**	**d5**
4	**♘f3**	**♗g7**
5	**♗g5** (95)	

This was the approach adopted by Seirawan against Kasparov at the Dubai Olympiad. Kasparov has employed the White side as well, against Smyslov in the Candidates' finals of 1984.

5   ...   ♘e4
6   cd

If White does not wish to give up the bishop pair then he can play 6 ♗h4, but after 6 ... ♘×c3 7 bc dc Black has a good game, for example:

(a) 8 e3 ♗e6 9 ♗e2 (9 ♖b1 b6 10 ♘d2 0-0 11 ♘×c4 ♗d5 12 ♕d2 ♕d7 13 ♘a3 c5 14 f3 ♕a4 ∞ Mecking–Fischer, Buenos Aires 1970) 9 ... 0-0 10 0-0 ♘d7 11 ♘g5 ♗d5 12 e4 h6 13 ed hg 14 ♗×g5 ♘b6 15 ♕d2 ♖e8 16 ♗h6 ♗f6 = Groszpeter–Ftačnik, Trnava 1983.

(b) 8 ♕a4+ ♕d7 9 ♕×c4 b6 10 e3 ♗a6 11 ♕b3 ♗×f1 12 ♔×f1 c5 13 ♔e2 cd 14 cd ♘c6 15 ♖hd1 0-0 16 ♖ac1 ♖ac8 = Foisor–W. Schmidt, Polanica Zdroj 1982.

6 ♗f4 is no more effective, e.g. 6 ... ♘×c3 7 bc 0-0 8 cd ♕×d5 9 ♕b3 a5 10 e3 c5 11 ♗c4 cd 12 ed ♘c6 = Bronstein–Suetin, USSR Ch. 1965.

	6	...	♘×g5
	7	♘×g5	e6
	8	♘f3	

8 ♕d2 is a major alternative, but it appears that after 8 ... ed 9 ♕e3+ ♔f8! White cannot obtain any advantage. An example is 10 ♕f4 ♗f6 11 h4 h6 12 ♘f3 c6 13 e3 ♗e6 14 ♗d3 ♘d7 15 0-0-0 ♕b8 16 ♕×b8 ♖×b8 = Bisguier–Korchnoi, Lone Pine 1979.

8 ♕a4+ c6 9 dc ♘×c6 10 ♘f3 deserves thorough practical testing.

| | 8 | ... | ed |
| | 9 | e3 | |

9 b4 ♕d6 10 a3 0-0 11 e3 c6 12 ♗e2 ♗f5 13 0-0 ♘d7 gave Black equality in Seirawan–Kasparov, Dubai Ol. 1986.

| | 9 | ... | 0-0 *(96)* |

96
W

10   b4

10 ♗e2 has fallen from favour. One secure equalizing line is 10 ... ♖e8 11 0-0 ♗f8 12 ♘e5 c6 13 ♗f3 ♗d6 14 ♘d3 ♗f5 15 ♖e1 ♘d7 16 ♘e2 ♕b6 17 ♘g3 ♗×d3 18 ♕×d3 ♘f6 19 ♖ab1 a5 = Gurgenidze–Zilberstein, USSR 1974.

| | 10 | ... | c6 |
| | 11 | ♕b3 | |

(a) 11 ♗e2 a5 12 b5 a4 13 0-0 ♕a5 14 ♕d2 ♗g4 15 bc bc 16 h3 ♗×f3 17 ♗×f3 ♘d7 was equal in Ostermeyer–Korchnoi, Biel 1984.

(b) 11 ♗d3 ♘d7 12 0-0 ♘b6 13 a4 ♗e6 14 b5 c5 15 dc ♗×c3 16 ♖c1 ♗b2 17 ♖b1 ♗f6 18 cb was seen in Seirawan–Korchnoi, Brussels 1986, where Black could have equalized with 18 ... ♕×b6.

| | 11 | ... | ♗e6 |
| | 12 | ♖c1 | |

12 ♗e2 ♘d7 13 0-0 g5 14 ♖ac1 a5 gives chances for both sides (Bogdanov–Gulko, USSR 1973).

| | 12 | ... | ♘d7 |
| | 13 | ♗d3 | |

13 ♗e2 f5 14 0-0 a6 15 ♖fe1 ♔h8 16 ♗f1 f4 17 ef ♖×f4 18 ♖×e6 ♖×f3! 19 gf ♕g5+ ∓ was seen in Cebalo–Kavalek, Reggio Emilia 1985/86. 18 ♘a4 would have limited the damage.

	13	...	♕e7
	14	0-0	♖fc8
	15	♘a4	b6

In this unclear position chances are about equal (Browne–Timman, Buenos Aires 1980).

VI

| | 1 | d4 | ♘f6 |

2	c4	g6
3	♘c3	d5
4	♘f3	♗g7
5	♕a4+ *(97)*	

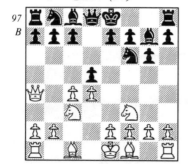

This is a thoroughly innocuous line, with which Kasparov has had no difficulty.

5	...	♗d7
6	♕b3	dc
7	♕×c4	0-0
8	e4	b5!
9	♘×b5	

9 ♕b3 c5 10 e5 ♘g4 11 ♗×b5 cd

12 ♘×d4 ♗×b5 13 ♘d×b5 a6 14 ♘a3 ♕d4! 15 ♕c2 ♘c6 16 ♕e2 ♕×e5! gave Black a substantial advantage in Hübner–Kasparov, Brussels 1986.

9	...	♘×e4
10	♘×c7	

Kengis points out that 10 ♕d5 c6 11 ♕×e4 fails to 11 ... ♗f5! ∓.

10	...	♘c6
11	♘×a8	♕a5+
12	♗d2	♘×d2
13	♘×d2	♘×d4
14	♕c7	♕×c7
15	♘×c7	♘c2+
16	♔d1	♘×a1
17	♗d3	♗×b2
18	♔e2	

In Bönsch–Jasnikowski, Harkany 1985, White obtained some compensation for his material after 18 ... ♖c8?! 19 ♖b1 ♗e5 20 ♘d5, but after 18 ... ♗c6! Black would have had a clear advantage.

9 Sicilian Defence

98

Kasparov has relied on the Sicilian Defence for most of his career. We will concentrate on two systems which have played a major role in his repertoire — the Scheveningen (including the Keres Attack) and the Taimanov Variations. We will also note some significant contributions to the theory of the Richter–Rauzer and Najdorf Variations.

1	e4	c5
2	♘f3	

I Scheveningen Variation

This variation was especially important in the first two Kasparov–Karpov clashes, before Karpov switched to 1 d4 as his primary weapon. Kasparov has written an entire book on the subject (available in an English translation by co-author Schiller),

together with his trainer Nikitin, who has been a leading Soviet expert on this system for many years, and who had already written profusely on the subject.

It is not really possible to give a full Sicilian repertoire for Black — such a task would require at least a full volume by itself. The authors have endeavoured to provide significant coverage of the major, popular lines. There are many good sources for the less familiar lines, some by Kasparov himself.

2	...	e6
3	d4	cd
4	♘×d4	♘f6
5	♘c3	d6
6	♗e2	(99)

6 g4, the Keres Attack, is generally sidestepped by Kasparov, who employs a variety of move orders to avoid it.

99
B

6 ... a6

Black can adopt a number of move orders, but this one, which can also arise from the Najdorf move order 2 ... d6 3 d4 cd 4 ♘xd4 ♘f6 5 ♘c3 a6 6 ♗e2 e6, is a solid one, as Black generally chooses to include the advance a7–a6 in his plans. One example where Kasparov omitted the move is his game against Kupreichik from Kislovodsk 1982: 1 e4 c5 2 ♘f3 e6 3 d4 cd 4 ♘xd4 ♘c6 5 ♘c3 d6 6 ♗e3 ♘f6 7 ♗e2 ♗e7 8 f4 0-0 9 ♕d2?! (intending 0-0-0) 9 ... e5! 10 ♘f3 (10 ♘f5 ♗xf5 11 ef ef 12 ♗xf4 d5! gives Black the initiative, according to Kasparov.) 10 ... ♘g4! 11 f5? (11 ♘d5! would have led to a level position according to Kasparov.) 11 ... ♘b4! 12 ♗d3 (12 0-0-0 d5! and 12 ♗g1 d5! both give Black a strong initiative.) 12 ... d5! 13 ♘xd5 ♘xd5 14 ed e4! 15 ♗xe4 ♖e8 ∓ 16 0-0-0 ♗f6 17 ♗g5 ♖xe4 18 h3 ♘e5 19 ♗xf6 ♕xf6 20 ♘xe5 ♕xe5 21 g4 ♗d7 and, as Kasparov noted, 'the rest was a matter of technique'.

7 0-0 ♗e7
8 f4 0-0
9 ♔h1 ♕c7 *(100)*

This is a typical starting point for the analysis of the Scheveningen material. White has developed his pieces, staked a claim in the centre, and shuttled his king to safety. Black has developed calmly and has maintained his flexibility with regard to the deployment of his queenside pieces.

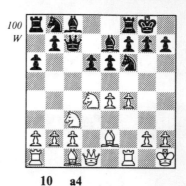

10 a4

This policy of restraining Black's queenside has occupied centre stage for the last ten years. White can, of course, delay this move, and Kasparov has faced three alternatives:

(a) 10 ♗e3 ♘c6 11 a4 just returns to the text.

(b) Karpov–Kasparov, (m/5) 1984–5: 10 ♗f3 ♘c6 (Kasparov has never employed the more passive 10 ... ♘bd7.) 11 a4 ♖e8 12 ♗e3 ♖b8 13 ♖e1 (Kasparov had an unpleasant experience with 13 ♗f2 ♗f8 14 ♖e1 in an encounter with Razuvayev in the 1978 USSR Ch.: 14 ... ♘d7 15 ♕e2 ♘xd4 16 ♗xd4 b6 17 e5!? de 18 fe ♗b4? 19 ♖ad1 ♘f8 20 ♖f1 ♘g6 21 ♘e4 ±, but 18 ... ♗c5! would have been much stronger.) 13 ... ♗d7 14 ♕d3 (This entails an old-fashioned idea of redeploying the White forces with ♖a1–d1 and ♗e3–c1. Kasparov experiences no difficulty in achieving full equality.) 14 ... ♘xd4 15 ♗xd4 e5! (A typical Kasparov counter-thrust. The previously standard 15 ... ♗c6 allowed White to obtain advantage with 16 a5.) 16 ♗a7 ♖bc8 17 ♗e3 (Karpov prevents Black from advancing his b-pawn, which would have been possible on 16 ♗e3.) 17 ... ♕c4 18 a5 h6 (A useful prophylactic move, as the immediate 18 ... ♗f8 would have been met by 19 fe de 20 ♗g5!) 19 h3 ♗f8 20 ♗d2 ♕d4 21 ♗e3 ♕b4 ½-½.

(c) Karpov–Kasparov, (m/43) 1984-5: 10 ♕e1 (This introduces a well-known offensive formation with 10 ... ♘c6 11 ♗e3 ♗d7 12 ♕g3, but Karpov actually intends to place his queen at f2. Kasparov chooses an active counter-strategy on the queenside.) 10 ... b5! 11 ♗f3 ♗b7 12 e5 ♘e8 (In their monograph, Kasparov and Nikitin suggested that 12 ... de 13 fe ♘fd7 is a playable, if risky alternative.) 13 f5 de 14 fe ♗xf3 15 ef+ ♖xf7 16 ♘xf3 ♘d7 17 ♗g5 (17 ♗e3 ♕c6 19 ♖d1 ♗b4 20 ♗d2 ♘d6 = Kasparov and Nikitin.) 17 ... ♗f8 18 a3 ♘d6 19 ♘d2 ♖xf1+ and a draw was agreed after a couple more moves. A rather relaxed 'book' game which was a sort of time-out in the gruelling marathon match. In game 7 the protagonists returned to consideration of the main line (below). But there was every reason for Karpov to respect Kasparov's ability to defend the main line, based on the following examples:

(c1) 9 ... ♘c6 (In the Scheveningen, it is often better to study positions grouped thematically,

rather than by specific move orders. In our book, all of our branchings refer to the boldfaced main move order. In other words, this line (c1) departs from the position after 9 ♔h1 in the boldfaced text.) 10 ♗e3 ♗d7 11 ♕e1 b5 12 a3 ♕b8! (Better than 12 ... ♕c7 where White could play 13 ♕g3 ♖ab8 14 e5! de 15 fe ♘xe5 16 ♖xf6! ♗xf6 17 ♗f4 ∓ Kasparov-Korsunsky, USSR 1978.) 13 ♕g3?! b4! 14 ab ♕xb4 15 ♖fd1 ♕xb2 16 ♘xc6 ♗xc6 17 ♗d4 ♕b7 18 ♖ab1 ♕c7 19 e5?! (Too late; better 19 ♗d3 ∓.) 19 ... de 20 ♗xe5 ♕c8 21 ♖d4 g6 22 ♖c4 ♕e8 23 f5!? ef 24 ♖b6 ♖c8! 25 ♖xa6 ♘e4 26 ♘xe4 ♗xe4 ∓.

(c2) 9 ♕e1 ♘c6 10 ♗e3 ♘xd4?! 11 ♗xd4 b5 12 ♖d1 ♕c7 13 e5! de 14 fe ♘d7 15 ♘e4 ♗b7 16 ♘f6+! ♔h8 17 ♕h4 (17 ♕g3! would have been more precise, for example 17 ... h6 18 ♕d3 ± or 17 ... gf 18 ef ♘xf6 19 ♗d3! with a strong attack.) 17 ... h6 18 ♕h3 ♖ad8! 19 ♕d3 ♘xf6 20 ef ♗xf6 21 ♖xf6 e5! and Kasparov successfully repelled the attack. Nevertheless, in his subsequent games in this line he avoided the premature capture at d4.

10	...	♘c6
11	♗e3	♖e8
12	♗f3	

Geller's 12 ♗g1!? was seen in Karpov-Kasparov, (m/10) 1985: 12 ... ♖b8! (improving on 12 ... e5? 13 ♘b3 ef 14 a5! ♘e5 15 ♖xf4 ♗e6 16 ♘d5 which allowed Geller to overrun Polugayevsky in the 1983 USSR Ch.) 13 ♕d2 (Kudrin–Arnason, Bor 1984, saw White gain an advantage with 13 ♕d3 after 13 ... ♘×d4?! 14 ♗×d4 e5 15 ♗a7 ♖a8 16 ♗e3, but after 13 ... ♘b4 Black would lay claim to equality, at the very least, for example 14 ♕g3 e5! or 14 ♕d2 d5!? 15 e5 ♘e4.) 13 ... e5 (The prosaic 13 ... ♘×d4 is good for White, while 13 ... ♗d7 14 ♘b3! gives Black a lot of trouble, since he has to contend with the threat of 15 a5, but 14 ... b6? fails to 15 ♗×a6 and 14 ... ♘a5 is met by 15 e5!) 14 ♘b3 ♘a5!? (Black must navigate these tricky waters with great care. This move must be played right now, as it creates the threat of capturing at b3, thus taking White's attention away from the centre. If, for example, 15 fe, then Black does not have to recapture immediately with 15 ... de, although that is playable provided that on 16 ♘d5 he plays 16 ... ♘×b3! and not 16 ... ♘×d5?? 17 ♕×d5, but he can also interpose 15 ... ♘×b3!, as 16 ed ♘×d2 is fully playable.) 15 ♘×a5 ♕×a5 16 ♗a7 ♖a8 17 ♗e3 ♕b4!? Once again, Kasparov heads for complications. In his comments, he gives 17 ... ef 18 ♗×f4 ♗e6 or 18 ♖×f4 ♗e6 19 ♗d4 ♘d7 as equal, but 18 ♗×f4 ♗e6 19 ♘d5 is, in our opinion, not so clear, since 19 ... ♕×d2 20 ♘×e7+ ♖×e7 21 ♗×d2 is better for White, e.g. 21 ... d5 22 e5 ♘e4 23 ♗b4 or 21 ... ♘d7 22 ♗b4 ♘c5 23 e5. Therefore the text move was,

at least from a psychological and perhaps from an objective viewpoint as well, the correct choice. The remainder of the game contained a number of errors by both players, but Kasparov managed to survive.

12 g4!? ♘×d4 13 ♕×d4 ♘d7 (13 ... e5!? =) 14 g5 b6 15 ♗f3 ♗b7 16 ♗g2 ♗f8 17 ♕d2 ♖ac8 18 f5 ♕c4 19 g6 hg 20 fg fg 21 ♕f2 ♘f6 22 ♕g3 e5 with a roughly level position which was agreed drawn (Tal–Kasparov, SWIFT Blitz 1987).

12 ♘f3 b6 13 ♕e1 ♘b4 14 ♖c1 ♗b7 15 ♗d3 e5 16 fe de = Tal–Hansen, Wijk aan Zee 1985. If 17 ♗f2!? then 17 ... ♗d8; if 17 ♕g3, ♖ac8 18 ♗h6 ♘h5 19 ♕g4 g6 ∞.

12 ... ♖b8 *(101)*

13 ♕d2

13 ♖e1 would transpose above to Karpov–Kasparov, (m/5) 1984–5.

13 ♕e1 e5 14 ♘f5 ♗×f5 15 ef e4 16 ♗e2 d5 17 ♕f2 ♘b4 18 ♖ac1 h5 19 h3 b6 20 g4 ♗c5 21 g5 ∞ with a slight initiative for White (Basanta–Hernandez, St. John 1988).

13 ... ♗d7

Karpov-Kasparov, (m/45) 1984-5, saw instead 13 ... ♘xd4 (A reasonable move. 13 ... ♘a5 should be met not by 14 ♕e2 ♘c4 15 ♗c1 e5! ∓, but by 14 b3 d5!? 15 e5 ♗b4 16 ♘de2 ♘e4 17 ♗xe4 de 18 ♘d5!, a possibility overlooked by the theoreticians and commentators.) 14 ♗xd4 e5 15 ♗a7! (Geller-Timoshchenko, USSR 1986, saw the eccentric 15 ♗g1!? ef 16 a5 ♗e6 17 ♗b6 ♕c8=, although the consistent 15 ... b5 is also worthy of consideration. Karpov's move was an innovation.) 15 ... ♖a8 16 ♗e3 ♗d7! (Taimanov suggested 16 ... ef 17 ♗xf4 ♗e6 but 18 ♖fd1 ♖ed8 19 ♘e2! intending 20 ♘d4 gives White a very pleasant position.) 17 a5 ♖ac8 18 ♗e2 (Preventing Black from transferring his queen to b4.) 18 ... ♗c6 (It is clear that this is a more active post for the bishop than e6. But what if White plays 19 ♗d3, intending to attack on the kingside? Dorfman suggested during the game the wild variation 19 ... ef 20 ♗b6 ♕b8? 21 ♖xf4 d5 *(21 ... ♘d7!?)* 22 ed ♘xd5 23 ♘xd5 ♗xd5 24 ♖f5 ♗c6 25 ♖h5 h6 26 ♗d4 with a formidable intiative. But 20 ... ♕d7! 21 ♖xf4 ♕e6 is a superior option.) 19 ♕d3 ♕d8!? (By threatening 20 ... ef 21 ♗xf4 d5, Kasparov encouraged the White rook to transfer to d1.) 20 ♖fd1. If 20 ♗b6 ♕d7 21 ♖ad1, as suggested by Taimanov, Black would obtain a playable game with 21 ... ef 22 ♖xf4 ♕e6 23 ♖df1 (23 ♗d4 ♘d7)

23 ... ♗d8 24 ♗d4 ♘xe4!? Kasparov has successfully solved his opening problems in the Scheveningen, even when he found himself in rather difficult situations.

14 ♘b3

It took Karpov some time to appreciate the value of this move. In Karpov-Kasparov, (m/2) 1985, he played 14 ♕f2 ♘xd4 (14 ... b6 is an interesting alternative.) 15 ♗xd4 e5 16 ♗e3 ♗e6?! (A rather bold and adventurous solution, leading to a position rich in positional and tactical possibilities which appeal to Kasparov's fighting spirit. 17 ♗b6 is playable for Black. Kasparov suggests 17 ... ♕c4 18 ♗e2! ♕c6 19 a5 and now 19 ... ♗d8! is best. Objectively, we must prefer 16 ... ef 17 ♗xf4 and now 17 ... ♗c6! followed by 18 ♖fd1 ♗f8 or 18 ♖ad1 ♖bd8. Sometimes psychological considerations override objective evaluation. In this game, it turns out for the best, as far as Kasparov is concerned.) 17 f5 ♗c4 18 ♗b6 ♕c8 and now we come to a position of considerable interest *(102)*.

19 ♖fc1 (Kasparov, as well as Averbakh and Taimanov, suggested 19 ♖fd1! as the refutation of Black's dubious plan initiated with 16 ... ♗e6. It is truly a powerful and logical move, but Black can survive his trials and tribulations if he avoids 19 ... d5 20 ed ♕xf5 21 b3 ♗b4 22 ♘a2! and

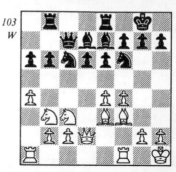

chooses instead 19 ... ♘d7! 20 b3 ♗×b3! or 20 ♗a7 ♖a8 21 ♗e3 b5 where White is only slightly better. Karpov's move created the immediate threat of 20 b3, but allowed Kasparov to create tactical counterplay.) 19 ... d5! 20 b3 ♗b4 21 ♘a2 ♗a3! (Kasparov either overlooked or underestimated this zwischenzug.) 22 bc ♗×c1 23 ♘×c1 ♕×c4! 24 ed e4 and Black was able to make good use of his strong passed pawn at e4.

14 ... b6 *(103)*

Now that White has eliminated the possibility of an exchange of knights in the centre, Black must determine what sort of queenside formation is appropriate. 14 ... ♘a5 would not be successful here, because 15 ♘×a5 ♕×a5 allows the strong break 16 e5!

15 g4!

In Karpov–Kasparov, (m/18) 1985, Karpov played 15 ♗f2, but after 15 ... ♗c8! (Not 15 ... ♘a5 because of 16 ♘×a5 ba 17 e5!) 16 ♗g3 (This manoeuvre seems a bit artificial and is in any event too slow. Now Kasparov managed to

without difficulty.) 16 ... ♘d7 17 ♖ae1 ♗b7! (Kasparov notes that 17 ... ♘a5 is met by 18 e5! with an initiative for White, and he is certainly correct, as after 18 ... ♘×b3 19 cb de 20 fe ♗b7 21 ♘e4 ♗×e4 22 ♗×e4 (Kasparov), Black's position is not pleasant, for example 22 ... ♖bd8 23 ♕f2 ♖f8 24 ♗f4. It is curious that Karpov managed to effectively restrict Black's plans involving ...♘c6–a5.) 18 e5 ♖bd8 19 ♕f2 ♖f8! (Now it was Karpov who had some problems to solve.) 20 ♗e4 de 21 fe ♘c5 22 ♘×c5 bc! 23 ♗f4 and here a draw was agreed even though Kasparov claims that his position would have been the stronger one after 23 ... ♘d4 24 ♕g3 ♔h8. Why agree to the draw, then? We know that psychological points can play a big role in a match, and Kasparov was no doubt content simply to survive once again with Black.

The text was introduced in the most critical game of the match — the final one. In Karpov–Kasparov, (m/24) 1985, the then World Champion made up his mind to adopt a classical attacking posture. This was no doubt due to the match situation, which required a win in order to retain the title. One notes that when Kasparov found himself in an identical situation in Seville, he chose a quite different approach, adopting the unambitious Réti Opening.

The advance of the g-pawn is in keeping with Karpov's general approach to the Scheveningen. He frequently employs the Keres Attack, which we will discuss below. The introduction of this move creates a typical, rich, Sicilian position which makes all of the previous examples pale by comparison. The game has been subject to so much scrutiny that we will concentrate on the main points and introduce a few new ideas of our own.

15	...	♗c8
16	g5	♘d7
17	♕f2!	

Both players were aware of the recent game between Sokolov and Ribli, where the Russian 'Sicilian Knight' played 17 ♗g2 ♘a5 18 ♕f2, allowing his lines of communication to be cut after 18 ... ♘c4 19 ♗c1.

| 17 | ... | ♗f8 |

17 ... ♘a5 is still not on, because of 18 ♖ad1!

| 18 | ♗g2 | ♗b7 |
| 19 | ♖ad1 | |

Perhaps 19 ♖ae1 is better, as Black cannot prevent the transfer of the rook to h3.

| 19 | ... | g6 |
| 20 | ♗c1 | ♖bc8?! |

Kasparov suggested 20 ... ♘c5 to stop ♖d3–h3, but 21 ♖de1!? is a reasonable try (Kasparov considered only 21 ♘xc5). Perhaps the rook would reach the h-file after all.

| 21 | ♖d3! | ♘b4 |
| 22 | ♖h3 | ♗g7 (104) |

Kasparov noted that 22 ... f5!? should give Black good chances to hold the draw. This means that White's attack initiated by 15 g4 is strong, but not necessarily decisive. Black is not lost even after the text, however, as we shall see.

104
W

| 23 | ♗e3 | |

All of the commentators, including Kasparov, criticised this move as too timid, and suggested 23 f5 instead. On the other hand, Kasparov himself demonstrated that White does indeed maintain an advantage with this move, thanks to the weakness of the d-pawn. Now 23 f5 is fully in the attacking spirit of this variation, but even so Black could maintain a shaky and unclear balance with 23

... ef 24 ef ♗×g2+ 25 ♔×g2 ♕b7+ 26 ♔g1 ♖c4! 27 fg ♖g4+ 28 ♖g3 ♖×g3+ 29 hg ♘e5 30 gh+ ♔h8 with compensation for the pawns. So White's choice in this position was more a matter of taste than an objective mistake.

23	...	♖e7!
24	♔g1	♖ce8
25	♖fd1!	f5!

Otherwise White will play 26 ♕d2, attacking the weak point at d6.

26	gf	♘×f6!

By sacrificing the pawn, Kasparov achieves full counter-play. The opening and early middlegame have come to an end, and Black is no worse for wear, so the attack with 15 g4 does not seem to have achieved its objective. The rest of the game is extremely interesting, but it has been extensively analysed elsewhere so we present the moves with just a few comments: 27 ♖g3 ♖f7 28 ♗×b6 ♕b8 29 ♗e3 ♘h5 20 ♖g4 (30 ♖f3 would have led to material loss for White after 30 ... ♗×c3 31 bc ♘a2!) 30 ... ♘f6 31 ♖h4 (Obviously a repetition of moves would have left Karpov without his title, so there really wasn't much choice. On 31 ♖g5 Black would have played 31 ... ♗h6 32 ♖g3 ♘h5 33 ♖f3 ♖ef8 34 ♗h3 ♗c8.) 31 ... g5! 32 fg ♘g4! 33 ♕d2 ♘×e3 34 ♕×e3 ♘×c2 35 ♕b6 ♗a8! 36 ♖×d6 (This hastens the end, but the title had already slipped away many moves ago.) 36 ... ♖b7

37 ♕×a6 ♖×b3 38 ♖×e6 ♖×b2 39 ♕c4 ♔h8 40 e5 ♕a7+ 41 ♔h1 ♗×g2+ 42 ♔×g2 ♘d4+ 0-1.

II   Taimanov Variation

1	e4	c5
2	♘f3	e6
3	d4	cd
4	♘×d4	♘c6
5	♘b5	d6
6	c4	

6 ♗f4, as seen in Fischer-Petrosian, match 1971, is no longer so popular. Kengis-Romanishin, Jurmala 1987: 6 ... e5 7 ♗e3 ♘f6 8 ♗g5 ♕a5+ (Petrosian's 8 ... ♗e6 was better.) 9 ♕d2 ♘×e4 10 ♕×a5 ♘×a5 11 ♗e3 ∞.

6	...	♘f6
7	♘1c3	a6
8	♘a3	*(105)*

This system is one of the Maroczy Bind formations which Kasparov has been willing to defend. In the next chapter we will examine another. If Black wishes to play the Scheveningen, but does not want to face the Keres Attack, then he must either adopt the Najdorf move order (see below),

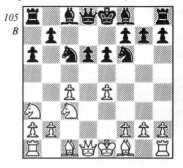

105
B

or allow White to seize the centre as in this line.

8   ...   ♗e7

A number of players, including co-author Shamkovich, prefer 8 ... b6, for example 9 ♗e2 ♗b7 10 0-0 ♗e7 11 f4 0-0 12 ♗e3 ♘b8! A recent example of this approach is Geller–I. Sokolov, Pančevo 1987, which saw 10 ... ♘e5 11 f4 ♘ed7 12 ♗f3 ♗e7 13 ♕e2 0-0 14 g4!? d5 15 ed ed 16 g5 ♖e8! 17 ♕g2 ♘e4 18 ♘xd5 ♗xd5 =. Geller gives 18 cd ±, but in our opinion Black actually has a fully playable game after 18 ... ♗xa3 19 ♘xe4 ♗f8.

But Kasparov's most striking contribution to opening theory is the so-called 'Gary Gambit' with 8 ... d5!? We will examine that line at the end of this section.

9   ♗e2   0-0
10 0-0   b6
11 ♗e3   ♗b7

Kasparov could still have chosen the strategy employed against Tseshkovsky, at Minsk 1979, if he had played instead 11 ... ♘e5. That game continued 12 f4 ♘ed7 13 ♗f3 ♗b7 14 ♕e2 ♕c7 (Kasparov criticised this move in *The Test of Time* and recommended 14 ... ♖e8 instead. We feel that 14 ... ♖c8 is a good alternative as well, for example Hebert–Shamkovich, Lone Pine 1981: 15 g4 ♘c5 16 ♕g2 ♘e8 17 g5 f5! with plenty of counterplay for Black.) 15 ♖ac1 ♖ac8 16 g4 ♘c5 17 ♕g2 d5!? (This is the consistent move, but Kasparov has also proposed

the fantastic variation 17 ... g5!? 18 fg ♘fd7.) 18 e5 (On 18 ed or 18 cd, 18 ... ♘d3! is very strong according to Kasparov.) 18 ... ♘fe4 19 cd ed 20 b4 ♘xc3 21 ♖xc3 d4! and even though Kasparov was not proud of his 14th move, he must surely have been happy with this position.

12   ♕b3 *(106)*

12 ♖c1 allows Black to play 12 ... ♘e5, e.g. 13 f3 ♖c8 14 ♕d2 ♕c7 15 ♖fd1 ♕b8 16 ♕e1 ♗d8 17 ♕f2 ♘ed7 18 ♗f1 ♗c7 and Black has secured d6 (Hernandez–Semkov St. John 1988).

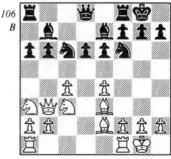

12   ...   ♘a5?!

This was introduced in the game Karpov–Kasparov, (m/3) 1984–5: Not all of Kasparov's departures from known theory are to he held as models of correct decision making. In this case, the more popular 12 ... ♘d7 would have been a better choice, but Kasparov decided that the terrain would have been too familiar to his rival.

13   ♕xb6   ♘xe4
14   ♘xe4   ♗xe4

15	♕×d8	♗×d8
16	♖ad1!	d5?!

An impatient move. White is already in possession of a clear advantage, thanks to the weakness of the Black pawns at a6 and d6. Nevertheless, Black does hold one trump card — the offside position of White's ♘a3. His position was therefore tenable, after, for example, Gufeld's 16 ... ♘b7 17 ♘b1 ♗f6, since 18 b3 (18 b4 a5 19 b5 a4! leads to a complicated position with chances for both sides.) 18 ... ♖fd8 19 f3 ♗c6 intending ... d4. The pseudo-active break 16 ... d5 created an unbalanced position which Karpov found uncomfortable.

17	f3	♗f5
18	cd	ed
19	♖×d5	♗e6
20	♖d6	♗×a2?

Polugayevsky showed that more resistance could have been offered by 20 ... ♗e7 21 ♖×a6 ♖×a6 22 ♗×a6 ♖b8 23 ♗d4 ♘c6 24 ♗c3 ♗c5+ 25 ♔h1 ♗×a2, but Black would still have been in deep trouble.

21	♖×a6	♖b8
22	♗c5	♖e8
23	♗b5!	

and White won after a few more moves. It was a rough defeat, particularly because it involved the failure of a prepared innovation. Kasparov did not try to improve this particular line. Instead, he developed a new idea, inspired by bitter experience.

In Karpov–Kasparov, (m/12) 1985, the bomb was dropped:

8 ... d5!? (107)

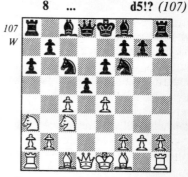

107
W

This remains the most sensational innovation of the Karpov-Kasparov matches. The idea of such a sacrifice is nothing new (indeed, the move was first played in Honfi–Dely, Hungary 1965, and promptly forgotten; Kasparov discovered the idea independently). Kasparov was surely aware of the line of the Dragon Sicilian: 1 e4 c5 2 ♘f3 ♘c6 3 d4 cd 4 ♘×d4 g6 5 ♘c3 ♗g7 6 ♗e3 ♘f6 7 ♗c4 0-0 8 ♗b3 a5 9 f3 d5!? 10 ed ♘b4, and also the games in the Taimanov which see this motif applied later in the game, a recent example of which is Haba–Mokry, Prague 1986: 8 ... b6 9 ♗e2 ♗e7 10 0-0 0-0 11 ♗e3 ♘e5 12 f3 ♗b7 13 ♕e1 ♕c7 14 ♕f2 ♘ed7 15 ♖fd1 ♖ac8 16 ♖d2 ♖fe8 17 ♖ad1 d5! 18 ed ed 19 ♘×d5 ♘×d5 20 cd ♗d6 21 ♔h1 b5! ∓. A similar idea also appears in the English Opening: 1 c4 c5 2 ♘f3 ♘f6 3 d4 cd 4 ♘×d4 e5 5 ♘b5 d5!? 6 cd ♗c5, with sufficient counterplay, e.g. 7 e3 0-0 8 ♘5c3 a6 9 ♗e2 e4 10 0-0 ♖e8 11 ♘d2 ♗f5 12 a3 ♘bd7 13 ♘b3 ♗d6 ∓/⊼, Antunas-Shamkovich, New York 1981. But the early advance of the d-pawn is still a striking original idea. Kasparov has noted that although it seems to lack sufficient foundation, one must keep in mind that the White ♘a3 is offside and will serve as one of the focal points of Black's attack.

Most of the members of the professional chess community have branded the experiment as a failure, on the basis of a single, impressive victory for White. But if the refutation were that simple, why did Kasparov and his team fail to find it during their extensive preparation for the match? Co-author Shamkovich devoted considerable effort to the investigation of this mystery, and the present section may be considered our 'interim report' on the subject, which we expect has not permanently disappeared from the public arena.

9   ed   ed
10   cd   ♘b4
11   ♗e2! *(108)*

Karpov-Kasparov, (m/12) 1985 saw 11 ♗c4 ♗g4! (11 ... b5 12 0-0 bc 13 ♖e1+ ♗e7 14 d6 ± was given by Kasparov, and T. Horvath-Szabolcsi, Budapest 1986, failed to improve: 12 ... ♗e7 13 ♗f4 ♗g4 14 ♗e2 ♘b×d5 15 ♘×d5 ♘×d5 16 ♗×g4 ♘×f4 17 ♕f3 ♘g6 – *17 ... ♕b8 18 ♖fe1 ± – 18 ♖fd1* with a decisive advantage for White.

Also inadequate is 12 ... ♗d6 13 ♖e1+ ♔f8 14 ♗f1 ±.) 12 ♗e2 (12 ♕d4!? was tested in Santo-Roman–Kouatly, Cannes 1986: 12 ... b5 and now instead of Kasparov's 13 ♗b3? ♗c5 ∓, White chose 13 ♘c×b5 ab 14 ♗×b5+ ♗d7 15 d6! ♘c2+? 16 ♘×c2 ♕a5+ 17 ♗d2 ♕×b5 18 0-0-0 with a strong attack. But Black could have played more strongly, for example 15 ... ♕a5! and now 16 ♕e5+ ♔d8 17 0-0 ♘d3! ∓ or 16 ♗d2 ♕×b5! 17 ♘×b5 ♘c2+ 18 ♔d1 ♘×d4 19 ♘c7+ ♔d8 20 ♘×a8 ♗c6 ∓. So Black is still in business here.) 12 ... ♗×e2 13 ♕×e2+ ♕e7 14 ♗e3 ♘b×d5 15 ♘c2 (15 ♘×d5 ♘×d5 16 0-0 ♕e6! = Kasparov.) 15 ... ♘×e3 16 ♘×e3 ♕e6 17 0-0 ½-½.

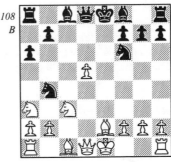

108
B

11   ...   ♗e7!
11 ... ♗c5?! was seen in Karpov-Kasparov, (m/16) 1985: 12 0-0 0-0 13 ♗f3 (13 ♗g5 leads to a roughly level position.) 13 ... ♗f5! 15 ♗g5 ♖e8 15 ♕d2? (15 ♘c4!? ♗d3 16 a3 would have given White counterplay, according to Kasparov.) 15 ... b5! (Black clearly has full compensation for his material and

probably stands better already.) 16
♖ad1 ♘d3! 17 ♘ab1? (17 d6!?
Kasparov.) 17 ... h6 18 ♗h4 b4 19
♘a4 ♗d6 ∓ 20 ♗g3 ♖c8 21 b3 g5!!
22 ♗×d6 ♛×d6 23 g3 ♘d7 24 ♗g2
(24 ♘b2 would have allowed the
brilliant reply 24 ... ♛f6!!
Kasparov.) 24 ... ♛f6 25 a3 a5 and
Black went on to win.

But, as Kostiuchenko pointed
out, 12 ♗e3! would give White a
substantial advantage. This was
confirmed in the famous game
Karpov–van der Wiel, Brussels
1986: 12 ♗e3! ♗×e3 13 ♛a4+ ♘d7
(13 ... b5 14 ♛×b4 ♗b6 15 0-0 ♗a5
16 ♗×b5+! with a winning attack,
or 13 ... ♗d7 14 ♛×b4 ♛b6 15
♛×b6 ♗×b6 and, according to
Kasparov, 'White's superiority is
obvious because Black is con-
demned to a difficult defence,
although the endgame can probably be held.' Van der Wiel gives
16 ♘c4 ♗d4 17 ♖d1 ± and 16 ...
♗c5! 17 ♗f3 ±, which is probably
an overstatement, since on 17 ...
0-0 18 0-0 Black might try 18 ...
♗b5!?, e.g. 19 ♘×b5 ab 20 ♘e5
♗d4 21 ♘d3 ♘e8! 22 a3 ♘d6 with
compensation. So this variation
may still be alive.) 14 ♛×b4? (The
correct line, as van der Wiel
pointed out, is 14 fe! ♛h4+ 15 g3
♛e7 16 ♖ad1 a5 ±, to which we
add 17 ♘c4 0-0 18 a3 ±.) 14 ... ♗c5
15 ♛e4+ ♔f8 16 0-0 b5 and van der
Wiel eventually saved the game.

There are still other options for
Black, but they do not seem to be
adequate:

(a) 11 ... ♘b×d5 12 0-0 ♗e6 (12
... ♗×a3? 13 ♛a4+! or 12 ... ♗e7 13
♘×d5 ♘×d5 14 ♗f3 ♗e6 15 ♘c2!
±/± Kasparov.) 13 ♗f3 ♗e7 14
♘×d5 ♗×d5 15 ♗g5 ±/±.

(b) 11 ... b5 12 ♘c2! (12 0-0?
♗d6 13 ♘c2 ♘×c2 14 ♛×c2 ♛c7
followed by either 15 ... ♗×h2+ or
15 ... b4) 12 ... ♘×c2+ 13 ♛×c2 ±
since 13 ... ♗d6 is met by 14 ♘×b5!
and 13 ... ♗b7 runs into trouble on
14 ♗f3.

12   0-0   0-0 *(109)*

We feel that this position may
be playable for Black.

13   ♗f3

13 ♘c2 ♘b×d5 and Black is not
worse.

13   ...   ♗f5
14   ♛d4   b5!

Now the ♘a3 is cut off and if 15
d6, Black can play 15 ... ♗×d6 16
♖d1 ♘d3! ∓. Further tests are still
needed to determine the validity
of Kasparov's idea, but in our
opinion rumours of its death have
been greatly exaggerated.

III   Najdorf Variation

1   e4   c5

2	♘f3	d6
3	d4	cd
4	♘×d4	♘f6
5	♘c3	a6 *(110)*

When Black chooses this method of avoiding the Keres Attack, he must be prepared to face the formidable main line of the Najdorf with 6 ♗g5. But Kasparov, like Fischer before him, is not afraid of fights! His opponents, however, have not been so bold, and only Najdorf guru John Nunn has dared to employ the main lines.

| 6 | ♗g5 | e6 |
| 7 | f4 | ♛b6 |

The dreaded Poisoned Pawn Variation.

| 8 | ♛d3 | |

We must wait for examples of the normal continuation 8 ♛d2, which Kasparov used as White in his younger days. At the time this game was played (Brussels 1986), White's 8th move was fashionable.

8	...	♛×b2
9	♖b1	♛a3
10	f5	♗e7!
11	♗e2	

As Kasparov has noted, 11 fe fe 12 ♛c4 0-0! 13 ♘×e6 b5! wins for Black, but 13 ♘f5!? ♘c6 is less clear.

11	...	♘c6
12	fe	fe
13	♘×c6	bc
14	e5!?	

14 0-0 is a more normal move.

14	...	de
15	♗×f6	gf
16	♗h5+	♚f8
17	♛d2	

Nunn's intended improvement on van der Wiel–Gavrikov, London 1985, which saw 17 0-0 e4! 18 ♛h3 f5 ∓.

Kasparov suggested that 17 ♛e3!? ♖g8 18 ♛h6+ ♖g7 19 ♖b3 ♛a5 20 0-0 f5 would lead to unclear complications. On 21 ♘e4!, Black must avoid 21 ... ♖a7? 22 ♖b8 ♛c7 23 ♛×e6 ++, but 21 ... ♗h4 22 ♘f6 is still messy.

| 17 | ... | ♚g7! |
| 18 | ♖b3 | ♛a5! |

Black must be careful; if 18 ... ♛d6 19 ♘d5! Black is in trouble (Kasparov).

| 19 | 0-0 | ♖g8! |
| 20 | ♚h1 | ♚h8 |

Black has fully consolidated his position.

| 21 | ♛h6 | |

The last chance, hoping to get in 22 ♖×f6.

21	...	♛d8
22	♘e4	f5
23	♗f7	

23 ♖h3 ♗g5!

| 23 | ... | ♛f8! |

24 ♕h5   ♖g7

Kasparov's only slip — even stronger, as he later remarked, was 24 ... ♖g4! 25 ♖h3 ♕g7, winning.

25 ♗e8   a5
26 ♗×c6   ♗a6
27 ♖f2   ♖d8
0-1

With this brilliant example of counter-attack we must conclude our brief foray into the forest of the Sicilian Defence.

10 Hedgehog

111

This is one of the most popular, but at the same time most mysterious opening systems. Its labyrinth of transpositions baffles opening classifiers and authors, and to date no monograph has appeared on this prolific line. Black seems to play passively during the opening, hoping for an explosive middlegame break. The variation is rather like a coiled spring, which can burst out at any moment. Black can play for breaks in the centre (with ... e5 or ... d5) or on the flank (usually with ... b5).

There is some resemblance to the Taimanov System of the Sicilian and other Maroczy Bind positions, but here Black has more pronounced pressure on the a8–h1 diagonal. The position was not considered playable until the 1970s, when it became clear that

White's vice-like grip on the centre was not of a permanent nature. Many players have adopted a positional approach as Black, but Kasparov has preferred to engage in tactical brawls. The defence played a significant role in his repertoire in the early 1980s.

As we have mentioned, this is not an opening which leads itself to clear organization and discussion of individual lines. We will present a selection of significant games by Kasparov, with some general discussion of the ideas behind the Hedgehog.

1	c4	c5
2	♘f3	♘f6
3	♘c3	b6
4	g3	♗b7
5	♗g2	

There are a number of paths into the Hedgehog complex, and the preceding moves represent a fairly pure move order which allows Black to choose between deploying his ♗f8 at g7 or e7. But this flexibility is rarely needed, as Black generally has a preference which he need not disguise in the opening. So in the examples below, we will show the actual move order used in each game and discuss the significance of each choice. We will place our commentary in the context of each game, rather than adopt a variation-based format, because the depth of transpositions and bewildering variety of move-orders cannot be captured in a brief chapter.

Karpov–Kasparov, USSR Team Ch. 1981, was the second meeting of the two giants and it started off with Karpov adopting the English move order:

1	c4	♘f6
2	♘c3	c5
3	♘f3	e6
4	g3	b6

Black could also opt for the Tarrasch Defence with 4 ... d5, but this game was played before Kasparov 'discovered' that opening.

5	♗g2	♗b7
6	0-0	♗e7 *(112)*

112
W

7	d4	cd
8	♕×d4	d6

Black can develop with tempo by 8 ... ♘c6, but after 9 ♕f4 followed by ♖d1 Black comes under some uncomfortable pressure.

9	♗g5	

This is just one of many strategies tried by White in the early 1980s. White must find some way of exploiting Black's only real weakness — the d-pawn.

9	...	a6
10	♗×f6	♗×f6
11	♕f4	0-0
12	♖fd1	♗e7
13	♘e4	♗×e4
14	♕×e4	♖a7
15	♘d4	♕c8
16	b3	♖e8!
17	a4	♕c5
18	♖a2	♗f6
19	♖ad2	♖c7
20	♕b1!	♗e7
21	b4!?	

This is the only way to obtain active play, but the c-pawn is weak, and Kasparov will be able to take advantage of this. This rather risky approach is not in keeping with Karpov's usual style, but even at this stage Karpov recognized in Kasparov a potential challenger who should be put in his place (in a 1981 interview, Karpov said of Kasparov that 'he does not play as well as he thinks he does.) It is not clear whether Karpov still holds this opinion.

21	...	♕h5

Not 21 ... ♕×c4?? which loses to 22 ♖c2.

22	♖c2	♖ec8
23	b5?	

Perhaps Karpov was trying to confuse his young opponent. The correct plan was 23 ♕b3, as White has nothing to fear from 23 ... d5 24 cd 🜚×c2 25 ♘×c2 ♕×e2, because White obtains an overpowering position with 26 ♘d4. At the same time, 23 ... e5 24 ♘f3 b5 is met by 25 🜚dc1. Black's best plan would be to settle for equality with 23 ... ♘d7, because the combinative 24 c5 bc 25 ♘×e6 fe 26 ♕×e6+ doesn't work, with 26 ... ♕f7 providing the refutation.

23	...	ab
24	ab	🜚×c4
25	🜚×c4	

On 25 ♘c6 Kasparov had prepared 25 ... 🜚×c2 26 ♘×e7+ ♚h8! (protecting the h-pawn) 27 ♗f3 ♕e5 28 ♘×c8 🜚×c8 ∓.

25	...	🜚×c4
26	♕a2!	♕c5
27	♕a8	🜚×d4
28	♕×b8+	♗f8
29	🜚a1	

Here, instead of 29 ... d5?!, Kasparov claimed that 29 ... h6! 20 🜚a8 🜚d1+ would have brought a clear advantage for Black. So far as the opening is concerned, Kasparov was clearly successful in one of his first attempts at defending the Hedgehog.

In the strong Tilburg International of 1981 Kasparov defended the Black side against Hübner, who varied with:

9 b3

White prepares to deploy his bishop on the queenside. He can choose to place it in the centre as well. 9 ♗e3 was seen in Korchnoi–Hjartarson, (m/4) 1988: 9 ... 0-0 10 🜚ad1 ♘bd7 11 ♘b5 d5 12 ♗f4 ♗c5 13 ♕d3 dc 14 ♕×c4 a6 15 ♘c3 b5 with plenty of counterplay for Black.

9	...	0-0

Korchnoi–Hjartarson, (m/6) 1988, saw instead 9 ... ♘bd7, to which Korchnoi chose a forceful and original reply: 10 ♘b5!? and now Hjartarson went wrong with 10 ... ♘c5?! (10 ... ♘e4 11 ♕×g7 ♗f6 12 ♕h6 ♗×a1 13 ♘g5 ±) 11 🜚d1 d5 (11 ... ♘fe4 12 ♕×g7 ♗f6 13 ♕h6 ♗×a1 14 ♘g5!! ♕f6 15 ♘×e4 ♘×e4 16 ♗×e4 ♗×e4 17 ♘×d6+ ±) 12 cd ed 13 ♗h3! 0-0 14 ♗b2 a6 15 ♘c3 🜚e8 16 🜚ac1 ♘e6?! 17 ♗×e6 fe 18 ♘a4 and Korchnoi easily won this critical match game. So Black had better castle immediately.

10	e4	

10 ♗a3 is a common alternative.

10	...	♘bd7
11	♕e3	a6 (113)

12	♘d4	

The Hedgehog is a slow-moving opening, and White can afford to take time out to redeploy his forces on more promising squares.

12	...	♛c7
13	♗b2	♖fe8
14	h3	♗f8

Black's position is already preferable in view of the potential breaks at d5 and b5 (or even e5). White must exercise caution here. For example, he would find himself in trouble after 15 f4? e5! 16 ♘f5 d5! (Kasparov).

15	♖fe1	♖ad8
16	♖e2	g6
17	♖ae1	♛b8
18	♛d2	♗g7
19	♛d1	♘c5
20	♗c1?	

20 ♖d2 was a more promising alternative, according to Kasparov. White is swimming, playing without a plan, and soon found himself in difficulty.

20	...	♖c8
21	♗g5	h6
22	♗c1	♖ed8
23	♗b2 *(114)*	

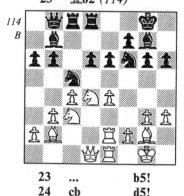

114
B

| 23 | ... | b5! |
| 24 | cb | d5! |

Two methodical breaks in a row — an unusual sight! Black has firm control of the initiative.

| 25 | ed | |

There is not much choice, since 25 e5 is met by 25 ... ♘fe4 ∓.

25	...	♘×d5
26	♘×d5	♗×d5
27	b4!	♗×g2
28	♔×g2	e5!
29	bc	ed
30	♖d2?!	

30 ♛d3 would have limited the damage, according to Kasparov.

30	...	♖×c5
31	ba	♛a8+
32	♔f3	♛×a6
33	♖ed1	♖f5
34	♛e4	♛a4! *(115)*

115
W

Black clearly stands better, even though material is still equal. His passed pawn at d4 is considerably stronger than White's a-pawn. Kasparov was able to convert his advantage into a full point:

| 35 | a3 | |

35 ♗×d4 is not on because of 35 ... ♖fd5!

| 35 | ... | ♖e8?! |

35 ... h5 would have been more effective, according to Kasparov.

| 36 | ♛b7 | ♖d8! |

37	♖d3	h5
38	♖1d2	♕e8!
39	♔f1?!	

After this move the win is simple. 39 ♔h2 should have been played.

| 39 | ... | ♖b8 |
| 40 | ♕c7 | ♖xb2! |

Hübner–Kasparov, Tilburg 1981, concluded 41 ♖xb2 ♕e4 42 ♕c4 ♕h1+ 43 ♔e2 ♕g1! 44 ♖b8+ ♔h7 45 f4 h4! 46 ♖b5 ♖xb5 47 ♕xb5 hg 48 ♕g5 ♕f2+ 49 ♔d1 ♕f1+ 0-1.

One of Kasparov's more impressive victories with the Hedgehog came at the expense of former World Champion Smyslov, at the 4-team Match tournament held in Moscow 1981.

| 1 | ♘f3 | c5 |
| 2 | c4 | |

White declines the invitation to the Sicilian Defence with 2 e4.

2	...	♘f6
3	g3	b6
4	♗g2	♗b7
5	0-0	e6
6	♘c3	♗e7
7	b3	

There is no reason why White cannot delay the advance of his d-pawn.

7	...	0-0
8	♗b2	d6
9	e3	

In this way White prepares to advance d2–d4, and if Black captures, then recapture with a pawn is possible, maintaining strong central pressure.

| 9 | ... | ♘bd7 |
| 10 | d4 | a6 *(116)* |

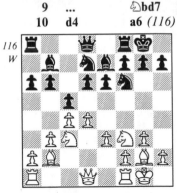

116
W

| 11 | ♕e2 | |

In a dramatic encounter at the World Youth Team Championship at Graz, 1981, Kasparov demonstrated his skill with the Black pieces against Jon Speelman, who chose 11 ♖c1. Now instead of the normal 11 ... ♖c8, Kasparov once again bravely entered a web of complications with 11 ... b5!? 12 d5 (On 12 dc Kasparov intended the wild 12 ... ♘xc5 13 cb ab 14 ♘xb5 ♖xa2 15 ♗xf6 ♗xf6 16 ♘xd6 ♗a6! 17 ♖xc5 ♗e2!! 18 ♕b1 ♖b2! and the result of the devastation is an overwhelming advantage for Black!) 12 ... ed 13 ♘xd5 ♘xd5 14 cd ♗f6 15 ♗xf6 ♘xf6 16 ♘h4 a5 and Kasparov exploited his advantage in the endgame.

| 11 | ... | ♘e4 |

This prevents White from playing e3–e4. 11 ... ♖c8 is also possible, as on 12 e4 Black can capture at d4, and White will have wasted a tempo in the slow march of his e-pawn.

12	🨂fd1	👑b8!?

A rather provocative choice. 12 ... 👑c7 is more cautious.

13	🨄xe4	🨗xe4
14	🨄e5!?	🨗xg2
15	🨄xd7	👑b7
16	🨄xf8	🨗f3
17	👑d3	

White hopes for 18 👑xh7+.

17	...	🨂xf8
18	🨂d2	f5

Kasparov sacrifices the exchange in order to obtain a strong attack along the a1-h8 diagonal. Still, this bold action may not be justified, and if Smyslov had chosen here 19 a3!, Kasparov might have regretted his decision. Instead, Smyslov embarks on a series of poor moves.

19	🨂e1?	👑c8
20	👑c3?	🨂f6
21	a3?	👑e8
22	dc	👑h5!
23	h4	👑g4
24	👑h2	bc
25	🨂h1	🨂g6
26	👑g1	🨗xh4
27	👑a5	h6

0-1.

Was Kasparov lucky? Sure, but fortune favours the brave!

Where does the Hedgehog stand in contemporary practice? It is still extremely popular, and White has been seeking improvements in a number of ways. One popular idea is the return to recapturing at d4 with the knight, after first supporting the centre. A recent example is Vaganian–Co.

Ionescu, Sochi 1986:

1	🨄f3	c5
2	c4	🨄f6
3	🨄c3	e6
4	g3	b6
5	🨗g2	🨗b7
6	0-0	a6

6 ... 🨗e7 7 🨂e1 d5 was seen in Vaganian–Portisch, match 1988, but we feel that 7 ... d6 is a more cautious approach, and play should therefore transpose below.

7	🨂e1	🨗e7
8	e4	d6
9	d4	cd
10	🨄xd4	*(117)*

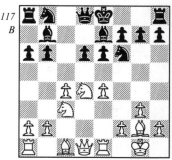

This is a classical Maroczy Bind position.

10	...	👑c7
11	🨗e3	0-0

11 ... 🨄bd7 was met in Ivanov-Shamkovich, St. John 1988: 12 🨂c1 🨂c8 13 f4 0-0 (13 ... 👑b8! is more accurate, and if 14 g4, then 14 ... h5 is a strong possibility.) 14 g4! 🨄c5 15 🨗f2 🨄e8 16 g5 g6 17 👑d2 🨄g7 18 f5!? gf 19 ef 🨗xg2 20 👑xg2 👑b7+ 21 👑g1 ef 22 🨂xe7 👑xe7 23 🨄d5 👑d8 24 🨄f6+ 👑h8 25 👑f4 and now Black should have

played 25 ... ♘e4 ∞/∓, instead of
25 ... ♘e8 26 ♘×h7 ♔×h7 27 ♕h4+
♔g8 28 ♖c3 ♘e4 29 ♖h3 ♕×g5+
30 ♖g3 f6 31 ♗e3 and now Black
blundered with 31 ... ♕×g3??
instead of 31 ... ♘×g3 ∞.

12	♖c1	♘bd7
13	f4	♖fe8
14	g4!?	

This is a typical Sicilian attacking idea.

14	...	h6
15	g5	hg
16	fg	♘h7
17	g6!	♘hf8
18	gf+	♔×f7
19	♖f1+	♔g8
20	♘d5!!	ed
21	cd	♕d8
22	♘c6	♗g5
23	♘×d8	♗×e3+
24	♔h1	♖a×d8
25	♖c7	

and after this spectacular display White managed to win after a few more moves.

Of course this game was hardly the refutation of the resilient Hedgehog, and Black still has a wide range of valid plans from which to choose. Kasparov's contributions to this opening are important, greater in quality than in quantity.

11 Spanish

Kasparov played the Spanish game a bit in his early years, but put it aside until 1985, when he started to play it for both sides. At the Hilversum match against Timman, co-author Schiller asked him how he had managed to absorb all of the theory so quickly as to be able to employ it in serious play. He replied that it was not necessary to know all of the latest moves in order to play the Spanish. An understanding of the underlying principles is sufficient, because the Spanish is primarily a positional opening.

To discuss even the Zaitsev variation alone in any depth would require an entire book (co-author Schiller has written such a book, published by Chess Enterprises in 1989) and so we will confine ourselves to the two principal variations which have featured prominently in the World Champion's play.

1	e4	e5
2	♘f3	♘c6
3	♗b5	a6
4	♗a4	♘f6
5	0-0	♗e7
6	♖e1	b5
7	♗b3	d6
8	c3	0-0
9	h3	♗b7
10	d4	♖e8
11	♘bd2	♗f8 (118)

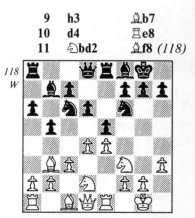

In this position we find the World Champion continuing with 12 a4 as White and often defending the Black side after 12 a3.

I   12 a4
II   12 a3

A dubious innovation is 12 ♘g5 ♖e7 13 f4?! h6 14 ♘df3 ♕e8 and White was on his way to being pasted in Arnason–Geller, Reykjavik 1986. After the more normal 13 d5, Black can play 13 ... ♘a5! 14 ♗c2 c6 15 b4 ♘c4 16 ♘×c4 bc 17 dc ♗×c6 with good play (Timman–Karpov, Bugojno 1980).

Against 12 d5 the best retreat is 12 ... ♘b8, e.g. 13 ♘f1 ♘bd7 14 ♘g3 g6 and now:

(a) 15 c4 ♗g7! 16 cb ab 17 ♗e3 ♕e7, as proposed by Lev Gutman.

(b) 15 ♘h2 ♗g7 16 a4 ♕e7! 17 ♘g4 ♘xg4 18 hg was seen in Elen–Gligorić, Portorož–Ljubljana 1977, where Gutman recommends 18 ... c6 19 ♘f1 with sufficient counterplay for Black.

On 12 ♗c2, then 12 ... g6 is playable, but Black can also choose to enter the Breyer Variation with 12 ... ♘b8.

I

12   a4   h6

Karpov tried 12 ... ♕d7 in Karpov–Kasparov (m/46) 1984–5, but after 13 ab ab 14 ♖xa8 ♗xa8 15 d5 ♘d8 16 ♘f1 h6 17 ♘3h2 he found himself in a difficult position. Convinced of the strength of the line, he later adopted it as White against Smejkal at the 1986 Olympiad in Dubai, obtaining a smaller, but still significant advantage after 15 ... ♘b8 16 ♘f1 ♘a6 17 ♗g5 ♗e7 18 ♘g3. Smejkal had previously defended 15 ... ♘e7 16 c4 ♖b8 against Popović at Zagreb 1985, but was probably afraid to repeat the line because of 16 ♘f1. In the meantime, however, Karpov found the improvement 15 ... ♘a5!, which he introduced in Karpov–Kasparov, (m/5) 1985: 16 ♗a2 c6 17 b4 ♘b7 (17 ... ♘c4? 18 ♘xc4 bc 19 ♗g5 cd 20 ♗xf6 de 21 ♘xe5 and 19 ♗xc4 cd 20 ed ♖c8 21 ♕b3 are both very good for White.) 18 c4 ♖c8 19 dc ♕xc6 with equal chances. But it is not clear that Black will be able to equalize against 18 ♘f1, as 18 ... cd 19 ed ♖c8 20 ♗g5 ♖xc3?! runs

into 21 ♗xf6 gf 22 ♘h4 with a strong initiative for White, so Black ought to play 20 ... ♗e7 with unclear complications after 21 ♕d2, according to Kasparov.

13   ♗c2 *(119)*

It is not wise to block the centre with 13 d5, because Black can then obtain favourable Breyer-type positions with 13 ... ♘b8 (13 ... ♘a7 14 ♘f1 c6 15 ♘3h2 left the initiative in White's hands in Nunn–Smejkal, Dubai Ol 1986, and 13 ... ♘e7 14 c4 allows White a free hand on the queenside, Jansa–Nikolić, Esbjerg 1982.) and now if 14 c4, then 14 ... c6! puts strong pressure on the White centre (but not 14 ... bc 15 ♘xc4 with a comfortable advantage for White in Kindermann–Greenfeld, Beersheva 1984.) If White then trades rooks with 15 ab ab 16 ♖xa8 ♗xa8, and then grabs the pawn with 17 dc, then Black obtains counterplay with 17 ... b4! (17 ... bc leads to a more prosaic equality after 18 ♘xc4 ♗xc6 19 ♗a4.) 18 ♗a4 ♘xc6 and now White's kingside play is balanced by

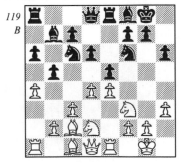

119
B

Black's queenside opportunities, for example 19 ♘f1 ♕b8 20 g4 (20 ♘g3 g6! followed by ... ♖c8 is better for Black.) 20 ... ♖c8 21 ♘g3 ♘d8 22 g5 hg 23 ♘×g5, as seen in Kasparov–Dorfman, USSR Ch. 1978.

13 ... ed

Karpov prefers to move pieces to b8 here, but he fails to equalize:

(a) 13 ... ♘b8 14 ♗d3 c6 15 ♘f1 ♘bd7 16 ♘g3 ♕c7 17 ♗d2! g6 (17 ... ♖ad8 18 ab ab 19 c4 △ ♗a5) 18 ♕c1 ♔h7 19 b3! ± Kasparov–Karpov, (m/9) 1985. After 19 ... ♗g7 20 ♕c2 ♘f8 21 ♗e3! ♘e6 22 ♖ad1 ♖ac8 23 ♗f1 ♗f8 24 ♖d2 ♕b8 25 ♕b1 ♗a8 26 b4 ♗b7 instead of 27 ab?! ab 29 ♖ed1 White should have played 27 ♕a2!, intending ♖b2, de, c4 (Kasparov).

(b) 13 ... ♖b8 allows White to open the a-file without exchanging rooks: 14 ab ab 15 ♗d3 ♗c8 16 ♘f1 and White was better in Timman–Karpov, Tilburg 1986.

(c) 13 ... ♕d7 seems out of place here, as after 14 d5 ♘e7 15 b3 Black is left without a clear plan (Spassky–Balashov, Toluca Zonal 1982).

14 cd ♘b4
15 ♗b1 *(120)* **c5**

Theory has settled on this as the best move in view of the failure of the alternatives to achieve a playable game for Black:

(a) 15 ... ♕d7 16 ♖a3 ba 17 ♖×a4 a5 18 ♖a3 ♕b5 19 ♘h2 g6 20 ♘g4 ♘×g4 21 ♕×g4 and despite the time wasted by the White rook,

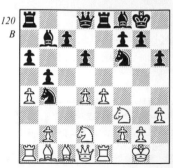

Black still lacks sufficient counterplay (Dvoris–Lerner, Kharkov 1985).

(b) 15 ... g6? allows the aggressive try 16 e5!? In Matulović–Lukacs, Vrnačka Banja 1985, play continued 16 ... de 17 de ♘h5 18 ab ab 19 ♖×a8 ♕×a8 20 ♘e4 ♖d8 21 ♕e2 ♘d5 22 ♕×b5 ♘hf4 23 ♗×f4 ♘×f4 24 ♘f6+ ♔g7 25 ♗e4 ♗×e4 26 ♖×e4 ♘d3 27 ♖a4 ♕b8 28 ♘e8+ ♖×e8 29 ♕×d3 ♕×b2 30 ♖c4 c5 ½-½. Therefore we prefer 16 d5, e.g. 16 ... ♗g7 17 ♕b3 ±.

(c) 15 ... ba 16 ♖×a4 a5 17 ♖a3 is also insufficient:

(c1) 17 ... ♖a6 18 ♘h2 ± Sax–Bañas, Balatonberenyi 1984, where Black committed suicide with 18 ... ♕a8? 19 ♖ae3 ♕a7 20 e5 ♘fd5 21 ♖g3 de 22 de ♖ae6 23 ♘e4 ♔h8 24 ♘f3 ♕b6 25 ♘fg5 hg 26 ♘×g5 g6 27 ♕h5+ 1-0.

(c2) 17 ... g6 18 ♖ae3 ± Sax–Belyavsky, Moscow Interzonal 1982.

(c3) 17 ... ♕d7 18 ♘h4 with an initiative for White (Ehlvest–Belyavsky, USSR Ch. 1984). The game continued 18 ... ♕b5 19 ♖f3

♘h7 20 ♖g3 ♘g5 21 ♘hf3 ♘xf3+ 22 ♘xf3 ♕h5 23 ♗d2 ♖e7 24 ♕c1 ♔h8 25 d5 c5 26 ♖g4 ♗c8 27 ♖f4 ♔g8 28 e5 g5 29 ♖f6 de 30 ♗xb4 ab 31 ♕c2 ♔g7 32 d6 ♔xf6 33 de ♗xe7 34 ♕e4 1-0.

16   d5

Kasparov tried 16 dc dc 17 e5 against Balashov in a game played in the Soviet Union in 1982, but after 17 ... ♘d7 he wasn't able to achieve anything.

16 b3 is also too slow, as after 16 ... cd 17 ♘xd4 ba 18 ♖xa4 a5 the game was level in Tseshkovsky-Balashov, Minsk 1982, a tournament notable for its contributions to the theory of the Spanish Game.

16   ...   ♘d7

The immediate fianchetto is also possible. After 16 ... g6 17 ♘f1 ♗g7 18 ♖a3! ba 19 ♖xa4 a5 20 ♖a3 ♗a6 21 ♘g3 Black was feeling the pressure in Aseyev-Dorfman, USSR Ch. 1984, although Sax and Hazai suggest here 21 ... ♘d7! and Black should be safe.

17   ♖a3 *(121)*

The standard plan with 17 ♘f1 runs into the surprising counter

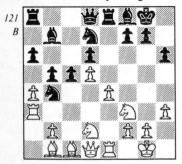

121
B

17 ... f5!, leading to an unclear position in which Black's chances are to be preferred (de Firmian-Belyavsky. Tunis Interzonal 1985).

17   ...   c4!

18   ♘d4

Kasparov-Karpov (m/14) 1986 saw 18 ab ab 19 ♘d4 ♖xa3 20 ba ♘d3 21 ♗xd3 cd 22 ♗b2 ♕a5 23 ♘f5 ♘e5 24 ♗xe5 (24 f4 is interesting: 24 ... ♘c4 25 ♘xc4 bc 26 ♘xh6+ gh 27 ♕g4+ = or 26 ♗xg7 ♗xd5!? 27 ♕a1 ♖xe4 28 ♖xe4 ♗xe4 29 ♗xf8 c3) with an unclear position with chances for both sides.

Sax-Short, match 1988, tried to improve with 22 ♖e3 ♘e5 23 ♘xb5 ♕a5 24 ♘d4 ♕c3 25 ♘2b3 ♗a6 26 ♗d2 ♕b2 27 ♗b4 g6 28 f4 (28 ♕d2 ♘c4 29 ♕xb2 ♘xb2 30 ♘c6 is better for White, but 28 ... ♕xd2 29 ♘xd2 ♗g7 is less clear.) 28 ... ♘c4 29 ♖xd3 ♖xe4 30 ♕f3 ♖e8 31 ♔h2 ♗g7 32 ♘c6 ♕e2 33 ♘bd4 ♕xf3 34 ♖xf3 ♖e4 35 ♘b3 ♖e2 36 ♘cd4 ♖e4 37 ♘c6 ♖e2 38 ♔g3 (An attempt to win, but it doesn't work) 38 ... ♘e3 39 h4 ♖xg2+ 40 ♔h3 ♗c8+ 41 f5 ♗xf5+ 42 ♖xf5 gxf5 43 ♗xd6 ♖b2 44 ♘e7+ ♔h7 45 ♘c5 ♗f6 0-1.

18   ...   ♕f6 *(122)*

Recent attempts to improve upon this advance have proven fruitless:

(a) 18 ... ♕b6?! 19 ♘f5! was crushing in Sax-Nikolić, Lugano 1987: 19 ... ♘e5 20 ♖g3 ♔h7 21 ♘f3 ♗c8 (21 ... g6 22 ♘xh6 ♗xh6 23 ♗xh6 ♔xh6 24 ♕d2 ±) 22 ♘xg7

♗×g7 23 ♕d2.

(b) 18 ... ♘e5 19 ab ♕b6 and now:

(b1) 20 ♘2f3 ♘bd3! (This is better than 20 ... ♘ed3 since 21 ♗e3!? ♘×e1 22 ♘×e1 ♕c7 23 ♕d2! a5 24 ♘ef3 ⯑ gives full compensation for the exchange.) 21 ♗×d3 ♘×d3 22 ♖×d3!? cd 23 ♕×d3 ab 24 ♕×b5 (Ernst-Bjerke, Malmö 1987-88) 24 ... ♕×b5 25 ♘×b5 ♖a1 (intending 26 ... ♗×d5) 26 ♘c3 ♗a6 ∓.

(b2) 20 ♘×c4!? was seen in Sax-Short, Subotica 1987. After 20 ... ♘×c4 21 ♖g3 ♗c8! (21 ... ab 22 ♘f5 g6 23 ♕h5! ♔h7 24 ♘×h6!! gh 25 e5+ wins for White) White has two options:

(b21) 22 ♗×h6?! ab 23 ♘f3 (Weaker is 23 ♘b3, suggested by Petran, since 23 ... ♘e5 24 ♕d2 ♘a6 25 ♗e3 ♕d8 26 ♗d4 ♘c5! ∓.) 23 ... ♖a1 (Sax-Short), and now, instead of 24 ♘g5, stronger would have been 24 b3 ♘e5 (24 ... ♘a3 25 ♕d2 ±) 25 ♕d2 ♘g6 26 ♗f4 ±/⯑ (Petran), but 24 ... ♘a6 seems more sensible to us.

(b22) 22 b3!? ♘e5 23 ♗e3 (intending 24 ♘c6) 23 ... ♘g6 24 f4! ♕d8 25 f5 ♘e5 26 ♕d2 a5 27 ♗×h6 ♕h4? (27 ... ♗d7!? ±) 28 ♔h2 ♗d7 29 ♗g5 ♕h5 30 ♖f1! ± (A. Sokolov-Portisch, Brussels 1988; move numbers given here differ from the actual game, in which there was an early repetition.).

This gambit line (20 ♘×c4!?) needs more detailed analysis and examination. Hence we cannot be sure that Black's opening strategy has been refuted by the knight sacrifice. It is interesting to note that Kasparov did not play 1 e4 at all in the fourth match against Karpov, but in the Amsterdam Options Exchange Tournament in 1988 he played it twice.

(b3) Pliester recommends 20 ♘f5, but we feel that Black will quickly gain the upper hand with 20 ... ♘bd3 21 ♗×d3 ♘×d3 22 ♖e3 ab ∓.

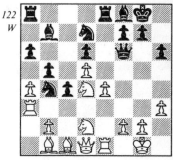

122
W

19　♘2f3　　♘d3

19 ... ♘c5 20 ab ab 21 ♘×b5 ♖×a3 22 ♘×a3 ♗a6 led to an unclear position where there is plenty of compensation for the material in Kasparov-Karpov, (m/16) 1986.

20　♗×d3

20 ♖×d3!? cd 21 ab!? is an interesting line which deserves practical tests. Black might be able to play 21 ... ♘c5, e.g. 22 b4 ♘×e4 23 ♕×d3 ♗×d5 24 ♘c6 ♗×c6 25 bc d5 ∓.

20　...　　　b4
21　♗×c4

21 ♖a1 cd 22 ♕×d3 ♘c5 23 ♕c4

a5! 24 ♘b5 ♖ac8 is definitely better for Black.

21 ... ba

22 b3

In this state-of-the-art position both sides have chances, according to analysis by Kasparov. It is entirely possible that White is slightly better here. For example:

(a) 22 ... ♘e5 23 ♗xa3 ♘xc4 24 bc g6 25 ♕d3 ♗g7 26 ♖b1 ±.

(b) 22 ... ♘c5 23 ♕c2 a2 24 ♗b2 ♕g6 25 ♘d2 ♖ac8 26 ♗c3 ♗e7 ∞.

II

12 a3 *(123)*

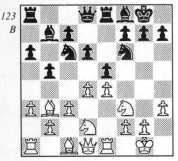

Kasparov has handled this position from the Black side. White does not attempt to attack the Black king but rather keeps his eye on the queenside, preparing the advance of his b-pawn.

12 ... h6

This transposition into the Smyslov system is considered the only playable option at present.

(a) 12 ... ♕d7 13 ♗c2 ♖ad8 14 ♘b3 h6 15 d5 ♘e7 16 ♘a5 c6 17 c4 gave White the advantage in Psakhis–Balashov, USSR Ch. 1980–81.

(b) 12 ... g6 13 ♗a2 ♗g7 (Black can try 13 ... ♕d7 now but it seems that after 14 b4 a5 15 d5 White has secured an advantage, for example 15 ... ♘e7 16 ba c6 17 c4 ♖xa5 18 dc ♘xc6 19 cb ♖xb5 20 a4 ♖a5 21 ♘c4 ♖a6 22 ♗g5 Lukin–Polovodin, USSR 1984.) 14 d5! with an initiative for White, for example 14 ... ♘b8 (14 ... ♘e7 15 c4! c6 16 b4 bc 17 dc ± Gutman.) 15 b4 c6 16 c4 ♖a7 (Gutman provides 16 ... bc 17 dc! ♘xc6 18 ♘xc4 ♘d4 19 ♗g5! and 16 ... cd 17 cd a5 18 ♘b3 ab 19 ab ±. 16 ... ♘bd7 17 dc ♗xc6 18 ♗b2 is slightly better for White.) 17 ♗b2 bc (17 ... ♘bd7 18 ♖c1 ♕a8 19 dc! ♗xc6 20 ♕c2! ± Gufeld–Aseyev, USSR 1986) 18 dc ♗xc6 19 ♗xc4 and White stands better.

13 ♗c2

13 ♗a2 can be met by the interesting move 13 ... ♘a7!?, or by 13 ... ♘b8 14 b4 ed (14 ... ♘bd7 15 ♗b2 g6 16 ♕b1 ♗g7 17 c4 was agreed drawn in Dobrovolsky–Plachetka, Trnava 1983.) 15 cd ♘xe4 16 ♕b3 ♕f6 17 ♕c2 ♘xd2 18 ♖xe8 ♘xf3+ 19 gf ♘c6 with compensation (Mortensen–Hjartarson, Copenhagen 1985). After 20 ♖xa8 Black should have simply recaptured, saving the knight move for later.

13 ... ♘b8

Probably best, although an interesting alternative is 13 ... g6!? 14 ♘f1 ♘a5 15 ♘g3 ♘c4 16 b3 ♘b6 17 ♗d3 ♗g7 with unclear complications (Aseyev–Timoshchenko,

Irkutsk 1986).

14 b4 *(124)*

14 b3 is a major alternative. Black plays 14 ... ♘bd7 and now:

(a) 15 ♗b2 g6 16 a4 might be met by Hjartarson's 16 ... ♘h5, while 16 ♖c1 c6 17 c4 ed 18 ♗×d4 ♗g7 19 b4 ♕c7 20 c5 dc 21 bc ♘h5 led to unclear complications in Romanishin-van der Sterren, Tallinn 1987.

(b) 15 d5 c6 16 c4 ♕c7 and now:

(b1) 17 ♗b2 ♖eb8 18 dc ♗×c6 19 cb ab was agreed drawn in Smyslov-Gligorić, Sochi 1986.

(b2) 17 ♘f1 ♖eb8 18 ♘g3 ♗c8 19 a4 is a bit slow, e.g. 19 ... bc 20 bc ♘c5 21 ♗a3 ♘fd7 22 ♘e2 cd 23 cd a5 24 ♘c3 ♗a6 with a decisive queenside advantage (Liang-Sun, China 1986).

(b3) 17 a4 ♖ec8 18 ♖a2 ba 19 ba a5 20 ♗a3 ♗a6 21 ♘h2 g6 22 ♘hf1 cd 23 cd h5 24 ♕f3 ♗e7 25 ♗d3 ♗×d3 26 ♕×d3 ♕c3 27 ♕×c3 ♖×c3 28 ♖b1 ♘c5 29 ♗×c5 ♖×c5 30 ♘e3 ♖ac8 31 ♖b7 ♗f8 32 ♘b3 ♖c1+ 33 ♘×c1 ♖×c1+ 34 ♔h2 ♗h6 35 g3 ♘×e4 36 ♔g2 ♘c3 37 ♖d2 ♘×a4 38 ♖d7 ♗f8 39 ♖a2 ♘c5 40 ♖c7 ♗h6 41 ♖c6 ♗×e3 42 fe ♖e1 43 ♖×d6 ♖×e3 44 ♔h2 ♖b3 ½-½ Sax-Short, match 1988.

14 ... ♘bd7

15 ♗b2 g6

It is hard to pass judgement on 15 ... ♖b8 16 c4 ed 17 cb ab 18 ♘×d4 c5, since the game was abandoned as drawn in Byrne-Geller, Reykjavik 1986.

16 c4

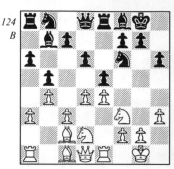

Unclear complications arise after 16 ♕b1 ♗g7 (16 ... ♘h5!? 17 g3 c5 is also unclear.) 17 ♘b3 ♖c8! 18 ♘a5 ♗a8 19 d5 ♘b6 20 a4 ♕d7 21 ab ab 22 ♗d3 (Psakhis-Portisch, Sarajevo 1986).

16 ... ed

17 cb ab

18 ♘×d4 c6 *(125)*

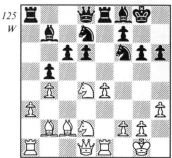

19 a4

Neither of the alternatives lend any clarity to the picture:

(a) 19 ♖c1 ♕b6 20 ♗d3 ♗g7 21 ♘2b3 Sokolov-Izeta, Bilbao 1987.

(b) 19 ♘2b3 ♖c8 20 ♘a5 ♗a8 21 ♕d2 ♕b6 22 ♘db3 c5 Klovan-Goldin (m/1) USSR 1987.

19 ... ba

20 ♗×a4 ♕b6

This was Kasparov's original contribution to the theory of the variation. Here Timman had to find methods of pursuing White's initiative.

21   ♘c2

21 b5?! was seen in the first game of Timman-Kasparov, match 1985, but after 21 ... cb 22 ♗xb5 d5! 23 ♖xa8 ♗xa8 Black had more chances in the unbalanced position.

21   ...   ♕c7
22   ♗b3   ♖xa1

This is more exact than 22 ... ♗a6 23 ♖c1 ♗g7 which led to an unclear position in Timman's third game against Kasparov: 24 ♘e3 ♗b5 and Black held the initiative.

23   ♗xa1

23 ♕xa1 ♗g7 24 ♗c3 ♘e5 led to equality in Hübner-Portisch, Tilburg 1986.

23   ...   ♗g7
24   ♘e3   c5
25   bc   ♘xc5
26   ♗xf6   ♗xf6

This unclear position was agreed drawn in Timman-Karpov, Bugojno 1986.

The Closed Variations of the Spanish Game are among the most profound in all of chess, and we can be confident that the World Champion will continue to enrich the theory of these lines.

12 Queen's Gambit

Kasparov has explored a variety of defences within the domain of the Queen's Gambit Declined. We will concentrate on two variations which have played a significant role in his repertoire – the Tarrasch Defence and the Tartakower Variation.

The Tarrasch Defence

This defence became unfashionable in the post-war years until Boris Spassky resurrected it for his match against Petrosian in 1969. It fell into disfavour again, until a few stalwarts, led by John Nunn, brought it back in the early 1980s, and Kasparov picked it up a bit later. The authors have written a monograph on the subject (*Play the Tarrasch*, Pergamon 1984.) References to 'Shamkovich' in the new edition of *ECO D* refer to that work. In this book we cover the basic variations and incorporate the critical developments of the last five years.

1	d4	d5
2	c4	e6
3	♘c3	c5
4	cd	ed
5	♘f3	♘c6
6	g3	♘f6
7	♗g2	♗e7

8	0-0	0-0 *(126)*

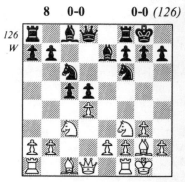

Kasparov's defeats at the hands of Karpov have put a damper on the general enthusiasm the Tarrasch enjoyed in 1983–84, although Icelandic GM Margeir Petursson and Murray Chandler remain faithful to the opening.

I	9 dc
II	9 ♗g5
III	9 b3
IV	9 ♗e3

I

	9	dc	♗×c5

9 ... d4 is now out of commission, and this is the only move seen in contemporary praxis.

	10	♗g5

10 ♘a4 has fallen from favour. After 10 ... ♗e7 11 ♗e3 (White should avoid 11 ♘d4 ♘e4! 12 ♘×c6 bc 13 ♗e3 ♕a5 14 ♖c1 ♗e6 15 a3 ♗f6 16 ♗d4 ♗×d4 17 ♕×d4

♘d2!, Weltmander-Aronin, 1958.)
11 ... 罝e8 12 罝c1 (12 ♘d4 ♗g4 13
♘×c6 bc 14 罝e1 ♗b4 15 ♗d2 ♗d6
16 罝c1 罝c8 17 a3 ♘e4 18 ♗e3
♗d7 ∓ Chamrak-Vaganian, USSR
1957.) 12 ... ♗g4 and now:
  (a) 13 h3 ♗h5 14 ♘d4 ♕d7
15 ♘×c6 bc 16 罝e1 ♗b4 17 ♗d2
♗f8 = Ree-Petursson, Reykjavik
1984.
  (b) 13 ♕b3 ♕d7 14 ♗c5 ♘e4 15
♗×e7 罝×e7 16 罝fd1 d4 led to
an unclear position in Kukuk-
Marjanović, Yugoslav Ch. 1984.
  (c) 13 ♘c5 ♗×c5 14 ♗×c5 (14
罝×c5 ♕d7 led to an equal position
in Szabo-Parma, Palma de
Mallorca 1969.) 14 ... ♕d7 (This is
the new line, replacing 14 ... ♘e4
15 ♗e3 ♕d7 16 ♕a4 罝ad8 17 罝fd1
h6 Hort-Ivkov, Palma de Mallorca
1970.) 15 罝e1 罝ad8 16 ♘d4 h5 17
♘c6 bc 18 ♗d4 ♘h7 19 ♕d2 ♘f8
20 f3 ♗f5 and chances were equal
in Partos-Petursson, Biel IZ 1985.

10 ...   d4 *(127)*

The older 10 ... ♗e6 is still
playable, but less frequently seen.

127
W

11   ♗×f6

This is now the standard move.
  (a) 11 ♘a4 ♗b6! 12 ♘×b6 ab 13
a3 h6 14 ♗f6 ♕×f6 15 ♘e1 罝e8 =
Bagirov-L. Grigorian, USSR 1967.
  (b) 11 ♘e4 ♗e7 12 ♗×f6 ♗×f6
13 罝c1 罝b8 (13 ... 罝e8 14 ♘e1
♗e7 15 ♘d3 ♗f8 16 ♕d2 a5 17
罝fd1 ♗g4 18 ♘dc5 ♗×c5 and now
19 罝×c5? ♕e7 gave Black the
advantage in Nikolić-Kasparov,
Nikšić 1983, so White must play
19 ♘×c5 with roughly level
chances.) 14 ♘e1 ♗e7 15 ♘d3 ♕b6
16 a3 ♗g4 ½-½ Adamski-Rogers,
Valjevo 1984. Or 13 ♕d2 ♗e7 14
罝fd1 ♗g4 15 ♕f4 ♗×f3 16 ♕×f3
♕b6 17 ♕b3 ♕×b3 18 ab ±
Palatnik-Klinger, Havana 1985.

11 ...   ♕×f6
12   ♘d5

12 ♘e4 ♕e7 13 ♘×c5 ♕×c5
does not bring White any
advantage, for example 14 ♕d2
♗f5 15 ♕g5 f6 16 ♕h5 ♘e7 with an
equal game, according to Keres.

12 ...   ♕d8

12 ... ♕d6!? is an alternative,
e.g. 13 ♘d2 ♗e6 14 ♘f4 ♗b6 15
罝c1 (15 ♕a4 罝ac8 16 罝fc1 ♘a5 17
♘×e6 ♕×e6 18 ♗f3 罝fd8 =
Trabattoni-Defize, Malta Ol.
1980.) 15 ... 罝fd8 16 a3 罝ac8 17 b4
a5 18 b5 ♘e5 19 ♗×b7 罝×c1 20
♕×c1 d3 21 e3 罝b8 22 ♘×e6 ♕×e6
and there is clear compensation
for the pawn (Dealune-Southam,
St. John 1988), although 23 ♘f3
罝×b7 24 ♘×e5 罝c7 25 ♘c6 ♕b3
26 ♕b1 ♕×a3 27 罝d1 would be
clearly better for White.

13   ♘d2 *(128)* 罝e8

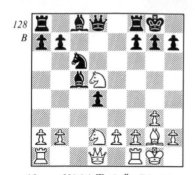

13 ... a6?! 14 ♖c1 ♗a7 led to one of the World Champion's most spectacular victories — Kasparov–Gavrikov, USSR Ch. 1981: 15 ♘c4! ♖b8 (15 ... ♗h3 16 ♗×h3 ♕×d5 17 ♗g2 ♕e6 ± would have been wiser.) 16 ♘f4! b5? (16 ... ♗f5!? 17 ♕d2 ♖c8!?) 17 ♘d6! ♕×d6 (Black is sliding rapidly downhill. 17 ... ♘e5 might have slowed the pace a bit.) 18 ♖×c6 ♕d8 19 ♕c2 ♖e8 20 ♖c1 a5 21 ♗d5! (Keep your eye on this peripatetic cleric!) 21 ... ♗b6 22 ♕b3! (22 ♗×f7+ would also have been good, e.g. ♔×f7 23 ♕×h7 d3 24 ♘×d3!) 22 ... ♖e7 23 ♗f3 ♖e5 24 ♗h5!! g6 25 ♗×g6! hg 26 ♖×g6+ ♔f8 27 ♖h6! ♔e7 28 ♖cc6! ♖f5 29 ♕f3! ♗c7 30 ♕e4+ ♖e5 31 ♘g6+!! fg 32 ♖h7+ ♔f8 33 ♕×g6 1-0.

14 ♖c1

14 ♖e1 is a major alternative, but after 14 ... a6 (14 ... ♗e6 is also playable, but Kasparov failed to equalize against Miles at Nikšić 1983, and it has fallen from favour.) 15 ♖c1 ♗a7 and now the alternatives are:

(a) 16 ♘c4 ♗e6 17 ♘f4 ♗f5!

where Black will equalize with ... ♗f5-e4;

(b) 16 ♘b3 ♗f5 17 ♕d2 ♗e4 18 ♗×e4 ♖×e4 = Øgaard-Petursson, Gausdal 1984.);

(c) 16 ♕b3 ♖b8 17 a3 (17 ♘f4 ♖e5! 18 ♘c4 ♖b5 19 ♕a3 ♘b4! = Miles–Hjorth, London 1984) 17 ... ♖e5! 18 ♘f4 ♖a5 19 ♕b3 ♖b5 20 ♕c2 ♗f5 Black has equalized (Miles–Chandler, West Germany 1984).

14 ... ♗b6
15 ♘b3

There are a few other moves which are seen in tournament play:

(a) 15 ♖e1 ♗e6 (15 ... ♗g4!? is an interesting alternative, e.g. 16 ♘c4 ♗a5 17 ♘×A5 ♕×a5 18 b4!? ♕×b4 19 ♕d2 ♘c6 20 ♕×a5 ♘×a5 21 ♘c7 d3! = Spraggett–Leski, San Francisco 1987.) 16 ♘f4 ♗×a2 and now:

(a1) 17 ♗×c6 bc 18 b3 ♗a5 19 ♖c2 ♗×b3 20 ♘×b3 d3 21 ♘×a5 dc 22 ♕a1 (Miles considers this position better for Black, while Ribli and Kasparov claim that it is better for White! We consider it equal.) 22 ... ♖e4 23 ♖c1 ♕g5 24 e3 (24 h4!? was suggested by Rogers.) 24 ... ♕b5! = Spraggett–Chandler, Hong Kong 1984.

(a2) 17 b3 ♗a5 18 ♖c2 (18 ♗d5 d3! 19 e3 ♘e5 20 ♔f1 ♖c8 21 ♖a1 ♖c2! 22 ♖×a2 ♖×a2 23 b4 ♗×b4! 24 ♗×a2 ♕a5 25 ♘×d3 (*25 ♕b3 ♗×d2 26 ♘×d3 ♗×e1 ∓∓*) 25 ... ♘×d3 26 ♕b3 ♕f5! 27 ♖e2 ♘c1 28 ♕c4 ♖c8 29 g4 ♖×c4 0-1 King-

Chandler, Reykjavik 1984.) 18 ...
♗xd2 19 ♖xd2 ♕a5 20 ♖b2 d3 21
♘xd3 ♖ad8 = Christiansen, or 18
... ♗xb3 19 ♘xb3 d3 20 ♖xc6!
♗xe1 (20 ... bc 21 ♘xa5 ♕xa5 22
♗xc6 d2 23 ♖f1 ++ Chandler) 21
♖c1 (Chandler) 21 ... d2 22 ♖b1 a5
23 ♘d3 ± Karpov-Chandler,
London 1984.

(b) 15 ♘f4 ♗g4 16 h3 ♗f5 17
♘b3 ♗e4 18 ♗xe4 ♖xe4 19 ♕d3
♖e5 20 ♘d2 ♘b4 = Seirawan-
Frey, Mexico 1980.

(c) 15 ♘c4 ♗e6 16 ♘f4 ♗f5 17
♖e1 ♖c8 18 a3 ♗e4 = Psakhis-
Lputian, USSR Ch. 1985.

| 15 | ... | ♗e6 |
| 16 | ♘f4 | |

No more effective is 16 ♘xb6
♕xb6 17 ♘c5 ♗g4 18 ♘a4 ♕b4 19
a3 ♕e7 = Palatnik-Legky, USSR
1981.

| 16 | ... | ♕d6 *(129)* |

129
W

| 17 | a3 |

This is the only move that
denies Black easy equality:

(a) 17 a4 ♖ad8 18 ♘xe6 ♕xe6
19 ♗xc6 bc 20 a5 ♗c7 21 ♘xd4
♕e5 22 e3 c5 23 ♕c2 cd 24 ed ♕xa5
25 ♕xc7 ♕d2! 26 ♕xa7 ♕xb2 =

Knaak-Groszpeter, Trnava 1983.

(b) 17 ♘xe6 ♕xe6 18 ♖c2 ♖ad8
19 ♖d2 h5 20 a4 (20 a3!? is an
interesting suggestion by Lputian,
aiming to redeploy the knight at
d3, but 20 h4 ♕f6 21 a3 ♘e5 22
♘c1 g5 23 hg ♕xg5 24 ♘d3 ♘g6
(24 ... ♘g4!? is a good alternative.)
25 ♖c2 h4 led to unclear
complications in Spiridonov-
Groszpeter, Polanica Zdroj 1985,
and we do not feel that Black's
chances are any worse.) 20 ... ♕c4
21 ♗xc6 bc 22 a5 ♗c7 23 ♕c2 (but
not 23 ♖d3?! h4 24 ♕d2 h3 which
gave Black the advantage in Knaak-
Lputian, Berlin 1982) 23 ... ♕xc2 24
♖xc2 ♖d5 25 ♖xc6 ♗xa5 =.

17	...	♖ad8
18	♖e1	♗g4
19	♘d3	♖e7
20	♘bc5	♗xc5
21	♘xc5	b6

The position holds chances for
both sides (Jansa-Chandler,
Plovdiv 1983).

II

| 9 | ♗g5 | cd |

The co-authors of this book
thought that 9 ... c4 had been
buried.

To begin with there is Kasparov-
Hjorth, Dortmund 1980: 10 ♘e5
♗e6 11 f4 ♘xe5 12 fe! ♘e4 13
♗xe7 ♘xc3 14 bc ♕xe7 15 e4 ♕d7
16 a4!, but Bekelman has come up
with 16 ... de 17 ♗xe4 ♗d5 where
Black is only slightly worse.

We had tried to resurrect 11 ...
♘g4, an old Lasker idea, but found
12 ♘xg4 ♗xg4 13 ♗xd5 ♗xg5 14

fg ♕×g5 15 ♖f4 ♖ad8 16 ♕f1! unpleasant. Nogueiras–Lputian, Sarajevo 1985, confirmed our judgement, but saw 16 ♕d2 instead. In either case one would not wish to be playing the Black pieces. But 15 ... ♗e6 16 ♗g2 ♖ad8 17 ♔h1 h6 18 ♕g1 ♘e7 19 e4 ♘g6 20 ♖af1 ♗g4 21 h4 ♕h5 led to unclear complications in Salov–Lputian, 1986–87, so it isn't dead yet.

White may therefore return to 11 ♘×c6 bc 12 b3 ♕a5 13 ♘a4, which is still very slightly better for him.

10   ♘×d4 *(130)*

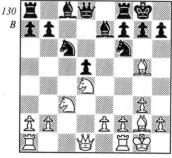

10   ...   h6

A popular alternative in the 1980s is Margeir Petursson's 10 ... ♖e8, although Kasparov does not seem to have much confidence in it.

(a) 11 ♕a4 ♗d7 12 e3 ♘e4 13 ♗×e7 ♘×e7 14 ♕a3 ♘×c3 15 ♕×c3 ♕b6 16 ♖fd1 ♖ac8 17 ♕a3 ♗g4 18 ♖d3 and White held a slight advantage in Suba–Zysk, Dortmund 1984.

(b) 11 ♖c1 h6 12 ♗f4 ♗g4 13 h3

♗e6 14 ♘×e6 fe 15 e4 d4 16 e5 dc 17 ef ♗×f6 18 bc ♕×d1 19 ♖c×d1 ♖ad8 20 c4 ♖×d1 21 ♖×d1 ♖d8 22 ♖×d8+ ♗×d8 = Lalic–D. Ross, St. John 1988.

11   ♗e3

The standard reply, as others fail to secure any sort of opening advantage:

(a) 11 ♗×f6 ♗×f6 12 ♘b3 d4! 13 ♘e4 ♗e7 14 ♖c1 ♕b6 15 ♘ec5 ♖d8 16 ♖c4 ♗×c5! 17 ♘×c5 ♕×b2 Seirawan–Kasparov, Nikšić 1983.

(b) 11 ♗f4 ♗g4 12 h3 ♗h5 13 ♘b3 a5 14 ♘×d5 ♘×d5 15 ♗×d5 a4 16 ♘c1 ♗f6 17 ♖b1 ♘d4 and Black has full compensation.

11   ...   ♖e8 *(131)*

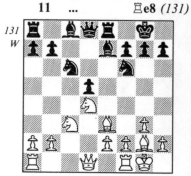

Here there are five significant paths:

A   12 ♕b3
B   12 ♕a4
C   12 ♕c2
D   12 ♖c1
E   12 a3

A

	12	♕b3	♘a5
	13	♕c2	♗g4
	14	♘f5	*(132)*

14 h3 and now:

(a) 14 ... ♗d7 15 ♖ad1 ♗e6 is an interesting line suggested by Mikhail Tal.

(b) 14 ... ♗h5 15 ♖ad1 (15 ♖fd1 ± Monokroussas) 15 ... ♗b4 16 g4 ♗g6 17 ♘f5 ♕c7! 18 ♗xd5?! (18 ♗d4! ♘e4! 19 ♕d3 ♗xc3 is roughly level.) 18 ... ♘xd5 19 ♖xd5 ♗xf5 20 ♕xf5 ♖xe3! 21 fe (21 ♖d7 ♕e5 =) 21 ... ♕g3+ 22 ♔h1 ♕xh3+ 23 ♔g3 ♕g3+ ½–½ Grivainis-Monokroussas, Las Vegas 1984.

132
B

14 ... ♗b4

14 ... ♖c8 15 ♗d4! (15 ♘xe7+ ♖xe7 16 ♖ad1 ♕e8 17 h3 ♗h5 18 ♗xd5 ♗g6 19 ♕c1 ♘xd5 20 ♖xd5 ♘c4 21 ♗d4 ♖ec7 = Karpov-Kasparov, (m/7) 1984–5) 15 ... ♗c5 16 ♗xc5 ♖xc5 17 ♘e3 ♗e6 18 ♖ad1 was better for White in Karpov-Kasparov, (m/9) 1984–5.

15 ♗d4

15 h3 is an alternative and now:

(a) 15 ... ♗xf5 16 ♕xf5 ♗xc3 17 bc seems slightly better for White, e.g. 17 ... ♘c4 18 ♗d4 ♖xe2 19 ♖fe1!? ±/= Kouatly-Martin, Thessaloniki Ol. 1984.

(b) 15 ... ♗h5 16 g4 ♗g6 17

♖ad1 ♖c8 = Korchnoi-Ivkov, Zagreb 1970.

15 ... ♗xc3
16 ♗xc3 ♖xe2
17 ♕d3

White stands better, for example: 17 ... ♖e8 18 ♘e3 ♗e6 19 ♕b5! b6 20 ♖ad1 a6 (Portisch-Chandler, London 1984) 21 ♕a4! = Timman.

B

12 ♕a4 *(133)*

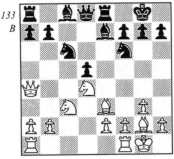

133
B

12 ... ♗d7
13 ♖ad1

13 ♖fd1 and now:

13 ... ♘b4 14 ♕b3 a5 15 ♘xd5 ♘fxd5 16 ♗xd5 ♘xd5 17 ♕xd5 ♗g4 ± La Plaza-Schiller, corr. 1983.

13 ... ♘a5 14 ♕c2 ♖c8 15 ♘f5 ♗e6 16 ♘xe7+ ♖xe7 17 ♗d4 ♖d7 18 ♖ac1 ♘e8 19 ♕d3 ♘c6 20 e3 ♘xd4 21 ♕xd4 ± Cvitan-Handoko, Zagreb 1985.

13 ... ♘b4
14 ♕b3 a5
15 a4! *(134)*

15 ♖d2 a4 16 ♕d1 a3 17 ♕b1 ♗f8 18 ba ♖xa3 19 ♕b2 ♕a8 (Belyavsky-Kasparov (m/2) 1983)

20 ♘c2! ♗xc2 21 ♖xc2 ♗c6 22 ♖d1 ♘e4 23 ♘xe4 de ±.
15 ♘xd5 ♘bxd5 16 ♗xd5 ♘xd5 17 ♕xd5 ♗h3 ∓ Vaganian–Ivkov, USSR v. Yugoslavia 1975.

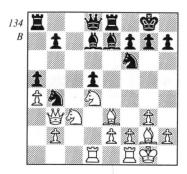

134 B

15 ... ♖c8
15 ... ♗f8 16 ♘c2 ♗e6 17 ♗d4 ♘e4 18 ♘xb4 ab 19 ♘b5 ♕a5 20 ♗xe4 de 21 ♕e3 (Vaganian–Nunn, Buenos Aires 1978) 21 ... ♕xa4 22 ♘c7 ♗b3 23 ♖c1 ♗c2 24 ♘xe8 ♖xe8 25 ♖a1 ♕b5! ⯈⯇ Shamkovich and Schiller (1984).
16 ♘db5
16 ♘c2 b5! 17 ♘xb4 ba 18 ♘xa4 ♗xb4 19 ♘b6 (19 ♘c3 ♗xc3 20 bc a4 ∓ Majorov–Ehlvest, USSR 1983) 19 ... ♖xe3! 20 ♕xe3 ♗c5 21 ♘xd7 ♗xe3 22 ♘xf6 ♕xf6 23 fe ♕xb2 24 ♗xd5 (Korchnoi–Kasparov, Herceg Novi Blitz 1983) 24 ... ♕xe2 (Keene).
16 ... ♗e6
The position is roughly equal.
C
12 ♕c2 *(135)* **♗g4**
13 ♖fd1 ♕d7?!
13 ... ♗f8 14 ♖ac1 ♖c8 15 ♘xc6 bc 16 ♗d4 ♗b4 17 ♖d2 ♕e7 18 a3

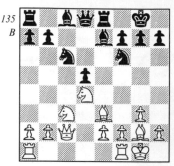

135 B

♗a5 was seen in Belyavsky–Kasparov, (m/6) 1983, and now with 19 h3! ♗h5 20 b4 ♗b6 21 e3 Belyavsky claims White could have claimed an advantage. But 14 ... ♖xe3!? 15 fe g6 intending ... ♗h6 deserves serious consideration, and may be Black's best option in this line.
14 ♘b3 ♖ac8
14 ... ♖ad8 15 ♖ac1 ♗e6 16 ♘c5 ♗xc5 17 ♗xc5 d4 18 ♘b5 ♘b4! = Sandström–Brojtigem, Berlin 1985.
15 ♖ac1
15 ♘xd5? is met by 15 ... ♘d4!
15 ... ♗d6
16 a3 ♗e5
17 ♘c5
17 ♘xd5!? is possible, for example 17 ... ♘d4? 18 ♕xc8!, or 17 ... ♘xd5 18 ♖xd5, where neither 18 ... ♘d4 19 ♕d3! ± nor 18 ... ♘b4 19 ♕xc8 ± are acceptable for Black, so it seems that 13 ... ♗f8 is a better choice for Black.
17 ... ♕e7
18 ♘xd5 ♘xd5
19 ♖xd5 b6
The position is unclear, according to Kasparov in *ECO D* II.

D

12   ♜c1 *(136)*

136
B

12   ...   ♝f8
13   ♕c2

The alternatives fail to provide White with any advantage:

(a) 13 ♞a4 ♛a5 14 a3 ♞e5 15 ♝d2 ♛d8 = Youngworth-Gligorić, Lone Pine 1980.

(b) 13 ♜e1 ♞g4 14 ♞xd5 ♞xe3 15 fe ♝d7 = Garcia Gonzalez-Gligorić, Buenos Aires Ol. 1978.

(c) 13 ♞b3 ♝e6 14 ♝c5 ♝xc5 15 ♞xc5 ♛e7 = Mecking-Spassky, Palma de Mallorca 1969.

(d) 13 ♞xc6 bc and now:

(d1) 14 ♞a4 ♞g4! 15 ♝c5 ♝a6! (Better than 15 ... ♝xc5?! 16 ♞xc5 ± Timman-Gligorić, Nikšić 1978.) 16 ♜e1 ♛f6 17 ♛d4 ♛xd4 18 ♝xd4 ♝xe2 = or 17 ♝xd4 ♛g6 18 ♞c5 ♝xc5 19 ♜xc5 ♜e6 =.

(d2) 14 ♝d4 ♝f5!? 15 ♛d2 and in Adorjan-Gligorić, Vršac 1983, a draw was agreed after 15 ... ♛d6 16 ♜fe1; Kasparov gives further 16 ... a5 17 b3 ♛e6 18 ♞a4 ♝a3 19 ♝b2 ♝b4 =.

13   ...   ♝e6
14   ♜fd1   ♛e7!?

An untested Kasparov suggestion in *ECO D* II. He gives further 15 ♞b3 ♞g4 16 ♝c5 ♛f6 ∞. We feel that after 17 e3 ♛h6 18 h3 ♞ge5 there is a double-edged position with chances for both sides. 14 ... ♞g4 is weak, because 15 ♞xe6 17 fe allows 16 ♞xd5 ±.

E

12   a3 *(137)*

137
B

This move was seen frequently in the Smyslov-Kasparov Candidates' final, 1983.

12   ...   ♝e6

Kasparov has analysed 12 ... ♝g4!?, but there is no practical experience as yet. Nevertheless, White should stand better after either 13 ♛b3 ♞a5 14 ♞a2 or 13 ♛a4.

In our opinion the best move is 12 ... ♝f8, e.g. 13 ♛b3 ♜e5 14 ♜ad1 ♜h5 15 ♝h3 ♞a5 16 ♛a2 ♝g4 ∞ Ki. Georgiev-Kindermann, Plovdiv 1984.

13   ♔h1

13 ♛b3 ♛d7 14 ♞xe6 fe 15 ♜ad1 ♝d6 16 ♝c1 ♔h8 ∞ Korchnoi-Kasparov, (m/2) 1983.

At present, 13 ♞xe6 fe 14 ♛a4 is

considered best, for example 14 ...
罩c8 15 罩ad1 ♚h8 16 ♚h1 a6 17 f4
♘a5 and now instead of 18 f5 b5
19 ♛h4 ♘g8 20 ♛h3 ♘c4 21 ♗c1
♗g5 22 fe ♗xc1 23 罩xc1 ♘e3 ∞
Smyslov-Kasparov, (m/12) 1984.
Kasparov recommends 18 ♗d4
followed by 18 ... ♘c4 19 ♛b3 ♗c5
20 e4!? ±.

| | 13 | ... | ♗g4 |

13 ... ♛d7 14 ♘xe6 fe 15 f4!
罩ed8! 16 ♗g1 罩ac8 17 ♛a4 ♚h8
18 罩ad1 ± Smyslov-Kasparov,
(m/2) 1984.

| | 14 | f3 | ♗h5 |
| | 15 | ♘xc6 | |

15 ♗g1 ♛d7 16 ♛a4 ♗c5! 17
罩ad1 ♗b6 18 罩fe1 ♗g6! =
Smyslov-Kasparov, (m/8) 1984.

	15	...	bc
	16	♘a4	♛c8
	17	♗d4	♛e6
	18	罩c1	♘d7
	19	罩c3	

and now instead of 19 ... ♗f6?!
20 e3 ♗g6 (Smyslov-Kasparov,
(m/10) 1984), where White could
have obtained an endgame
advantage with 21 ♗xf6 ♛xf6 22
♛d4! ♛xd4 23 ed, 19 ... ♗g6!
would have equalized, according
to Kasparov.

III

| | 9 | b3 | |

The variation with 9 b3 has
been an infrequent visitor to the
tournament scene ever since a
new defence with an early ... b6
appeared.

| | 9 | ... | ♘e4 |
| | 10 | ♗b2 | ♗f6 *(138)* |

138
W

| | 11 | ♘a4 | |

11 ♘xe4 de 12 ♘d2 ♗xd4 13
♗xd4 cd 14 ♘xe4 ♗f5 15 ♛d2
罩e8 = Mestel-Nunn, London 1984.

| | 11 | ... | b6! |
| | 12 | 罩c1 | 罩e8 |

12 ... ♗a6 13 dc ♗xb2 14 ♘xb2
bc 15 ♘d3 罩e8: see 12 ... 罩e8 13 dc
♗xb2 14 ♘xb2 bc 15 ♘d3.

	13	dc	♗xb2
	14	♘xb2	bc
	15	♘a4	

15 ♘d3 ♗a6 16 ♘f4 ♘b4 (16 ...
d4!?) 17 ♘d2 ♘xa2 18 ♘xe4 ♘xc1
(18 ... de 19 ♛xd8 罩axd8 20 罩xc5
罩d2 ∞) 19 ♘c3 g5 20 ♛xc1 gf
21 ♘xd5 (Arencibia-Perez, Cien-
fuegos II 1984) 21 ... ♗xe2! ∞.

	15	...	♗a6
	16	罩e1	c4
	17	♘h4	

(a) 17 ♘d4 ♘e5! ∞ Kasparov.

(b) 17 ♘d2 ♛f6 18 ♘xe4 de 19
bc 罩ad8 20 ♛b3 (20 ♛c2 e3!?) 20
... e3! 21 fe ♘e5 22 罩f1! ♛h6 23
罩f4 (Novikov-Sturua, USSR
1984) 23 ... g5! 24 罩d4 罩xd4 25 ed
♘g4 26 h3 ♘e3 ∞ Sturua. 27 ♘b2
would be met by 27 ... ♛d6!

| | 17 | ... | ♛a5 |

| 18 | ♘f5 | g6 |
| 19 | ♘d4 | ♖ac8 |

This position was reached in Larsen–Kasparov, Nikšić 1983, where 20 ♘xc6 ♖xc6 21 ♗xe4 de 22 ♕d7 would have brought a level position.

IV

| 9 | ♗e3 | c4!? *(139)* |

This move has moved in and out of fashion over the past two decades.

| 10 | ♘e5 | h6! |

Black's fortunes have been greatly improved by this recent discovery.

11	b3	cb
12	♘xc6	bc
13	ab	a5
14	♕c2	

Timoshchenko–Kasparov, USSR 1983, saw Black gain the upper hand after 14 ♗c1 (14 ♗d2 ♗f5!=) 14 ... ♗b4 15 ♘a4 ♖e8 16 ♗d2 ♗a6 17 ♖e1 ♗f8 18 ♕c2 ♘e4 19 ♘c3 ♘xd2.

| 14 | ... | ♗a6 |
| 15 | ♘a4 | ♗b5 |

Black has equalized (Kasparov).

The Tartakower Defence

1	d4	d5
2	c4	e6
3	♘c3	♘f6
4	♗g5	♗e7
5	e3	0-0
6	♘f3	h6
7	♗h4	b6 *(140)*

This defence has featured prominently in the World Championship matches of the last decade. In the most recent match in Seville, there were two games in a row played with the line, with Karpov and Kasparov changing sides!

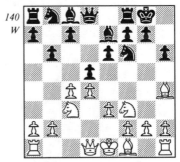

I	8 ♗e2
II	8 ♕c2
III	8 ♕b3
IV	8 ♖c1
V	8 ♗d3
VI	8 cd

I

| 8 | ♗e2 |

We begin with the most popular line, seen in the Seville match.

| 8 | ... | ♗b7 |

8 ... dc is premature, e.g. 9 ♗xc4 ♗b7 10 0-0 ♘e4 11 ♘xe4 ♗xe4 12

♗g3 c5 13 dc ♗xc5 14 ♘e5 ±
Groszpeter–Lein, St. John 1988.

9	**♗xf6**	**♗xf6**
10	**cd**	**ed**
11	**b4**	

This principled move sets up a characteristic of the Tartakower Variation, by establishing 'hanging pawns' for Black.

11 0-0 was Karpov's choice in the 19th game of the 4th match.

(a) After 11 ... ♘d7 12 b4 c5 13 bc bc he avoided transposition below (14 ♖b1) by introducing 14 ♕b3!? Kasparov replied by simplifying the central situation with 14 ... cd 15 ♘xd4 ♗xd4! 16 ed ♘b6 and after 17 a4 ♖b8 18 a5 ♘c4 19 ♗xc4 dc 20 ♕xc4 ♕d6 Karpov found the only move which preserved the advantage − 21 ♕c5! After the exchange of queens White held a slight advantage, but Karpov–Kasparov, (m/19) 1987, was eventually drawn after excellent defensive play by Kasparov.

(b) Another popular reply is 11 ... ♖e8, for example 12 ♕b3 c6 13 ♖ad1 ♘a6 14 ♖fe1 ♘c7 15 ♗d3 ♘e6!? (15 ... g6 is safer) 16 ♗b1 g6 but White is better after 17 ♕c2 (Belyavsky–Karpov, Tilburg 1986). Or 12 b4 c6 13 ♕b3 ♕d6 13 ♘e1 ♘d7 14 ♘d3 ± Torre–Lalić, St. John 1988.

11	**...**	**c5**

There are two alternatives:

(a) 11 ... c6 12 0-0 ♕d6 13 ♕b3 ♘d7 14 ♖fd1 ♖fd8 15 ♖ac1 ♗e7 = Farago–Ki. Georgiev, Wijk aan Zee 1988.

(b) 11 ... ♘c6 12 ♕b3 ♘e7 13 0-0 ♕d6 14 ♖ac1 a6 15 b5 ± Groszpeter–Garcia, St. John 1988.

12	**bc**	**bc**
13	**♖b1**	**♗c6**

13 ... ♕a5 14 0-0 cd 15 ♘xd4 ♘c6 16 ♘db5 ♘e7 17 ♕a4 ♕xa4 18 ♘xa4 ♗c6 19 ♘c5 ♖fc8 20 ♖fc1 ♗xb5 21 ♗xb5 d4 22 ♘d7 de 23 ♘xf6+ gf 24 fe ♖ab8 25 ♗a4 ♔g7 26 ♖xb8 ♖xc1+ 27 ♔f2 ♖c7 ½-½ Timman–Karpov, Amsterdam 1988.

14	**0-0**	**♘d7** *(141)*

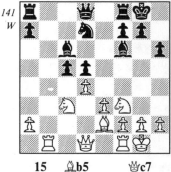

15	**♗b5**	**♕c7**
16	**♕d3**	

16 ♕c2 was seen in games from the marathon match:

(a) 16 ... ♖fd8 17 ♖fc1 ♖ab8 18 a4 ♕d6 19 dc ♘xc5 20 ♗xc6 ♕xc6 21 ♘b5 ♗e7 22 ♘xa7 (22 ♕f5 ♕e8 23 ♘e5 ♖b7 24 ♘d4 ♖c7 25 ♘b5 ♖b7 ½-½ Kasparov–Karpov, (m/38) 1984–85) 22 ... ♕a6 23 ♘b5 ♕xa4 24 ♕xa4 ♘xa4 25 ♘fd4 ± Karpov–Kasparov, (m/39) 1984–85.

(b) Kasparov–Karpov, (m/42) 1984–85: 16 ... ♖fc8 17 ♖fc1 ♗xb5 18 ♘xb5 ♕c6 19 dc ♘xc5 20 ♕f5 ♕e6 21 ♘fd4 ♕xf5 22 ♘xf5 ♘e6 23 ♖xc8 ♖xc8 24 ♘xa7 ♖c2 25

♘b5 ♖×a2 26 h3 ♖a5 ½–½.

16 ...   ♖fc8

This was Karpov's innovation in the 18th game of the Seville match. Until then Black had preferred the other rook move: 16 ... ♖fd8 17 ♖fd1 ♖ab8 18 ♗×c6 ♕×c6 19 ♖×b8 ♖×b8 20 dc ♗×c3 21 ♕×c3 ♕×c5 brought Black equality in Karpov–Kasparov, (m/18) 1985.

17 ♖fc1   ♖ab8

Kasparov gives 17 ... ♗×b5 18 ♘×b5 ♕c6 with no evaluation. We feel that White has the advantage here.

18 h3   cd

Kasparov's suggested improvement on Karpov–Kasparov, (m/18) 1987, which saw 18 ... g6? 19 ♗×c6 ♖×b1 20 ♕×b1! ♕×c6 21 dc ♕×c5 22 ♘e2 ♕f8, where Karpov missed 23 ♘f4 ♘b6 24 h4! which would have given him a significant initiative.

II

8   ♕c2 *(142)*

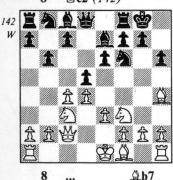

8	...	♗b7
9	♗×f6	♗×f6
10	cd	ed

11	0-0-0	c5
12	dc	♘d7
13	♘×d5	♘×c5
14	♗c4	b5
15	♘×f6+	♕×f6
16	♗d5	

Not 16 ♗×b5? ♗e4 17 ♕c3 ♖fc8! ∓∓.

16	...	♖ac8
17	♔b1	♘a4
18	♕e2	

± Kasparov–I. Zaitsev, Baku 1980.

III

8   ♕b3 *(143)*

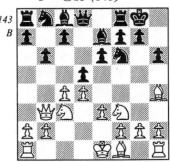

8	...	♗b7
9	♗×f6	♗×f6
10	cd	ed
11	♖d1	♖e8
12	a3	

12 ♗d3 c5 13 dc ♘d7 14 c6 ♗×c6 15 0-0 ♘c5 16 ♕a3 d4? 17 ♘×d4 ♗×d4 18 ed ♕g5 19 d5 succeeded in Kasparov–Belyavsky, USSR Ch. 1978, but Black can equalize with 12 ... ♘c6 13 0-0 ♘a5 14 ♕c2 c5! Polugayevsky–Tal, Alma Ata 1980.

12 ♗e2 c6 13 0-0 ♘d7 transposes to Variation I.

12	...	c6

12 ... c5 13 dc ♘d7 14 cb ♕×b6 15 ♕×b6 ♗×c3+ 16 bc ab 17 ♗b5 ± Petursson-Li, Biel IZ 1985.

13	♗d3	♘d7
14	0-0	♘f8
15	♗b1	g6
16	♖fe1	♘e6
17	♗a2	♗g7!

17 ... ♕c7 18 ♕a4 ♖ad8 19 b4! ♕b8 20 ♕c2 ± (Korchnoi-Kasparov, (m/10) 1983.

18	♕a4	b5!
19	♕c2	a5

Black has a good game, for example 20 ♘e2 b4 21 ab ab 22 ♘c1 ♕b6 23 ♗b3 ♖ac8 24 ♘d3 c5 = Agzamov-A. Petrosian, USSR Ch. 1985.

IV

| 8 | ♖c1 | *(144)* |

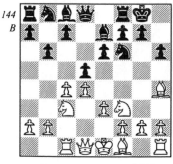

144
B

8	...	♗b7
9	♗e2	♘bd7

Black can also capture immediately: 9 ... dc 10 ♗×c4 ♘bd7 11 0-0 c5 12 ♕e2 (12 dc ♘×c5 13 ♕e2 a6 14 ♖fd1 ♕e8 15 ♘e5 b5 ∞ Szilagyi-Bönsch, Bundesliga 1987) 12 ... a6 13 a4 cd 13 ♘×d4 ♘c5 and now:

(a) 15 ♖fd1 ♕e8 16 ♗g3 ♘fe4

17 ♘×e4 ♘×e4 18 ♗e5 ♗f6 19 ♗×f6 ♘×f6 20 ♕c2 ♖d8 21 ♗e2 ♖d6 22 ♕c7 ♕b8 23 h3 was agreed drawn in Yusupov-Karpov, Bugojno 1986.

(b) 15 f3 ♘h5!? 16 ♗f2 ♗d6 17 ♖fd1 ♕e7 with an unclear position in Portisch-Hjartarson, Reykjavik 1987, or 15 ... ♕e8 16 ♕c2 ♖c8 17 ♗a2 ♘d5 = Portisch-Vaganian, match 1988.

| 10 | cd | |

10 0-0 c5 11 ♗g3 a6 12 cd ♘×d5 13 ♘×d5 ♗×d5 14 dc ♘×c5 15 b4 ♘e4 16 ♗c7 ♕e8 17 a3 a5! = Karpov-Kasparov, (m/17) 1984-85.

10	...	ed
11	0-0	c5
12	dc	bc
13	♗g3	

13 ♕c2 ♖c8 14 ♖fd1 ♕b6 15 ♕b1 ♖fd8 16 ♖c2 ♕e6 17 ♗g3 ♘h5 18 ♖cd2 ♘×g3 19 hg ♘f6 20 ♕c2 g6 ∓ Korchnoi-Karpov, (m/1) 1981.

13	...	♕b6!?
14	♘a4	♕a5

Safer is 14 ... ♕e6 15 b4! c4 16 ♘d4 ♕a6 = Timman-Belyavsky, Thessaloniki Ol. 1984.

| 15 | ♘h4 | g6 |

Karpov evaluates this position as unclear.

| 16 | ♕c2! | ♗c6 |

16 ... ♔g7 17 ♗d3 threatening ♗×g6 gives White a strong attack.

17	♘×g6!?	fg
18	♕×g6+	♔h8
19	♕×h6+	♔g8
20	♗g4!	♘×g4
21	♕×c6	♘gf6

22   ♘c3

White has more than sufficient compensation for his material.

V

8   ♗d3 *(145)*

This is presently a very popular line.

145
B

8   ...   ♗b7
9   0-0

9 ♗×f6 ♗×f6 10 cd ed 11 0-0 c5 12 dc bc 13 ♕b3 ♗c6 14 ♗e2 ♘d7 15 ♖fd1 ♖b8 16 ♕c2 ♕a5 17 ♘d2 was better for White in Portisch-Vaganian, (m/3) 1988.

9   ...   ♘bd7
10   ♕e2

10 ♗g3!? c5 11 ♖c1 a6 12 cd ♘×d5 13 ♘×d5 ♗×d5 14 e4 ♗b7 15 ♗b1 ± Romanishin-Ki. Georgiev, Leningrad 1987.

10   ...   c5
11   ♖fd1

11 ♖ac1 ♘e4 12 ♗g3 ♘×g3 13 hg = Torre-M. Gurevich, Leningrad 1987.

11   ...   ♘e4
12   ♗g3   cd
13   ♘×d4   ♘×g3
14   hg   ♘f6
15   ♖ac1   ♗b4

16   cd   ♗×c3
17   ♖×c3   ♘×d5
18   ♖cc1   ♖c8
19   ♗a6

and a draw was agreed in Novikov-Lputian, USSR Ch. 1984.

VI

8   cd   ed *(146)*

8 ... ♘×d5 is also playable:

(a) 9 ♗×e7 ♕×e7 10 ♘×d5 ed and now Winants-Kasparov, Brussels 1987, saw 11 ♖c1 ♗e6 12 ♕a4 c5 13 ♕a3 ♖c8 14 ♗e2 ♔f8 15 dc bc 16 0-0 a5 with chances for both sides.

(b) 9 ♘×d5 ed 10 ♗g3 ♗g4 11 a3 c5 12 dc bc 13 ♗e2 ♗f6 = Agdestein-van der Sterren, Wijk aan Zee 1988.

146
W

9   ♗d3   ♗b7

This is an old and traditional line which Karpov feels offers the best chances for White to gain the advantage (*ECO* 1987).

10   0-0   c5

10 ... ♘e4 11 ♗×e7 ♕×e7 12 ♕b3 (12 ♘e5 ♘d7 13 f4 ♘×e5 14 fe c5! 15 ♕e1 ♖ad8 16 ♖d1 ♕g5 17 ♖f3 f6! equalized in Kasparov-Belyavsky, (m/7) 1983.) 12 ... ♖d8

13 ♖ac1 c5 14 ♗b1 ♘c6 15 ♖fd1
♘xc3 16 ♕xc3 cd = Gligorić-
Kurajica, Rovinj/Zagreb 1970.

The text was seen in games 1, 3
and 5 of the 1983 Kasparov-
Belyavsky Candidates' match.

11 ♘e5!   ♘bd7

Kasparov–Belyavsky,   (m/1)
1984 continued 11 ... ♘c6 12 ♗a6!
♕c8 13 ♗xb7 ♕xb7 14 ♗xf6!
♗xf6 15 ♘g4! ♗d8! 16 ♘xd5
♘xd4! 17 ♘df6+ White held a
slight advantage.

12 ♗f5!

12 ♕f3?! cd 13 ed ♘xe5 14 de
♘d7 15 ♗xe7 ♕xe7 16 ♘xd5
♕xe5 17 ♘e7+ ♔h8! led to
equality in Kasparov–Belyavsky,
Moscow (m/3) 1984.

12 ...   ♘xe5?!

12 ... ♖e8 would have been only
slightly better for White.

13 de   ♘e8
14 ♗g3   ♘c7
15 ♕g4

This gave White a large advantage in Kasparov–Belyavsky,
(m/5), 1983.

13 Keeping Up with Kasparov

Keeping up with the World Champion is quite a task! As this book proceeded through the production stages, many interesting developments have taken place. Rather than rewrite entire chapters, we have placed the new material here, at the end of the book.

Sicilian Defence

Important developments have occurred in both the Scheveningen and Keres Attack.

Scheveningen

1 e4 c5 2 ♘f3 d6 3 d4 cd 4 ♘×d4 ♘f6 5 ♘c3 e6

6 f4

Kasparov has also faced the popular systems with ♗e3 and ♕d2: Khalifman–Kasparov, USSR Ch. 1988: 1 e4 c5 2 ♘f3 e6 3 d4 cd 4 ♘×d4 ♘f6 5 ♘c3 d6 6 ♗e3 a6 7 ♕d2 ♗e7 8 f3 ♘c6 9 0-0-0 0-0 10 g4 ♖b8 11 h4 ♘×d4 12 ♗×d4 ♘d7 13 g5 b5 14 ♔b1 ♕c7 15 h5 b4 16 ♘e2 ♘e5 17 ♘g1 f5 18 gf ♗×f6 19 h6 g6 20 b3 ♗b7 21 ♗h3 ♕e7 22 ♖h2 a5 23 ♖e2 ♘f7 24 ♗×f6 ♕×f6 25 f4 ♖bc8 26 ♘f3 ♕c3 27 ♖e3 ♕×d2 28 ♖×d2 ♖c3 29 ♖×c3 bc 30 ♖d3 ♗×e4 31 ♖×c3 ♗×f3 32 ♗×e6 ♗h5 33 ♖c7 g5 34 fg ♖e8 ½-½.

6 ... a6

7 ♗e2

In Yudashin–Kasparov, USSR Ch. 1988, White tried a more aggressive plan, but it did not meet with success: 7 ♗e3 b5 8 ♕f3 ♗b7 9 ♗d3 ♘bd7 10 a3 ♖c8 11 0-0 ♗e7 12 ♖ae1 0-0 13 ♕h3 ♘c5 14 ♗f2 ♘fd7 15 ♔h1 ♗f6 16 ♖d1 ♖e8 17 ♗g1 g6 18 ♘de2 ♗g7 19 f5 ♕e7 20 ♗d4 ♘f6 21 ♕g3 e5 22 fg hg 23 ♗e3 ♘f×e4 24 ♗×e4 ♘×e4 25 ♘×e4 ♗×e4 26 ♘c3 ♗b7 27 h4 ♖c4 28 ♗g5 ♕e6 29 ♖d2 ♖g4 30 ♕d3 f6 0-1.

7 ... ♗e7

8 0-0

Ehlvest–Kasparov, USSR Ch. 1988, saw instead 8 a4 ♕c7 9 0-0-0 0-0 10 ♕e1 ♘c6 11 ♗e3 e5 12 ♘b3 ♘b4 13 ♕f2 ♘×c2 14 ♗b6 ♕b8 15 ♖ad1 ♗e6 16 fe ♘d7 17 ♘d5 ♗×d5 18 ♖×d5 ♘b4 19 ♖dd1 ♘×e5 20 ♘d4 g6 21 ♗a5 ♘bc6 22 ♗c3 ♘×d4 23 ♖×d4 ♕a7 24 ♔h1 ♖ac8 25 ♗d1 ♕b6 26 a5 ♕d8 27 ♖b4 ♘d3 28 ♕d4 ♖×c3 29 bc ♘×b4 30 cb d5 31 ♗b3 de 32 ♕×e4 ♕d7 33 ♕d5 ♕×d5 34 ♗×d5 ♗×b4 35 ♗×b7 ♗×a5 36 ♗×a6 h5 37 ♗c4 ♔g7 38 ♖a1 ♗b6 39 ♖b1 ♖d8 40 g3 ♖d6 41 ♗e2 ♗c7 42 ♖c1 ½-½.

8 ... 0-0

9 ♔h1 ♕c7

10 a4 ♘c6

Kasparov delayed this move in van der Wiel–Kasparov, Amsterdam 1988, and equalized comfortably: 10 ... ♖d8 11 ♕e1 b6 12 ♕g3 ♗b7 13 f5 e5 14 ♗h6 ♗f8 15 ♗g5 ♗e7 16 ♗h6 ♗f8 17 ♗g5 ♗e7 ½–½.

| 11 | ♗e3 | ♖e8 *(147)* |

147
W

12   ♗g1!?

This is Geller's idea from the 10th game of the 1985 Karpov–Kasparov match (see p. 98).

In van der Wiel–Kasparov, Amsterdam 1988, Kasparov again expanded his repertoire, greeting 12 ♗f3 with the old fashioned 12 ... ♗d7 intead of his trusty 12 ... ♖b8. Play continued 13 ♘b3 (13 ♘de2!? is an interesting alternative.) 13 ... ♘a5!? 14 ♘×a5 (Against 14 e5 Kasparov suggested 14 ... ♘c4! 15 ef ♘×e3 16 ♕e2 ♘×f1 17 fe ♘×h2 18 ♔×h2 ♗c6 with unclear complications, an evaluation with which we agree.) 14 ... ♕×a5 15 ♕d3 ♖ad8 16 ♕d2 ♖c8 17 e5 de 18 fe ♕×e5 19 ♗×b7 ♖cd8 20 ♗f4 ♕a5 21 ♕e2 ♗c8 22 ♗c6 ♖f8 23 ♗f3 ♕b4 24 ♗c7 ♖d7 25 ♗e5 ♗b7 26 a5 ♖fd8 27 ♖a4 ♗×f3 28 ♕×f3

♕c5 29 ♗×f6 gf 30 ♖h4 f5 31 ♖h3 ♕c4 32 g4 f4 33 g5? (time pressure) 33 ... ♖d4 34 ♖f2 ♗×g5 35 ♕g4 f6 36 ♖hf3 ♔h8 37 ♖g2 ♖d2 38 h4 ♖×g2 39 ♔×g2 ♗h6 40 ♔h3 ♖g8 41 ♕h5 ♕c6 42 ♔h2 ♗f8 43 ♖f2 f5 44 ♕e2 ♖g4 0–1. This was a very complicated tactical game, with White's central advance being countered with play along the c- and d-files.

| 12 | ... | ♖b8 |
| 13 | ♗f3 | |

This is a novelty, replacing 13 ♕d2.

13	...	♗d7
14	♘b3	b6
15	g4	♗c8
16	g5	♘d7
17	♗g2	♗f8
18	♕f3	

Sokolov is regrouping his forces in a novel manner, choosing ♗g1 and ♕f3 instead of ♕d2–f2.

| 18 | ... | ♘a5 |

For his part, Kasparov has chosen a classical plan since White does not have 19 ♗e3 available because of 19 ... ♘c4 20 ♗c1 ♗b7 with a big edge for Black.

19	♘d2	♗b7
20	♕h5	g6
21	♕h3	♖bc8
22	f5	♘e5 *(148)*
23	fe?!	

After this exchange Black could easily repel all threats and grab the initiative. A more promising plan would have been 23 ♖f4!? for example 23 ... ♘ac4 24 ♘×c4 ♘×c4 25 ♖af1 (25 ♖h4 is not on because

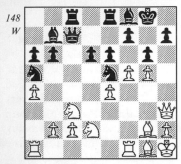

148
W

of 25 ... h6 26 gh ♔h7) 25 ... ♘e5 26
♗d4! and Black is in considerable
danger, e.g. 26 ... ♕c4?! 27 fg fg 28
♗xe5 de 29 ♖f7 and White wins,
or 26 ... ♗g7 27 ♖f4! But 23 ... ♕e7!
is playable, as well as 24 ... ♕xc4!
in the previous variation.

23	**...**	**fe**
24	♖f4	♕e7!
25	♖af1	♗g7

If 25 ... ♕xg5 then 26 ♖xf8+!
♖xf8 27 ♕xe6+ ♔h8 29 ♖xf8+
♖xf8 29 ♕xd6 with an attack that
provides plenty of compensation
for the exchange.

26	♖h4	♗h8

Now after 27 ♗d4 ♘ac4 28
♘xc4 ♖xc4 29 ♗e3 ♖cc8 30 ♗c1
b5 Black had an excellent game.

Keres Attack

**1 e4 c5 2 ♘f3 e6 3 d4 cd 4 ♘xd4 ♘f6
5 ♘c3 d6 6 g4**

Kasparov seems to have been
ducking the Keres Attack ever
since his 1984/85 marathon match,
employing the Najdorf and
Taimanov move orders. But
recently he has shown a willingness to defend the Black side, for

example Ljubojevic–Kasparov,
Belfort 1988:

6	**...**	♘c6

Kasparov follows his own
advice as he calls this move 'the
most logical answer to White's
flank attack' in his book on the
Scheveningen.

7	g5	♘d7
8	♖g1	♗e7
9	♗e3	0-0

An interesting choice, consid-
ering that Kasparov recommends
9 ... ♘b6! in his book, giving 10
♕h5 g6 11 ♕e2 e5 12 ♘b3 ♗e6
with a better game for Black, and
he also examined 10 ♖g3, 10 f4
and 10 ♗b5. But here, for some
reason, he chose to go another
way.

10	♕d2	a6
11	0-0-0	♘xd4
12	♗xd4	b5
13	f4	b4

A typical Sicilian strategy.

14	♘e2	

This is a novelty. Kasparov has
provided analysis only of 13 ♘a4
♕a5 14 b3 ♗b7 15 ♗g2 e5! with
good counterplay for Black.

14	**...**	♕a5
15	♔b1	e5

Black has achieved a very good
game, which is aided by a series of
blunders by Ljubojevic: 16 ♗f2
♘c5 17 ♕e3 ♗e6 18 ♘c1 ef 19
♕xf4 ♖ac8 20 ♗d4 ♖fe8 21 ♘b3
♕a4 22 ♗f6 ♗f8 23 ♖g3 ♕c6 24
♘xc5 dc 25 ♗e5 c4 26 ♗d6 b3 27
c3 ♖cd8 28 e5 ♗xd6 29 ed ♖xd6
30 ♖c1 ♕c5 31 ♔a1 ♖ed8 32 ♖e3

♖d1 33 ♖e1 ♖xe1 34 ♖xe1 ♕a5 35 a3 ♕d5 36 ♗e2 g6 37 h4 ♕d2 38 ♕f1 ♗h3 39 ♕g1 ♖e8 0-1.

Grünfeld Defence

Not surprisingly, Kasparov's favourite reply to 1 d4 has seen quite a bit of action, and there are a number of new developments to report.
1 d4 ♘f6 2 c4 g6 3 ♘c3 d5 4 cd ♘×d5 5 e4 ♘×c3 6 bc ♗g7 7 ♗c4 c5 8 ♘e2 ♘c6 9 ♗e3 0-0 10 0-0 *(149)*

149
B

Instead of 10 0-0, Polugayevsky's idea 10 ♖c1 is fashionable, e.g. Polugayevsky-Kudrin, New York Open 1989: 10 ... cd 11 cd ♕a5+ 12 ♔f1 ♗d7 13 h4 ♖ac8 14 h5 e5! 15 hg hg 16 d5 ♘d4! 17 ♘×d4 ♖×c4? 18 ♖×c4 ♕a6 19 ♕d3! ed 20 ♗×d4 ♗b5 21 ♕h3! and White won. Huzman and Vainerman found a significant improvement, however: 17 ... ed 18 ♗×d4 ♗b5!, for example 19 ♗×g7 ♖×c4 20 ♖×c4 ♗×c4+ 21 ♔g1 ♔×g7 22 ♕d4+ f6 23 ♕×c4 ♕e1+ 24 ♕f1 ♕×e4 and Black is better. Another interesting idea was seen in Nogueiras–Ljubojevic,

Barcelona World Cup 1989: 13 ... ♖fc8!? 14 h5 ♘d8! 15 hg hg 16 ♗d2 ♕a3 17 ♗b3 ♕a6 18 ♔g1 ♕d3! where Black is clearly better. Kasparov is not convinced, apparently, since he gives 10 ... ♘a5! 11 ♗d3 e5 followed by 12 d5 b6 13 0-0 ♘b7 14 c4 ♘d6 with equal chances, though this has not yet been tested. In any event, we can conclude that Polugayevsky's idea is not particularly dangerous for Black.

Korchnoi–Kasparov, Reykjavik World Cup 1988, saw a different new try for White in the form of 10 ♖b1!? (The point of this move is clear. After 10 ... cd 11 cd ♕a5+ 12 ♔f1 Black will have to expend an important tempo to protect his pawn at b7.) 10 ... ♘a5! 11 ♗d3 cd 12 cd b6 13 0-0 (On 13 h4, Kasparov suggested 13 ... e5! 14 d5 f5.) 13 ... e6! ♕a4?! (14 ♕d2 looks more logical here, for example 14 ... ♗b7 15 ♖fc1 ♕d7 =) 14 ... ♗b7 15 ♖fd1 ♖c8 16 ♗d2 ♘c6 17 ♗c3 ♕h4! 18 ♗e1 ♖fd8 19 f3 ♕e7 20 ♗b5?! (20 ♗f2 ♗h6!? was suggested by Kasparov, while 21 ♗b5 ♘a5 gives Black full equality.) 20 ... a6! 21 ♗×a6 ♗×a6 22 ♕×a6 ♘×d4! and Black's initiative is significant. Kasparov then demonstrated his tactical mastery and brilliant intuition in the middlegame, following on from the opening in a thoroughly logical manner, collecting the point against yet another world class player.

| 10 | ... | ♗g4 |
| 11 | f3 | ♘a5 |

Here there are two popular lines:

A   12 ♗d3
B   12 ♗×f7+

A

12	♗d3	cd
13	cd	♗e6
14	♖c1	♗×a2
15	♕a4	♗e6
16	d5	♗d7
17	♕b4	e6 *(150)*

150
W

This has become the main line of this subvariation, replacing 17 ... b6, though that move has not been refuted and is still considered to lead to unclear play.

18 ♘c3

Here Yusupov uncorked the novel 18 ♖fd1 in Yusupov-Kasparov, USSR Ch. 1988, and the game continued 18 ... ed 19 ed ♖e8 20 ♗f2 b5 (20 ... ♗f5 is not so strong because of 21 ♗×f5 ♖×e2 22 ♗e4 ♖b2 23 ♕e1 followed by 24 d6, according to Kasparov.) 21 ♘d4! ♘c4! 22 ♘c6 (22 ♗×c4 a5! 23 ♕c5 bc 24 ♕×c4 a4 25 ♘c6 ♕f6 = and 22 ♘×b5 ♘b2! are given by

Yusupov.) 22 ... ♗×c6 23 dc ♘b2 24 ♗×b5 (not 24 c7?? ♕×d3!!) 24 ... ♘×d1 25 c7 ♕d5 26 ♗×e8 ♘×f2 27 c8(♕) ♖×c8 28 ♖×c8 ♘h3+ 29 gh ♕d1+ 30 ♔g2 ♕e2+ 31 ♔g1 ½-½.

This was a very important game for opening theory, but Kasparov withstood the difficult test provided by his well-prepared opponent. Another test lay ahead, involving the text continuation 18 ♘c3.

18 ... ed

18 ... b6 comes strongly into consideration.

19 ed

For some reason the commentators neglected 19 ♘×d5 ♗e6 20 ♖fd1 ♗×d5 21 ed ♕×d5 22 ♗e4 ♕b3 23 ♗d2 b6 24 ♗×a8 ♖×a8 25 ♕e7 ♘c4 26 ♗f4 h5 27 ♕e4 ♖c8 28 ♖d7 ♕b5 29 ♖×a7 ♕c6 30 ♕e7 ♕c5+ 31 ♗e3 ♕×e7 32 ♖×e7 ♖c6 33 ♗×b6 ♗h6 34 ♖e8+ ♔h7 35 ♗d4+ f6 36 ♗×f6 1-0 Wilder-Kudrin, U.S. Ch. 1988. Instead of the risky 21 ... ♕×d5, a stronger move is 21 ... ♖e8, for example 22 ♗f2 ♗f8! 23 ♕a4 a6! 24 ♗h4 ♕b6+ 25 ♗f2 =.

19 ... ♖e8
20 ♗f2 *(151)*

On 20 ♘e4 Yusupov suggested 20 ... f5! 21 ♗g5 ♕b6 22 ♕×b6 ab 23 ♘f6+ ♗×f6 24 ♗×f6 ♔f7 and Black stands quite well, for example 25 ♗g5 ♖e5 26 ♗d2 ♖ac8.

This is one of the positions of the gambit system initiated by 14 ♖c1. 20 ... b6, 20 ... b5 and 20 ... ♗e5!? have all been seen here, but

151
B

Kasparov, contrary to his usual practice, followed the most conservative path with

    20 ...   ♗f8
    21 ♕b2

If 21 ♕f4 then 21 ... g5!? 22 ♕g3 ♘b3 23 ♖b1 ♘c5 24 ♗c2 f5 with a clear advantage for Black according to Belyavsky, but we find this analysis unconvincing in view of 23 ♘e4 ♘×c1 24 ♘×g5! ♗g7 25 ♖×c1 with a very strong attack for White, so 21 ♕f4 deserves further consideration.

    21 ...   ♗g7
    22 ♕b4   ♗f8
    23 ♕b2   ½-½

Belyavsky-Kasparov, USSR Ch. 1988. Truly a game which raised more questions than it answered.

B

    12 ♗×f7+   ♖×f7
    13 fg   ♖×f1+
    14 ♔×f1   ♕d6
    15 e5   ♕d5
    16 ♗f2   ♖d8
    17 ♕c2

Discussion of the Seville Variation of the Grünfeld continued in Karpov-Kasparov, Belfort 1988, where the former World Champion introduced 17♕a4!? to which Kasparov did not react correctly, playing 17 ... b6?! and after 18 ♕c2 ♖f8 (18 ... ♕c4?! 19 ♕e4! prevents 19 ... ♘c6.) 19 ♔g1 ♕c4 20 ♕d2 ♕e6 21 h3 ♘c4 22 ♕g5! and Kasparov was unable to hold the position. The game concluded 22 ... h6 23 ♕c1 ♕f7 24 ♗g3 g5 25 ♕c2 ♕d5 26 ♗f2 b5 27 ♘g3 ♖f7 28 ♖e1 b4 29 ♕g6 ♔f8 30 ♘e4 ♖×f2 31 ♔×f2 bc 32 ♕f5+ ♔g8 33 ♕c8+♔h7 34 ♕×c5 ♕f7+ 35 ♔g1 c2 36 ♘g3 ♗f8 37 ♘f5 ♔g8 38 ♖c1 1-0.

So Karpov won the most recent, but by no means last, set in this theoretical match. The move 17 ♕a4! was highly praised, but we feel that 17 ... ♖f8! should provide adequate counterplay, for example 18 ♔g1 (18 ♕×a5 ♕f7!) 18 ...♕f7 19 ♗h4 (19 ♗g3 is met by 19 ... ♗h6) 19 ... ♘c4 20 h3 ♘e3 with the deadly threat of 21 ... ♘×g2! The obvious drawback to 17 ♕a4 is the decentralization of the white queen.

Thus it should come as no surprise that Karpov has since reverted to 17 ♕c2 in his game against Timman from the Rotterdam World Cup 1989.

    17 ...   ♕c4
    18 ♕b2   ♗h6
    19 h4   ♖f8!? *(152)*

Timman introduced this novelty but it did not work out as he had planned.

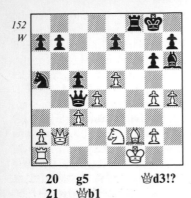

152
W

20	g5	♕d3!?
21	♕b1	

21 gh ♘c4 22 ♕c1 also favours White, e.g. 22 ... ♕f5 23 ♘f4! or 22 ... ♘e3+ 23 ♔g1 ♘xg2 24 ♕g5!

21	...	♕e3
22	♕e1	♗g7
23	♔g1	♕e4
24	♘g3	♕xh4
25	♘e4	♖xf2

If 25 ... ♕g4 26 ♘xc5 b6 then 27 ♕e4! ±. After 26 ♘xf2 cd 27 ♖d1! Karpov prevailed.

The last word on the Seville Variation remains to be said, and perhaps Kasparov will make the next contribution.

Dutch Defence

There is not too much to report here. In the Modern Stonewall, Kasparov achieved an advantage against Short at Brussels SWIFT 1987 after 1 d4 f5 2 g3 (avoiding lines with ... ♗f8–b4+) 2 ... ♘f6 3 ♗g2 e6 4 ♘f3 ♗e7 5 c4 d5 6 0-0 0-0 7 ♘bd2 (7 b3 is normal.) 7 ... c6 8 ♘e5 ♘bd7 9 ♘d3 ♘e4 10 ♕c2 ♗f6 11 ♘f3 ♔h8 12 b3 ♕e8 13 ♗a3 ♖g8 14 ♖ac1, where control of e5

and the spatial advantage play a significant role.

In the Leningrad, Kasparov tried a new move which did not prove much of a success: 3 ... g6 4 ♘f3 ♗g7 5 0-0 0-0 6 b3 (More common is 6 c4 d6 7 ♘c3) 6 ... d6 7 ♗b2 ♕e8 8 c4 ♘a6 9 d5 ♗d7 10 ♘c3 c6 11 ♖c1 h6 12 e3 ♖c8 13 ♘d4 ♕f7 and in Kasparov-Malanyuk, USSR Ch. 1988, Black had a fully playable game which was eventually drawn. One assumes that Kasparov will be better prepared next time he meets this opening!

English Opening

1 c4 ♘f6 2 ♘f3 g6 3 ♘c3 d5 4 cd ♘xd5 5 ♕a4+ is a modified Grünfeld which was seen in Korchnoi-Kasparov, Brussels SWIFT 1987: 5 ... ♗d7 6 ♕h4!? (6 ♕d4 and 6 ♕b3 both come into consideration) 6 ... ♗c6 7 g3 (Kasparov-Kouatly, simul. 1988, saw instead 7 ♕d4 f6 8 e4 ♘xc3 9 bc ♕xd4 10 ♘xd4 ♗d7 11 f4 c5 12 ♘b3 e6 13 d4 ♗c6 14 ♗d3 f5 15 ♘xc5 ♗xc5 16 dc fe) 7 ... ♗g7 8 ♗g2 ♘d7! (Korchnoi had probably prepared some innovation in the main line with 8 ... 0-0, but the World Champion equalized quickly on 9 ♘d4 (9 0-0 is well met by 9 ... e5! and Black is better.) 9 ... ♗xd4 10 ♘xd5 (10 ♕xd4 is also met by 10 ... e5! while on 10 ♗xd5, 10 ... ♘f6 gives Black the edge.) 10 ... ♗g7 11 0-0 e6 12 ♕xd8+ ♔xd8 13 ♘c3 ♗xg2 14 ♔xg2 ♘e7 15 d3 ♖hc8 16 ♗g5+

♔f8.

On the White side, Kasparov has slacked off a bit in his enthusiasm for the English, but he can still be devastating at times: Kasparov–Ivanchuk, USSR Ch. 1988: 1 c4 ♘f6 2 ♘c3 e5 3 ♘f3 ♘c6 4 g3 ♗b4 5 ♗g2 0-0 6 0-0 e4 7 ♘g5 ♗xc3 8 bc ♖e8 9 f3 ef 10 ♘xf3 d5 11 d4 ♘e4 12 ♕c2 dc 13 ♖b1 f5 14 g4 ♕e7 15 gf ♘d6 16 ♘g5 ♕xe2 17 ♗d5+ ♔h8 18 ♕xe2 ♖xe2 19 ♗f4 ♘d8 20 ♖be1 ♖xe1 21 ♖xe1 ♗d7 22 ♗xd6 cd 23 ♖e7 ♗c6 24 f6 1-0

Kasparov–Sokolov, Belfort 1988: 1 c4 ♘f6 2 ♘c3 e6 3 e4 c5 4 e5 ♘g8 5 ♘f3 ♘c6 6 d4 cd 7 ♘xd4 ♘xe5 8 ♘db5 a6 9 ♘d6+ ♗xd6 10 ♕xd6 f6 11 ♗e3 ♘e7 12 ♗b6 ♘f5 13 ♕c5 d6 14 ♕a5 ♕e7 15 0-0-0 0-0 16 f4 ♘c6 17 ♕a3 e5 18 g4 ♘fd4 19 ♘d5 ♕f7 20 f5 g6 21 ♖g1 gf 22 g5 ♔h8 23 gf ♗e6 24 ♕xd6 ♗xd5 25 cd ♕xf6 26 ♕xf6+ ♖xf6 27 ♔b1 ♘d8 28 ♗c5 ♖c8 29 ♗e7 ♖f7 30 ♗d6 ♘f3 31 ♖g3 e4 32 ♗e2 ♖f6 33 ♗f4 ♖g6 34 ♗xf3 ♖xg3 35 ♗xe4 fe 36 hg ♔g7 37 ♖d4 ♘f7 38 ♖xe4 ♖d8 39 ♖e7 ♖xd5 40 ♖xb7 h5 41 ♖a7 a5 42 a4 1-0

King's Indian Defence

As Black, Kasparov has returned to his old stomping ground, and has been stomping plenty of opponents along the way! He has been scoring points with both colours. Let's begin with the Classical System:

1 d4 ♘f6 2 c4 g6 3 ♘c3 ♗g7 4 e4 d6 5 ♘f3 0-0 6 ♗e2 e5 7 0-0

A battle of the greatest theoreticians took place in Kasparov–Nunn, Reykjavik 1988: 7 ♗e3 h6 8 0-0 ♘g4 9 ♗c1 ♘c6 10 d5 ♘e7 11 ♘d2 f5 12 ♗xg4 fg 13 b4 b6 14 ♘b3 g5 15 a4 ♘g6 16 a5 ♗d7 17 c5 bc 18 bc a6 19 ♘d2 ♘f4 20 ♖b1? (As Nunn points out, 20 c6! would have given Kasparov a significant advantage.) 20 ... dc 21 ♗a3 ♖f7 22 ♘c4 ♕f6 23 ♗xc5 ♗f8 24 ♗xf8 ♖axf8 25 ♖b4 h5 26 d6 ♗e6 27 ♘d5 ♗xd5 28 ed cd 29 ♖b6 ♖d7 30 ♖xa6 ♕g6 31 ♖e1 ♘d3 32 ♘xe5 ♘xe5 33 ♖xe5 ♕f6 34 ♖e2 ♖e7 35 ♖c6 ♖xe2 36 ♕xe2 ♕a1+ 37 ♕f1 ♕xa5 38 ♖xd6 ♖e8 39 ♖e6 ♖xe6 40 de ♕e5 41 ♕c1 ♔g7 ½-½.

Yusupov played 7 d5 against Kasparov at the Barcelona World Cup 1989. After 7 ... a5 8 ♗g5 h6 9 ♗h4 ♘a6 10 ♘d2 ♕e8 11 0-0 ♘h7 12 a3 ♗d7 13 b3 Kasparov introduced 13 ... f5!? instead of the more normal 13 ... h5. Kasparov achieved plenty of play after 14 ef gf 15 ♗h5 ♕c8 16 ♗e7 ♖e8 17 ♗xe8 ♕xe8 18 ♗h4 e4 19 ♕c2 ♕h5 20 ♗g3 ♖e8 21 ♗f4 ♕g4 22 g3 ♘g5 when instead of 23 ♔h1?, Yusupov should have played 23 ♗xg5 hg 24 f3 ef 25 ♘xf3 f4 26 ♕g6 with an unclear game, but Kasparov later blundered away his position and lost.

7	...	♘c6
8	d5	♘e7
9	♘d2	a5
10	a3!	

Improving on 10 b3 c5 11 a3 ♘e8 12 ♖b1 f5 13 b4 ab 14 ab b6 15

♕b3 ♘f6 with equality in Karpov–
Kasparov, (m/17) Seville 1987. After
16 ♗d3 ♗h6 17 ♖b2 Tal suggests
17 ... f4! instead of 17 ... ♖a1.

10 ... ♘d7

10 ... c5 11 ♖b1 is better for
White, as is 10 ... ♗d7 11 ♖a2 ♘e8
12 b4 f5 13 c5 ab 14 ab ♖×a2 15
♘×a2, Salov–Khalifman, USSR
Ch. 1988.

11 ♖b1 f5
12 b4 ♔h8!

This frees the g8-square for the
♘e7. 12 ... b6 13 f3 f4 14 ♘a4 was
seen in the complicated game
Kasparov–Smirin, USSR Ch. 1988,
but Kasparov and Nikitin point
out that after the simple 14 ♘b3!?
ab 15 ab g5 16 c5 White would
stand better. Of course such
positions are embraced by
Kasparov for their strategical and
tactical richness, and even if an
objective advantage cannot be
obtained, the complex nature of
the middlegame favours his style.
So in what follows, we find him on
the Black side of the same line!

13 f3 (153)

153
B

13 ♕c2 b6 14 ♘b3 ab 15 ab fe!?

(15 ... ♗h6 also comes into consideration.) 16 ♘×e4 ♘f6 17 ♗d3
♘×e4 18 ♗×e4 ♘f5 19 ♕d3 ♕h4
provided Black with good counterplay in Gavrikov–Kasparov, USSR
Ch. 1988.

13 ... ♘g8!

A fantastic conception on the
part of the World Champion. 13 ...
♗h6 14 ♘b3 ♗×c1 15 ♖×c1 ab 16
ab ♘f6 17 c5 g5 is considered to
provide Black with adequate
counterplay, for example 18 ♘d2?!
f4 19 ♘b5 g4! 20 fg ♖g8 21 ♗f3
♗×g4 22 ♔h1 ♗×f3 23 gf ♘h5 24
♖g1 ♘g3+!! 25 hg fg 26 ♖g2 ♘g6
and Black won quickly in Lukov–
Sznapik, Tbilisi 1988. But perhaps
Sznapik's suggested 18 ♕c2! was
convincing to Kasparov in home
analysis. We follow Karpov–
Kasparov, Skelleftea World Cup
1989.

14 ♘b3 ab
15 ab ♘df6
16 ♗d2 ♘h5

Already White's position is
near collapse.

17 g3

17 c5 ♘f4 18 ♗c4 ♕g5! 19 g3
♘h3+ 20 ♔g2 f4 gives Black a
strong attack.

17 ... ♘hf6
18 ♖f2 ♘h6
19 ♖a1 ♖×a1
20 ♕×a1 ♘f7!
21 ♕c1 f4!
22 g4

If 22 gf ef 23 ♗×f4, then Black is
still on the warpath after 23 ... ♘h5.

22 ... h5

23	h3	♘h7!
24	♗e1	♗f6
25	♔g2	♔g7
26	♖f1	♘hg5
27	♖h1 *(154)*	

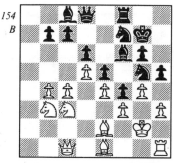

154
B

27	...	♘×h3!!
28	♖×h3	♘g5

Black has sacrificed the piece for a single pawn, but he has a very strong attack.

29   ♖h2

The point is that after 29 ♖h1 hg 30 fg f3+! 31 ♗×f3 ♘×f3 32 ♕h6+ ♔f7 33 ♔×f3 ♖h8 Black is winning.

29	...	hg
30	fg	♖h8
31	♗h4	

White is willing to return the material, but 31 ♖×h8 ♕×h8 was hopeless. His real problem is that his pieces are disorganized.

31	...	f3+
32	♗×f3	♘×f3
33	♗×f6+	♕×f6
34	♖×h8	♔×h8
35	♔g3	

And now instead of 35 ... g5?, Kasparov should have played 35 ... ♔g7!, for example:

(a) 36 ♘e2 ♕h4+! 37 ♔×f3 ♗×g4+ 38 ♔e3 ♕h3+ 39 ♔d2 ♕×b3;

(b) 36 ♕e3 ♘d4! 37 ♘d2 g5 38 ♘e2 ♕f4+! or simply 37 ... ♘c2.

Now let's take a look at Kasparov on both sides of the Sämisch: **1 d4 ♘f6 2 c4 g6 3 ♘c3 ♗g7 4 e4 d6 5 f3 0-0**

Before proceeding further, we take note that the sacrificial idea to be seen below has its origins in Spassky-Bronstein, Amsterdam 1956: 5 ... e5 6 d5? (6 ♘ge2!?) 6 ... ♘h5 7 ♗e3 ♘a6 8 ♕d2 ♕h4+ 9 g3 ♘×g3 10 ♕f2 ♘×f1 11 ♕×h4 ♘×e3 12 ♔f2? (12 ♔e2!?) 12 ... ♘×c4 13 b3 ♘a3 14 ♘ge2 ♘c5 with good counterplay for Black.

6	♗e3	e5
7	d5 *(155)*	

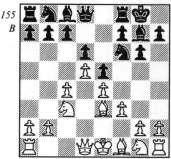

155
B

7	...	♘h5!?

As Black in Timman-Kasparov, Reykjavik 1988, the World Champion chose 7 ... c6 8 ♗d3 b5 9 cb (9 ♘ge2 gives White a slight advantage, according to *ECO*) 9 ... cd 10 ed (Here, too, 10 ♘ge2!? is probably best.) 10 ... e4! Kasparov is in his element and introduces a fine new move. The methodical pawn sacrifice frees his long diagonal and the e5-square.) 11 ♘xe4 ♘xd5 12 ♗g5 ♕a5+ 13 ♕d2 ♕xd2+ 14 ♗xd2 ♗xb2 with a good game. Play continued 15 ♖b1 ♗g7 16 ♘e2 ♘d7 17 ♘xd6?! ♘c5 18 ♗c2 ♗e6 (Black has full compensation here.) 19 ♘e4 ♖ac8 20 0-0 ♘xe4 21 ♗xe4 f5 22 ♗d3 ♘b6 23 ♘c1 ♖fd8 24 ♗g5 ♖d7 25 ♖e1 ♔f7 26 ♗e2 h6 27 ♗h4 ♘d5 28 ♗d1 ♗d4+ 29 ♗f2 ♗xf2+ 30 ♔xf2 ♘c3 31 ♗b3 ♗xb3 32 ♖xb3 ♘d1+ 33 ♖xd1 ♖xd1 34 ♘d3 ♖d2+ 35 ♔e3 ♖xg2 36 ♖a3 ♖e8+ 37 ♔d4 ♖e7 38 ♘e5+ ♔f6 39 ♘c6 ♖d7+ 40 ♔c4 ♖c2+ 41 ♔b4 ♖xh2 42 ♖a6 ♔g5 43 a4 h5 44 ♖xa7 ♖xa7 45 ♘xa7 0-1.

Gheorghiu–Kasparov, Thessaloniki Ol. 1988, varied with 8 ♕d2 cd 9 cd ♘bd7 10 ♘ge2 a6 11 ♘c1?! ♘h5 ♗d3 (a novelty) 12 ... f5 13 ♘1e2 ♘df6 13 ef gf 15 ♘g3 and the same theme re-emerged: 15 ... e4! 16 ♘xh5 ♗xh5 17 fe f4 18 ♗f2 ♗g4 19 h3! ♗d7 20 0-0-0 ♗e5 21 ♔b1 ♕f6 22 ♗e2 ♘g3 23 ♗xg3 (23 ♖he1 would have maintained the balance.) 23 ... fg 24 ♗f3 ♖ac8 25 ♘e2 and here with 25 ... ♖c5! Black would have had a clear advantage.

8	♕d2	♕h4+
9	♗f2	♕f4
10	♗e3	♕h4+
11	g3	♘xg3
12	♕f2	♘xf1
13	♕xh4	♘xe3
14	♔e2	♘xc4

15	♖c1	♘a6
16	♘d1	♘b6
17	♘e3	♗d7
18	♘h3	f6

This is the critical position. According to theory, White stands better.

| 19 | ♘f2 |

19 ♖hg1 ♖ad8 20 b3 c6 21 dc bc? 22 ♘f5! gf 23 ♖xg7+! is well known from Karpov–Velimirovic, Skopje 1976. But better is 21 ... ♗xc6!, where Black can follow up with ... d6–d5.

19	...	♘c8
20	♖c3	♘e7
21	♖hc1	♖ac8
22	♖b3	♖b8
23	♘d3	

Here, in Kasparov–Seirawan, Barcelona World Cup 1989, White had a clear advantage. After 23 ... ♖f7 24 ♕e1 ♘c8 25 ♕a5 ♘b6 26 ♖xc7! f5 he misplayed with 27 ♖c2? fe 28 fe ♖bf8 29 ♖xb6 and a draw was agreed, although there was the possible continuation 29 ... ab 30 ♕xb6 ♗h6! 31 ♕xd6 ♖f3 32 ♕xd7? ♖xe3+ 33 ♔d2 ♘b4! winning for Black. Instead,

Kasparov should have played 27 ♖c1 fe 28 fe ♖bf8 29 ♖g1 with a clear advantage, for example 29 ... ♗h6 30 ♖×b6! ♗×e3 31 ♔×e3 ♖f3+ 32 ♔e2 ab 33 ♕×b6, where Black lacks sufficient compensation for the material.

Kasparov started off in the fashion of the Modern Defence in Ljubojevic–Kasparov, Thessaloniki Ol. 1988: 1 c4 g6 2 ♘c3 ♗g7 3 g3 d6 4 d4 c5 5 ♗e3 cd 6 ♗×d4 but transferred to a more normal King's Indian with 6 ... ♘f6 7 ♘d5 ♘bd7 8 ♘f3 0-0 9 ♗g2 e5 and the game continued 10 ♗c3 ♘×d5 11 cd ♘c5 12 0-0 ♗d7 13 ♘d2 ♖c8 14 ♖c1 f5 15 ♘c4 ♗b5 16 ♘a3 ♗e8 17 ♕d2 ♖f7 18 ♗b4 ♘fc7 19 ♖c2 ♘a6 20 ♗c3 e4 21 ♗×g7 ♔×g7 22 ♖fc1 ♗f7 23 g4 fg 24 ♗×e4 ♕f6 25 ♘b5 ♖×c2 26 ♖×c2 ♖×c2 27 ♕×c2 ♘c5 28 b4 ♘×e4 29 ♕×e4 h5 30 a3 g5 31 ♘d4 a6 32 ♘e6+ ♔h6 33 ♔g2 ♗g6 34 ♕e3 ♕f5 35 ♕d4 ♕e4+ 36 ♔g1 ♕×d4 37 ♘×d4 ♗e4 38 f3 gf 39 ef ♗b1 40 ♔f2 ♔g6 41 b5 ♗a2 42 ba ba 43 ♘c6 ♔f5 44 ♘b4 ♗c4 45 ♔e3 a5 46 ♘c6 ♗×d5 47 ♘d4+ ♔e5 48 ♘e2 ♗f7 49 ♘g1 ♗c4 50 ♘h3 ♔f5 51 ♘f2 d5 0-1

Queen's Indian

Kasparov–Ehlvest, Belfort 1988: 1 d4 ♘f6 2 c4 e6 3 ♘f3 b6 4 a3 ♗b7 5 ♘c3 d5 6 cd ♘×d5 7 ♕c2 ♘×c3 8 bc ♗e7 9 e3 ♕c8 10 ♗b2 c5 11 ♗b5+ ♘c6 12 0-0 0-0 13 ♗d3 ♔h8 14 ♕e2 ♕c7 15 ♖ad1 ♖ad8 16 e4 ♘a5 17 ♖fe1 ♗f6 18 e5 ♗e7 19 ♘d2 cd 20 cd ♗d5 21 ♘e4 f5 22 ef

♗×f6 23 ♘×f6 ♖×f6 24 ♗c1 ♖df8 25 f3 ♘c6 26 ♗e4 ♗×e4 27 fe e5 28 d5 ♘d4 29 ♕d3 ♕f7 30 ♗b2 ♘f3+ 31 gf ♖×f3 32 ♖e3 ♕g6+ 33 ♔h1 ♖f2 34 ♖g1 ♕h6 ½-½.

Queen's Gambit

Probably the big news here is the addition of the Exchange Variation to the repertoire as White. The attacking play characteristic of his style flows naturally in the middlegames which arise from this venerable line. It should come as no surprise that he prefers to keep the play to the kingside rather than go after the minority attack on the queenside. We ought to point out that this approach to the Exchange Variation was successfully employed by Botvinnik back in the 1950s and 60s, especially in his well known games against Pilnik (Budapest 1952), Keres (USSR Ch. 1959) and Larsen (Nordwijk 1965). The Keres game is particularly close to Kasparov's spirited play. In the examples below, Kasparov displays a great deal of flexibility in his approach to the positions, attacking wherever circumstances permit, on the queenside, in the centre, or on the kingside.

1	d4	d5
2	c4	e6
3	♘c3	♘f6
4	♗g5	

Kasparov has also played (by transposition) the quiet system with 4 ♘f3 and an early ♗c1-f4;

Kasparov–Eingorn, USSR Ch. 1988:
1 ♘f3 ♘f6 2 c4 e6 3 ♘c3 d5 4 d4
♘bd7 5 cd ed 6 ♗f4 ♘b6 7 ♕c2 g6
8 e3 ♗f5 9 ♗d3 ♗xd3 10 ♕xd3 c6
11 0-0 ♗g7 12 b4 0-0 13 b5 ♖e8 14
bc bc 15 ♗g5 ♕d6 16 ♘d2 ♘fd7 17
a4 ♕e6 18 ♗f4 a5 19 ♗g3 ♗f8 20
♘e2 ½-½.

But he was more successful in
Kasparov–Short, Thessaloniki Ol.
1988: 1 c4 e6 2 ♘c3 d5 3 d4 ♗e7
4 cd ed 5 ♗f4 c6 6 ♕c2 g6 7 e3 ♗f5
8 ♕d2 ♘f6 9 f3 c5 10 ♗h6
(a novelty) 10 ... cd 11 ed a6 12 g4!
♗e6 13 ♘ge2 ♘bd7?! 14 ♗g2 ♘b6
15 b3 ♖c8 16 0-0 ♖c6 17 h3!, where
White already held a clear
advantage. After 17 ... ♘fd7 18
♘d1 ♖g8? 19 ♘f2 f5? Black could
not recover: 20 ♖ae1 g5 21 gf ♗f7
22 ♘g4 ♗h5 23 ♘g3! 1-0.

    4   **...**   **♗e7**
    5   **cd**

Of course the World Champion
has not entirely abandoned the
non-Exchange systems: Kasparov–
Timman, Amsterdam 1988 1 d4
♘f6 2 c4 e6 3 ♘f3 d5 4 ♘c3 ♗e7 5
♗g5 h6 6 ♗xf6 ♗xf6 7 ♕b3 c6 8 e3
0-0 9 ♖d1 ♕b6 10 ♕c2 dc 11 ♗xc4
c5 12 ♘e4 ♗e7 13 dc ♗xc5 14 0-0
♗e7 15 ♗e2 ♗d7 16 ♘e5 ♖c8 17
♕d3 ♗e8 18 ♘c4 ♕c7 19 ♘ed6
♖d8 20 ♘xe8 ♖xe8 21 ♗f3 ♖d8
22 ♕b3 ♘c6 23 g3 ♗f6 24 ♔g2
♖ab8 25 ♖xd8+ ♖xd8 ½-½.

    5   **...**   **ed**
    6   **e3**   **0-0**

Black was not so quick to
commit himself in Kasparov–
Smyslov, USSR Ch. 1988, and was

rewarded with an early declaration
of peace: 6 ... c6 7 ♘f3 ♘bd7 8 ♕c2
♘h5 9 ♗xe7 ♕xe7 10 0-0-0 ♘b6 11
h3 g6 12 g4 ♘g7 13 ♗d3 ♗e6 14
♘e2 0-0-0 15 ♘f4 ♔b8 16 ♗e2 ♘e8
17 ♘d2 ♘d6 18 h4 ♗c8 19 ♘b3
♘e4 20 ♗f3 f5 ½-½.

    7   **♗d3**   **♘bd7**
    8   **♘ge2**

The most aggressive continuation.

    8   **...**   **♖e8**
    9   **♕c2**   **♘f8**
   10   **0-0-0**

In Kasparov–Andersson, Belfort
1988, White castled kingside: after
9 ... c6 10 0-0 ♘f8 11 f3! (improving
on Botvinnik's 11 ♖b1.) 11 ... ♗e6
12 ♖ae1 ♖c8 13 ♔h1 ♘6d7 14
♗xe7 ♖xe7 15 ♘f4 ♖c7 16 ♕f2
♘f6 17 e4 de 18 fe ♖cd7 19 d5 cd 20
♗b5 ♖c7 21 ed ♗d7 22 ♗e2 ♖c8
23 ♕xa7 b6 24 ♕a6 ♘e4 25 d6
♘xd6 26 ♘fd5 ♖e5 27 ♕xb6 ♘f5
28 ♕xd8 ♖xd8 29 ♗d3 ♖xe1 30
♖xe1 ♘g6 31 a4 ♘d4 32 a5 ♔f8 33
♗xg6 hg 34 ♖d1 ♘e6 35 ♘b6 ♗c6
36 ♖xd8+ ♘xd8 37 b4 ♘e6 38 b5
1-0

   10   **...**   **♗e6**
   11   **♔b1**   **♘g4**

11 ... ♖c8!? would have been
wiser. With the kings on opposite
wings time is of the essence, and
the attacks must be launched
without delay.

   12   **♗xe7**   **♕xe7**
   13   **♘f4**   **♘f6** *(157)*
   14   **f3!**

Again, as in the Andersson
game, this move is the prelude to

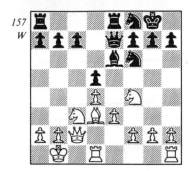

5 e4 b5 6 e5 ♘d5 7 a4 e6 8 ♘g5 ♗b4
9 ♕h5 ♕e7 10 ♗d2 h6 11 ♘ge4
♗a6 12 ♗e2 0-0 13 0-0 ♖d8 14 ab
cb 15 ♗×h6 gh 16 ♘×d5 ed 17
♘f6+ ♔g7 18 f4 ♕b7 19 ♖f3 ♕c6
20 f5 ♖h8 21 ♖af1 ♗d2 22 e6 ♖f8
23 ♘g4 ♕b6 24 f6+ ♔h7 25 e7
♕×d4+ 26 ♔h1 ♘c6 27 ♖h3 ♕×b2
28 ♘×h6 1-0

Other recent games of interest

Nimzoindian
In the Nimzoindian, Kasparov has
not escaped the lure of the popular
4 ♕c2, which has proven such an
effective weapon in the hands of
his arch-rival Karpov. Kasparov-
Sax, Reykjavik 1988, saw 1 d4 ♘f6
2 c4 e6 3 ♘c3 ♗b4 4 ♕c2 0-0 5 a3
♗×c3+ 6 ♕×c3 d6 7 f3 d5 8 ♗g5
♘bd7 9 e3 ♖e8 10 ♘h3 h6 11 ♗h4
c6 12 cd ed 13 ♗f2 c5 14 ♘f4 cd 15
♕×d4 ♕a5+ 16 b4 ♕b6 17 ♕d2 a5
18 b5 ♘c5 19 ♖d1 ♘b3 20 ♕b2 a4
21 ♗e2 ♕a5+ 22 ♔f1 ♗d7 23 ♗h4
d4 24 ♗×f6 gf 25 ed ♗×b5 26 ♔f2
♗×e2 27 ♘×e2 ♕g5 28 ♖d3 ♖e7
29 ♖hd1 ♖ae8 30 ♘g3 f5 31 ♔f1
♕h4 32 d5 ♘c5 33 ♖d4 ♕×h2 34
d6 ♖e3 35 ♔f2 ♖×f3+ 36 ♔×f3
♖e3+ 37 ♔×e3 ♕×g3+ 38 ♔d2 1-0

French
One doesn't find Kasparov on
either side of the French Defence
very often, so the following
game is of interest: Kasparov-
Kharitonov, USSR Ch. 1988: 1 e4
e6 2 d4 d5 3 ♘d2 c5 4 ♘gf3 ♘f6 5
ed ed 6 ♗b5+ ♗d7 7 ♗×d7+

---

a strong attack.

| | 14 | ... | c5 |
| | 15 | g4 | cd |

As Kasparov notes, 15 ... c4 16
♗f1 ♕d7 17 e4! de 18 d5 ♗×g4 19
fg ♕×g4 20 ♕f2 gives White a
crushing game.

	16	ed	♕d6
	17	♕d2	a6
	18	♘ce2	♖e7
	19	♘g3	♘g6
	20	♘g2!	♘d7
	21	♖hg1	♖ee8
	22	♖df1!!	

And now Black's position was
very shaky. After 22 ... ♘gf8 23
♘e3 ♔h8 24 ♘h5! g6 25 f4! gh 26 f4
h4 27 fe fe 28 g5 ♖e7 29 ♘g4 ♖g7
30 ♘h6 ♕b6 31 g6 hg 32 ♘f7+ ♔g8
33 ♕h6! ♖h7 34 ♖×g6+ ♘×g6 35
♕×g6+ ♖g7 36 ♕h6 1-0 in
Kasparov-Campora, Thessaloniki
Ol. 1988.

Tolush-Geller Gambit
We have a rare example of
Kasparov playing against a non-
human opponent in Kasparov-
Computer, Rotterdam simul. 1987:
1 ♘f3 c6 2 c4 ♘f6 3 ♘c3 d5 4 d4 dc

♘bxd7 8 0-0 ♗e7 9 dc ♘xc5 10 ♘d4 ♕d7 11 ♕f3 0-0 12 ♘2b3 ♘ce4 13 ♕f5 ♖fc8 14 ♖e1 ♗f8 15 c3 ♕xf5 16 ♘xf5 g6 17 ♘e3 ♖e8 18 ♖d1 ♘c5 19 g4 h6 20 h4 ♘xb3 21 ab ♗c5 22 g5 hg 23 hg ♘e4 24 ♘g4 ♗b6 25 ♔g2 ♔g7 26 ♗f4 ♖ad8 27 f3 ♘c5 28 b4 ♘b3 29 ♖a3 ♖e2+ 30 ♔g3 ♖xb2 31 c4 ♖e8 32 c5 ♗d8 33 ♖xa7 ♖ee2 34 ♖xd5 ♗e7 35 ♖xb7 1-0

Torre Attack

How does the World Champion handle the Torre Attack? A clear example was provided in Torre–Kasparov, Thessaloniki Ol. 1988:

1 d4 ♘f6 2 ♘f3 g6 3 ♗g5 ♗g7 4 c3 d5 5 ♘bd2 ♘bd7 6 e3 0-0 7 b4 c6 8 ♗e2 ♖e8 9 0-0 e5 10 a4 h6 11 ♗h4 a5 12 b5 c5 13 de ♘xe5 14 ♘xe5 ♖xe5 15 ♗xf6 ♗xf6 16 ♖c1 b6 17 ♗g4 ♗b7 18 ♗f3 ♕e7 19 c4 ♖d8 20 ♕c2 d4 21 ♗xb7 ♕xb7 22 ed ♖xd4 23 ♖ce1 ♖xe1 24 ♖xe1 ♕d7 25 ♘f1 h5 26 g3 h4 27 ♘e3 ♕e6 28 ♕e2 ♖e4 29 gh ♗c3 30 ♖d1 ♖xh4 31 ♕f3 ♗d4 32 ♘g2 ♖h3 33 ♕d5 ♕f6 34 ♘e3 ♗f3 35 ♔h1 ♖xf2 36 ♘g4 ♕f3+ 37 ♕xf3 ♖xf3 38 ♖e1 ♖a3 39 ♖e8+ ♔g7 40 ♖b8 ♖xa4 41 ♖xb6 ♖xc4 42 ♖a6 ♖b4 0-1